Tin Soldiers on
Jerusalem Beach

There were once five and twenty tin soldiers, all brothers. . . . Each soldier was exactly alike but one. . . .
There had not been enough tin to finish him—he had
but one leg.

—Hans Christian Andersen,
The Steadfast Tin Soldier

Tin Soldiers on Jerusalem Beach

_____ Amia Lieblich

Pantheon Books
New York

Lieblich, Amia. 1939–
Tin Soldiers on Jerusalem Beach.

Bibliography: pp. 305–7
1. Soldiers—Israel—Interviews. 2. Israel History, Military. 3. War—Psychological aspects case studies. 4 Gestalt therapy—Cases, clinical reports, statistics. I. Title.
DS119.2.L53 1978   956.94′05 78–51810
ISBN 0–394–42738–6

Design by Irva Mandelbaum

Manufactured in the United States of America

First Edition

Contents

Foreword

This book is a profile of Israel, a real-life profile.

I thought it needed no introduction, nor any opening, interpretation, or background. I wanted its stories, the "cases" of the people and the groups, to stand as separate units, as in a collection of photographs combined into an album. The documents could speak for themselves, and the readers would find their own personal meaning in each. It may be a bad habit, but in art books or photograph collections I rarely want to read the instructions written by others, who have already gone through what I am going to experience. Sometimes, however, I am interested in the introduction afterward.

Presenting the material of this book to readers of a foreign culture made some words of explanation indispensable, to be read either before or after the cases and interviews. The reader may choose his or her own preferred order, starting with the emotional account ("The Unfinished Business of War in Israel"), the descriptive report ("Peaceful Conversations About the War"), or the more intellectual discussion (the introduction to each section, and the first part of the book).

In the records collected and presented for the book, I served in at least two distinct roles: that of the therapist, group leader, or interviewer on the one hand, and that of the observer, recorder,* and writer of the group encounters on the other. A third unmanifested role I frequently took was that of the client, with whom I identified and through whom I sometimes coped with my personal dilemmas, with or without total awareness of this process. This is, apparently, the situation of the participant

*One year, in 1975, Aliza Leventhal was an observer who took down a complete record of all the group sessions. The other clinical material is based on my post-session notes. The interviews were all tape-recorded. In addition, part of the material is based on written records and papers of my group members.

observer in its greatest complexity. It would be, therefore, naïve to present the following material as objective in the strict sense of the word. My personality, my therapeutic background and considerations, my bias as a human being and as a therapist, certainly influenced the interactions I had and the way I recorded them. If this is, then, a photograph album, the photographer certainly selected the camera, the colors, and the settings, and decided what pictures to take and which of the taken pictures to exhibit publicly. There is an infinite number of pictures not taken, and many others were taken and not presented. Still, the small number of profiles chosen represent true instances of our reality.

This is not an easy book to read—neither was it easy to write. It is emotionally very demanding. Simultaneous with my inner urge to tell these stories were my doubts about the wisdom of this decision. The main reason for these doubts was that I did not wish to use this highly personal material to serve my own needs, to exploit for my own benefit people who confided in me. I would never have published this book were I not sure of its value as a human document, depicting, from a very unique angle, the reality of a people at war.

A note should also be made concerning the style and language of this book. The vast majority of the sessions recorded here actually took place in Hebrew. When I translated the stories into English, I searched for a style which would best convey the conversational tone of the Hebrew-speaking individuals. A direct translation would be too awkward for the English-speaking reader, so much so that the impact of the material might be lost. On the other hand, an attempt to transfer the Israeli colloquialisms and slang into the parallel style of speech used by Americans of the same age groups would be so foreign as to distort the message. I finally hit upon a mid-course that would be both comprehensible to the reader and not foreign to the speakers. Yet a problem remains. Israelis have developed terms to fit our reality; and since it is a rather unique reality, some of our words are missing from other languages. One example will suffice. Israelis refer to people who were killed in war as people who "fell" while on duty, or simply, "the fallen." Although other terms, more explicit in their reference to death, are also used, "the fallen" is the most common one. This is how Yael referred to her brother and boyfriend, and Tamar and Dana to their husbands. It is a word that has become sort of sacred with us; it conveys respect toward the heroes and, simultaneously, manages to avoid overt expression of their being dead. It is thus less blunt than any comparable English term. For this expression, as well as several others, approximations were the best we could achieve in a foreign language.

A couple of nights ago, on Yom Kippur* night, I had a dream. In my dream I am with a group during a session. I am one of the group members, a tall, dark woman with a long purple dress. I am also an invisible observer, watching me and all the rest. I see the many faces of people I wrote about, and some strangers as well. It is the last meeting of our group. Very moving. I feel how sad it is to say good-bye. Searching for the group leader, I realize she has gone already. Now it's my turn to leave, too.

The morning after, I recalled the dream and realized that I had said good-bye to this book. It is ready to go.

Jerusalem
September 1977

*The Jewish Day of Atonement

Acknowledgments

A word for all the people who made this endeavor possible. The list is practically endless.

My parents taught me respect for the written word and, in respecting and saving my earliest creative products, have built in me the knowledge that I could write. My husband and children provided me with warmth and courage, thus creating the conditions I needed for this work. Jim Simkin of Big Sur, California, has been my constant guide in Gestalt therapy. My conversations with him, in real life and on the empty chair, have repeatedly given me a renewed sense of direction.

The deepest gratitude I owe is, naturally, toward my clients, group members, and interviewees. In confiding in me and in giving me permission to write, they laid the path upon which I am treading. This book is theirs as much as it is mine.

People who read the manuscript in its different phases were also of great help to me. In Amherst, Massachusetts, where I started to write during my sabbatical, colleagues from the Psychology Department, in particular Harold Raush and Sheldon Cashdan, made some very helpful comments, while my friends and group members of the Everywoman Center—Ute, Arleen, and many others—shared my progress and crises as only sisters can.

As various ideas about the final conception of the book were evolving, I got immensely important suggestions from David and Sheila Rothman of New York and from André Schiffrin of Pantheon Books, all of whom visited Jerusalem in the spring of 1977. This started a long correspondence relationship with André Schiffrin, joined later by Donna Bass, who edited the book with great care and understanding, and helped me in overcoming the barriers of writing in a foreign language for a foreign audience.

In Israel, my co-workers—Amalia Koriat, Anat Ninio, Zev Klein, and Charles Greenbaum—were more than willing to support, review, encourage, and comment throughout the long process. Chaim Kuperman and Ruth Butler made extremely worthwhile revisions, Meir Perlow greatly helped in editing first drafts of the manuscript, and Elisheva May was the ever-loyal typist. Karen Sitton, our librarian, assisted in preparing the reading list for the book, and the Frankel Fund of the Psychology Department, the Hebrew University of Jerusalem, financed the final preparation of the manuscript.

To all these people and agencies I am deeply indebted for making this book a reality.

_____ Part **1**

When Cannons Are Stilled, Let Voices Be Heard

Six Wars _____

Presently, it is the fall of 1977. My work on the book is almost done. Will this book be of interest in the fall of 1978, when it will, presumably, appear in print? Just as for people living on a volcano, the answer is definitely: "Yes." All eruptions are the same: the lava pours down the slopes, sweeping whatever stands in its path, covering fields with ashes and debris. Lives are suddenly terminated. After a while, people come back, and life returns to normal. "Normal" here means waiting for the next convulsion.

This is a book about Israel, about people living their normal lives constantly in the shadow of war. Co-existence with war has been a central factor in Israel's history from its establishment in 1948, and even earlier, but the threat of defeat and individual loss has grown dramatically since the Yom Kippur War of 1973. The presence of war permeates all facets of life, while the promise of peace seems far from actualization.

But the book is not only about Israel, for most of the people of the world share, in principle, the same or similar fate. Furthermore, living with war probably does not differ from life under other ongoing stress conditions, like living near a volcano or suffering from a chronic disease. Experiences such as terror and mourning, and avenues of recovery from them, are universal, although different individuals of different nations or cultures express and deal with them in different ways.

What are the psychological effects of the presence of war on people who live and grow in this country? What are the best means of coping with this reality?

It would be very difficult to receive answers to these questions from the "professional" writers about war. The generals have to aggrandize their deeds; the politicians must cover up their blunders; the journalists need to search for the exciting; and the social scientists try to impose structure where chaos reigns. It is relatively rare that those who actually do the fighting, or their families—people without any ulterior motives except their own survival and the fulfillment of their duties—get the right of speech. Moreover, when this right is granted to people who are psychologically trained to be aware of their feelings and experiences, as well as sensitive to and observant of others, we might get a different story, as yet untold.

•   •   •   •

The war of October 1973 was the sixth war I have experienced in my lifetime. These different wars will creep into the story again and again, so I will put them down in chronological order.

There was World War II, of course, which shook the whole world from 1939 to 1945. In those days, Palestine, or "Eretz Israel," was under the British mandate. Jews living there were not as bothered by the actual war in the Middle East as by the whispered rumors, and later by the widespread news, about the genocide of our people in Europe. The holocaust is still a part of our present awareness in Israel. I have but vague memories of this period. My parents, in Tel Aviv, moved me, a baby, to safety in a village nearby. Later, right after the war, my father went on a rescue mission, spending a whole year in Europe, leaving my mother with us, three infants, in Jerusalem. I remember only the day of his return.

The War of Independence immediately followed the U. N. decision to establish the sovereign Jewish state of Israel, in November 1947. It continued off and on until the winter of 1949, when Egypt signed a cease-fire agreement, which was followed, that same year, by similar agreements with Lebanon, Jordan, and Syria. I was nine years old at the time and distinctly remember the nightly trips from our home in Tel Aviv to the neighborhood underground shelter, where we went when the town was bombed from the air. I also recall my father accompanying the first convoy to break the siege of Jerusalem—the Burma Road—and us children collecting bullet shells in the streets.

Then, the Sinai campaign in 1956 against Egypt. We were victorious, occupying the Sinai Desert and handing it back to the Egyptians a few months later. My parents were then on board a boat, returning from Europe; and I recall our anxiety, three teenagers alone at home, when the news of war was broadcast. A kind aunt rushed over to take care of us, and we spent the night in the shelter at her house.

My fourth war was the Six-Day War of 1967, a glorious victory following a long, anxiety-ridden waiting period. This was the third shelter I got to know intimately, this time with my three-year-old son. It was a huge shelter shared by about fifty women and children who lived in our apartment house. The men were all mobilized, of course. Together we calmed the children down, waiting for news, listening to the cannons and mortar shells fighting the battle of Jerusalem.

Immediately afterward, the War of Attrition started, a static, somewhat undeclared war that continued through 1970. Daily, our soldiers on the east bank of the Suez Canal exchanged fire with the Egyptians on the west bank. Similar conditions existed on the Syrian and Jordanian fronts, and people were being killed in a slow, constant succession—day in and day out. We spent a year in California during that period and discovered that anxiety grows with distance from the battlefield, and that the need to return home is stronger than all the attractions of a peaceful yet foreign land.

The Yom Kippur War of 1973, or the October War, is the last war I have been through. My husband and son praying in the synagogue, I was resting with my three-year-old daughter, exhausted from the fast, when the sudden siren woke us up. Dazed and half-dressed we ran into our new shelter to share the surprise with an old couple and an Orthodox family. The striking scene of Orthodox Jews driving their cars on the holy day while still fasting greeted me in the streets. The command to preserve life overrides the Sabbath restrictions.

The Yom Kippur War was my first as a psychotherapist, trained to listen to and help others rather than to tend to my own needs. Yet, I was fully aware that in others I found many reflections of myself, of my various selves. This is the source of my deep involvement in this business of war and peace, and of my attempt to finish it, partially, through this book.

Yet finishing this business, like finishing the business of life itself, is impossible. War is part of our daily life here; one can accept it or reject it, cope with it or deny it—it is still right here. I have met people who claim they accept the war as a fact of life, a problem of living. I have met many people who revolt against this fact and look for political solutions or a way to escape. I have met even more people who repress the whole matter and lead their lives as if all were normal. But I have never met one Israeli who loves war or fully enjoys it. As for me, carrying my memories of these four different shelters, I violently hate wars and am frightened by them. I hope for peace in our area and am afraid to hold on to this hope. Yet, after all is said and done, I accept war as an inseparable element of my life. One of the things I have learned from my therapy work is that I may revolt and accept at the same time.

On War and Sanity

As much as we accept that this is our destiny for now in this country, that in order to live in Israel one must take war in stride, the psychological reality of our existence here is rather intricate. Not only do people have to face war as soldiers, risking their lives, or as soldiers' relatives, waiting for their dear ones to return safely, but, here in Israel, people have to face a series of wars, none of which seems to be final. This repetitive occurrence of wars in one's lifetime, the certainty of another approaching war, is probably unique to our area. Psychologically, I believe this is different from experiencing one war as an isolated event, which is part of one's past. In Israel, war is part of the past, present, and future of each individual. One has to prepare for the next one, hoping to postpone it as long as possible, yet waiting. Questions like "If I was lucky the last few times, won't my luck run out the next time?" and "Will my son have to be a combat soldier, too?" are very real and painful for Israelis, not just invented future catastrophes we all carry within us.

The need to adjust to this reality raises the questions: What is necessary for the welfare of the country? What is best for the well-being of the individual citizen? Sometimes it may seem as if the answers are incompatible. The country needs efficient soldiers and builders; it encourages superior performance. Individuals need a climate in which to grow, to become what they can and wish. There is, however, one very basic common ground; namely, society must be interested in the sanity of its members, so that they, in turn, will be able to contribute more to it. This is frequently forgotten or neglected in reality.

Sanity and its requirements can also be debated. I believe that it involves being able to admit and experience the negative aspects of our life as well as the positive ones. To experience fear, grief, or even despair is better than total denial; it may start the building of inner strength. For that, one has to be aware of one's weak parts as well as the strong and the confident. In my work, I've always felt some progress has been achieved when "heroes" admitted feelings of inadequacy of some kind, as much as when heartbroken people have established contact with their hidden strength. This is the way of becoming sound and prepared for whatever may come.

One question, of course, is that of timing; everything in its proper time. The full-fledged emotional experience may, indeed, be more appropriate after the battle than during the time of its occurrence. When army psychiatrists are quoted as saying that a certain indifference is "functional" for a soldier, they may be right for the limited period of fighting. But it is doubtful whether this "functional indifference" would be helpful in preparing this soldier for the next war he may have to fight, or whether it produces sound citizens between the wars. My sense of timing prescribes that when the guns are silent, it is time for people to speak.*

Consequently, a friend, a relative, or a group of people with whom it is permissible to share those feelings—even if they are highly unpopular and counternormative—to express them and receive reactions to them is essential for psychological survival in our part of the world. This has become more evident after the Yom Kippur War, in which we suffered very heavy casualties and our so-called invulnerability was seriously shaken. Expressing the bad feelings involved with the war is not dangerous for the morale of the people or for the excellence of our military performance. If anything, the opposite is true. Blocking and

*A similar literary attempt with this aim in mind is *The Seventh Day: Soldiers' Talk About the Six-Day War.* Avraham Shapira, ed. (New York: Charles Scribner's Sons, 1971). In contradistinction to my work, it is based completely on interviews and deals largely with political and directly war-related topics.

repression lead to an enormous increase in hidden sorrows and fears, the end result of which may be the turning of people into aimless robots lacking inner devotion.

This belief has not been commonly accepted in Israel. I have heard of army commanders who have developed the idea of soldiers without feelings, who talk about education for the control, even the repression, of all emotions. I have never accepted this as a feasible goal nor one I would like to see accomplished.

Advocating the expression of feelings, one must not neglect the other aspect of the process of growth, the integration of these feelings with the total personality. This is what my group work has been leading to, a difficult aim that is sometimes reached but often missed.

Other points of view see additional elements as necessary for the sound coping with our conditions. People mentioned the importance of support from one's group—the famous camaraderie of warriors—as well as political awareness, education for a love of Israel, Jewish faith, and a knowledge of our origins and history. Theirs might be alternative approaches to sanity or, perhaps, something that can eventually be combined with the psychological outlook.

● ● ● ●

The attitudes and beliefs of the people whose stories make up this book vary as much as their experiences and personalities. These are the stories of people who live in Israel and who, in their own ways, talk about its wars.

The "language" of the sessions, as well as the manner in which they evolve, derives from Gestalt therapy, an approach to human growth that I learned from Dr. James Simkin of California. The work was done almost exclusively in groups, which were conducted from 1970 to 1977 and recorded immediately following each session.

One point should be made very clear: since the term Gestalt *therapy* will be repeatedly used, it might create the impression that our stories deal with "maladjusted" or "abnormal" individuals and can, therefore, be considered as marginal experiences not characteristic of the Israeli society at large. This was certainly not the case. Except for two individuals who came with the admitted motive of seeking help (cases recorded in "With an Intact Body" and "A Silent Gap"), all the records of the sessions are based on work with psychology and social-work students in training for psychotherapy, or with young mental-health professionals in growth/training workshops.

All names, as well as identifying details, have been changed, and the people I could contact have gladly given me permission to write about them. "It is an important story to tell," they said. "The world should know of the other aspect of war, the private aspect that is not measured by victories, territories, or numbers; war as experienced by real people rather than impersonal nations or international leaders." To be the group leader of these people has been my greatest privilege.

Overview of Gestalt Therapy ___

Gestalt therapy is a name for a philosophy, a psychological theory, and a therapeutic technique based on the contribution of Fritz Perls.* Since its main forte is *doing* rather than *talking about,* many of the available theoretical formulations of this approach lack clarity, and the best way to fully comprehend Gestalt therapy is through the experiential mode. Though reading the records of the sessions to be presented in Part II of the book is some way to experience Gestalt therapy, albeit vicariously, and is thus, from what would be assumedly the opinion of Fritz Perls, preferable to an attempt to describe the approach in any systematic manner, some readers may profit from an overview of the assumptions, aims, and techniques that underlie the present work.

Recently, there has been a growing number of books and papers that provides comprehensive explications of Gestalt therapy. Since the focus of the present book is on Israel rather than on therapy or psychological theory, the following section on Gestalt therapy is merely a shorthand presentation.

Gestalt is a German word meaning "whole" or "configuration." It was used by Perls to convey his belief that people are total organisms functioning as wholes; that there is no sense in dividing mind from body, consciousness from unconsciousness, knowing from feeling, etc. According to German Gestalt psychology, the gestalt as a whole is more than the sum total of its

*The references to the books upon which this review is based are listed in the suggested reading section at the end of the book. This review stems also from my personal training in Gestalt therapy with Dr. James S. Simkin.

elements; and in Perls's translation into therapy, that is the sense of integration of the various personal elements, of becoming a centered being who is smoothly functioning and flowing, in contact with himself and his surroundings rather than split and fractioned into uncoordinated parts. On a different level, following the Gestalt-school laws of perception—where it could be demonstrated that the incomplete gestalt creates pressure for closure; and once this is achieved, it fuses with the background, letting another figure emerge—Perls claimed that human needs keep exerting influence as long as they are not met. Therefore, unrecognized, unexpressed needs become "unfinished business" that tie down attention, thus reducing the flexibility of the person and his ability to cope with and adapt to new situations and demands.

The aim of therapy is, therefore, to bring to closure incomplete gestalten by focusing awareness in the now and leading people to experience how they block themselves. Awareness leads to growth, namely, the re-owning of split-off parts of the personality. Furthermore, directing the individual to maintain maximal awareness, stressing feeling and sensing the body and the surroundings rather than thinking about past events or future plans, would lead, according to Gestalt therapy, to a continuous flow of figure-ground need-satisfaction processes, thus ensuring healthy functioning. Awareness is, therefore, both the aim and the means of Gestalt therapy. It is the primary tool for effecting change, leading to closure, and thus clearing the scene for a new gestalt; it is also the basic characteristic of the healthy personality. From a different point of view, awareness is the path toward personal responsibility or, as Perls put it, "response-ability." Once we become aware of the various alternatives before us and the way we make our choice from them, we assume responsibility for ourselves.

By now it must be pretty clear that, with all his originality, Perls drew heavily from several sources. Briefly, from Freudian psychoanalysis Perls adopted the notion of the organism as driven toward need satisfaction and the important mechanisms of introjection and projection. From Reich Perls drew upon bringing the body into psychotherapy, using body language and body symbolism. From the existentialists he incorporated the basic concept of responsibility, the focus on the experience of the present moment, and the preference for "what is" rather than what "should be." Finally, from Gestalt psychology Perls borrowed his terms and accepted the approach to the organism as a whole and the basic claim that gestalten are dynamic, that they press toward closure. To all these, one must add the impact of Eastern philosophies, which helped shape many of Perls's ideas, such as the direction to slow down and get in touch with basic processes, and the seeming paradox of changing through becoming more of what one is rather than through trying to be different.

The actual practice of Gestalt therapy, which is largely based on the above-mentioned assumptions, is usually carried out in groups rather than individually and is characterized by direct communication that is present-centered and focuses on the awareness continuum between an active therapist and a responsible participant who volunteers to "work." The therapist may use various games and techniques designed to enhance awareness and bring external situations into the here and now of the group, yet by no means are these strict rules to be followed. In fact, the therapist is encouraged to be spontaneous and creative, and to express his/her personal reactions freely.

The following are some samples of Gestalt therapy techniques. "Centering" is achieved through working with splits and polarities. It is believed that as long as the person experiences only the extremes of any continuum, he has no center; there is a repeated struggle without resolution. The work of the therapist is to let the person experience his polarities, and then to facilitate integration and reconciliation of the opposing parts. Providing for the dialogue between the two alien or hostile roles is one of the routes toward achieving this aim.

Using the dialogue technique, the therapist suggests that the patient experiment by taking each part of the conflict or split in turn and having a confrontation between them (e.g., the strong me and the weak me, the "top dog" making demands and the "underdog" ever promising to comply in the future), switching and shuttling between the two polarities until a sense of balance or compromise is achieved. Another use of the dialogue technique is for re-enacting past unfinished business in expressing blocked feelings toward significant others, then changing roles and responding. A similar technique is used for working on dreams and fantasies, which are considered to be extremely important in providing existential messages in disguise. In dream work people are asked to re-live the dream as if it were happening in the present, then to identify with several of the objects which appear in the dream by becoming each one in turn or by having encounters between them. In this way people may advance toward an understanding of their various parts, re-owning projected, missing aspects of their personality, integrating the opposites, and developing a center.

With these techniques in mind, some of the apparent outstanding features of Gestalt therapy can now be understood, namely, the "hot seat" and the "empty chair." The hot seat was used by Perls as a place near him one volunteered to take in order to work with the therapist in the presence of the group. Although it may look like a gimmick, it designates in a nutshell some of the main characteristics of this approach, namely, the availability of the therapist (contrary to his/her initiative or control) and the responsible act of a willing participant to open up, share, and interact with the therapist in the here and now.

The empty chair's roles are manifold in helping to dramatize the "presence" of specific parts of the individual or significant others in his life when he creates his dialogues, switches roles, etc. Both actual "chairs"—as well as other technical aspects of the approach—can, of course, be dispensed with at the therapist's preference. Presumably it is possible to carry out Gestalt therapy with the aims and assumptions described above with or without the chairs or any such external features of the approach.

More significant than the techniques are some of the basic attitudes of Gestalt therapists toward their clients. These attitudes may be all presented under the heading of taking responsibility, and they stand out particularly vis-à-vis other therapeutic schools. The Gestalt therapist rejects the role of the helper, except in the sense of being with the client and available for work. The therapist is trained to be aware of how the patient tries to get support from others rather than to provide his/her own. The therapist tries to avoid getting sucked in and taking care of the patient, and to let the patient discover how he avoids taking responsibility for himself. (It is illuminating to change "I can't" into "I won't" and "I need" into "I want.") This involves, according to Perls, the necessity of timely "skillful frustration" of the client's manipulative roles, devising behavior that stops him from his usual roles—e.g., helplessness—and attempts to make him act out of his own creativity on his own behalf. This focuses frequently on arriving at the point of impasse, the place where the client realizes that he cannot move on, while he is prevented from taking refuge in his accustomed roles. By encouraging the person to let be and to allow himself to be stuck, including all the painful feelings involved, many people will discover new awareness and ways of being, and some of them may make the fundamental shift into self-reliance.

As the reader follows the transcripts of the sessions in Part II of the book, the actual way in which these concepts materialize into events taking place in the therapeutic encounter will be unfolded, and some deviations from the outlined theory and techniques may also be occasionally detected.* One point must be further clarified. As was elaborated above, Gestalt therapists differ from many of the therapists we know in certain important ways. In Gestalt therapy, we do not interpret or ask why; we concentrate on the awareness-focusing question of "how." "Why" is considered a "dirty" word; it leads to an endless

---

*As I judge myself against the principles outlined above, I often arrive at the verdict that I sinned in being too human, namely, more supportive and tolerant than a Gestalt therapist "should" be. At the same time, I recall that all external "should's" are questioned by Perls and his followers, who advise to accept no "should" or "ought" other than one's own. Presently, I accept my style of conducting Gestalt therapy as my own way, the way in which I want to act and through which I can accomplish more than in any dictated form.

chasing after reasons and explanations, frequently concentrating on the past and always detracting energy and attention from real initiative for change into intellectual reasoning. (Simkin named it, appropriately, "jump on the why-because merry-go-round.") Furthermore, the Gestalt approach is characterized by an utmost valuation of actuality in terms of stressing the body and the senses, and in terms of accepting images and utterances for what they are rather than as accepted symbols for hidden meanings known to the therapist. The therapist is therefore not leading (or not supposed to lead) into the deep, concealed realms he/she has learned about, such as sex or aggression drives, dependence or alienation problems, or any such basic domains that he/she believes to be generally significant for human beings. Rather, as Simkin put it, the therapist is like a midwife, following a process, facilitating it, but not dictating its course or goal. Following whatever the person sets up without previous assumptions, maps, or plans is the state of mind of the Gestalt therapist, hereby again indicating respect and appreciation for the client, his self-reliance, and his responsibility.

Yet presuming complete non-theory is, of course, naïve. In the moment of interaction, the therapist reacts to what stands out mostly in his/her eyes, according to his/her personality and the salience of certain momentary needs, values, or interests in the therapist's mind. But, to say the least, if—following the popular stereotypes of psychotherapy—the reader expects to find in the present work an exploration of sexual frustrations or riddles of early childhood complexes, he will need to look elsewhere.

In the records of the Gestalt sessions presented in this book, several other issues will be repeatedly encountered and explored: the expression of fear, guilt, and grief concerning personal situations resulting from the wars; the split of heroism versus weakness; and attending to the needs of the individual versus the public aims. These are, mainly, major dilemmas in the life of Israelis, put before the reader in the Gestalt manner. At the same time, they are probably reflections of some of my personal unfinished business, which added importance to these figures when they were emerging in the foreground.

Finally, although we explored with the reader Gestalt therapy to some extent, it should be repeated that this book is not aimed as a study of psychological theory or technique, nor is it a set of success stories of Gestalt therapy. Rather, it is an attempt to use the therapy context for an intimate, sincere angle of observation of Israelis in their coping with life and war in Israel.

The Groups

Tuesday afternoon: my new group is coming. I am the leader now, very alone. Am I good enough? And who expects me to be that good? "You top dog, sit quietly now, I am not going to have any arguments with you today. I want to be in full contact with these people." Top dog, the part within us which is always making demands, takes his place under the chair, hiding for a while. He can be controlled, thank heavens—no, thanks to me. I can control. I am responsible.

We have a long red room. The curtains are orange-red, and the afternoon sun shines through the western windows, coloring the room in warm red. The ceiling is made of large squares, white and gray, and some of the light bulbs are missing. I never look at the ceiling unless the group is silent and I withdraw. We learn that silence is acceptable and more worthwhile than small talk. A large picture hangs on the wall. Ruth says it looks like vegetable soup, Yuval says it is paradise, and Orit says it does not mean a thing. We are all different and unique.

Sometimes we are out on the grass or at home. We play Alice in Wonderland. Explore your wonderland, Alice; what do you find? We play being blind, letting another be our guide. We learn to trust. We make things of clay; we imagine, we play— now be the inverted tower that you have made or the wild horse. "Lose your mind and come to your senses." "Be in the moment." "Stay with it, don't push."

The group is a serious thing. People work here; work and games are not that different. I am sad and glad, playful and serious—these are all my parts. Can I put the puzzle together?

Being these parts is "working"—being in the now, with yourself, with me. Putting the parts together is "integration" and discovery of our own inner "center."

Sometimes there is silence and boredom and futility. A sense of losing the way. People sense my pressure, my demand: if you come here, you are supposed to work.

—I am not ready to work. The reasons—several. I am afraid.

—I don't have problems [could happen] and what is "problems" anyway?

—I deserve to be loved here even if I don't do a thing.

—I don't hear what you said. I hear the sound you are making. Can you produce some more?

Ron takes the hot seat, which is just another chair, next to me. His gesture means: I want to work now. As people volunteer to work, they use this chair and leave it when they feel they have finished. This becomes the rhythm of our work. Often we stay in our places and use the hot seat as a term only; the hot seat is, then, wherever a working person happens to be sitting.

We have a second distinguished chair in the room, the empty chair, for parts or people who are not actually there. Our empty chair hosts many: Father, Mother, the Wise Therapist; the stupid me, the demanding me, the child in me. All these, and many more, come and go in this reconstructed reality, in our long red room. Sometimes people change, all of a sudden, and sometimes they drop out. We become more aware, and gradually share more of our inner and outer realities.

Michal reports a dream about the group. In her dream she walks by old palaces and fancy castles until she finds our group in a white, modern house that has just been built on a hill in Jerusalem. It stands all alone in an uncultivated field. The group meets on the first floor, in a great white expanse. All the windows are wide open, fresh air and sunlight penetrate, flood the room. There are many people in the group, more than we really have in it. Yet Michal knows them all and feels close to and familiar with them. All she remembers is the warm open space, the feeling of closeness, and the fact that we scheduled our meeting for the next week at the same place.

Each dream is different, a separate reality. In our work we touch on many topics, as there are many individuals. Yet we are also similar in many ways. We all live in Israel, and our personal lives reflect the stormy happenings of our country. War, peace, fear, fate, and religion—all are frequently presented in the groups before, and mostly after, the war of October 1973. But also, as in other parts of the world, women ask: What is it like to be a woman? And youths ask: What is it like to be grown-up? We are all searching for our identity in the midst of stress, crisis, and simple everyday reality. As we grow, we find out that the answers are not out there; they are here and now. And sometimes there aren't any.

I see these people for a year or for very intensive weekends. We become very close, and separation is difficult. Some of them write to me: poems and papers, dialogues and dreams. Some sort of an integration. And out of these, and my notes and tapes of our sessions, I have written this book.

Reactions

Before broaching the presentation of the various parts of this book, a word of caution is needed regarding the generality of the issues or the conclusions which may be drawn.

This book is by no means a scientific summary of objective material, the number of cases is not great, and the points which were chosen for elaboration reflect my own approach and personality. I am fully aware that another individual may have created different interactions with the same people of my tales. Another person may have reacted to other needs of theirs, may have led an exploration of different areas, and, thus, another story might have emerged. I take responsibility for my share in producing these interactions and, therefore, these tales.

Yet there is a broader notion to be considered; namely, to what extent were the members of my groups, or the people I have chosen to interview, so-called typical Israelis, representative of the various subgroups of our society? Clearly, they were not. As previously mentioned, they are university students and young mental-health professionals, therefore of relatively high educational and socioeconomic levels. Their ability for verbal expression is superb, and they admire openness and self-exploration. Some may consider them oversensitive or spoiled, the lucky ones for whom war is the "only" hardship in life. It may very well be so; it is difficult to guess if similar profiles would emerge from conversations with laborers or housewives. Personally, I imagine they would. I believe that these students were willing and able to express the issues which, in many variations, are indeed the basic issues of our life in Israel. Yet, obviously, this book is not meant to verify this belief.

Finally, the problem of generalization has another aspect that must be considered. This book is a set of cases and interviews which are centered around the war. In focusing on this, and taking as a starting point the problem of adaptation to a prolonged war situation, the book may have erred in creating, perhaps, an impression of a constant preoccupation with war, death, and the difficult conditions of life in Israel. A book based on a collection of material that was originally scattered in terms of people and time may foster an illusion of one concentrated, continuous rap session of immense intensity. This was not the case in reality; and if it were, I guess it would have been too hard to bear. As much as war and peace are central to our lives in this troubled area, we are not constantly under the shadow of this awareness. Normal life, in reality and in fantasy, goes on in all spheres as in other parts of the world. The heroes of this book work and study, form intimate relationships, have babies, and travel—and, with all these, the painful aspects of their life exist as well.

The book has two main parts. One (Part II: "The Unfinished Business of War in Israel") consists of selected transcripts of work done in Gestalt therapy groups from 1970 to 1977, and includes eight sections, grouped according to similarity of content or to proximity in time of the sessions. They cover many topics, ranging from war, death, and bereavement, as well as the holocaust and its associations with the current situation, to wider manifestations and repercussions of the prolonged war in the family and in the attachment of Israelis to their country. The permeation of war themes into our psychological reality is further exemplified by several dreams about war, which—as discovered in working on them—actually stood for inner struggles and personal conflicts.

The second part (Part III: "Peacetime Conversations About War") is based on interviews conducted in 1977,* a relatively

---

*All interviews were conducted between March and July, before peace talks between Sadat and Begin started to take place.

peaceful year. Whereas all the casework mentioned above dealing with the topic of war was spontaneously started by the group members themselves, indicating their need to express, and arrive at clarification of, these issues, the interview material was initiated by me. Out of the special atmosphere of the group, Israelis of the same age group and background as those of the group participants, men and women, were confronted with direct questions regarding the effects of war on their lives. This method made it possible to uncover additional perspectives and points of view which were not in focus in the group work, and these were recorded in the last part of the book.

Tin Soldiers on
Jerusalem Beach _____

"Tin Soldiers on Jerusalem Beach" is the name of Chana's dream. It has become, for me, a name of many meanings.

Tin soldiers are here for good. Made of tin, they are permanent and functional. They never die. They certainly do not feel. Do they exist? And what is inside them?

Jerusalem Beach is not to be found on any geographic map. It is a dreamland where even tin soldiers have a life of their own. Here on earth, Jerusalem Beach is an improbable location, perhaps as improbable as this country we are trying to defend and which exists in spite of all rational calculations.

Real soldiers in Jerusalem alleys are our daily reality. This book deals with a separate reality, one of inner-space experience, fantasy, and emotion. Can these two realities be united?

There is no beach in Jerusalem, and soldiers are full-sized human beings. Yet Jerusalem exists, and Chana exists, and dreams exist as well.

_____ Part **2**

The Unfinished Business of War in Israel

War as a Symbol _____

Introduction

The salience of war in the Israeli reality, the daily vision of armed soldiers in the streets, the frequency of being called to reserve duty, the constant awareness of the need to defend and prepare for possible war—all these, and many other signs of this reality, render war inseparable from our mental life. This opening section will provide three examples of the infiltration of war into the inner space in terms of representing other psychological issues. It will demonstrate the fact that war is not only a reality with which Israelis must cope but also a symbol that conveys their inner struggle with strength, anger, freedom, and other apparently non-war-related concepts. Although the images of the following dreams and fantasies derive from our daily reality of soldiers, refugees, and physical danger, their personal meaning, as revealed through Gestalt work, is of a much broader and universal nature.

In the cases selected to exemplify this phenomenon, three different personal issues are explored: the apparent contradiction between the schlemiel—physically clumsy and inefficient yet craving for poetry, music, and philosophy—and the tough, courageous, adaptable command-car driver in the desert; the search for a stable identity challenged by the urge to become a freedom-seeking wanderer; and the conflict between the adult's constant preoccupation with daily chores and future trifles and the child's wish to be spontaneous and enjoy the present. All these are instances of the search for an integrated identity, a combining of one's various parts; indeed, they are clear manifestations of well-known dilemmas of internal growth.

Yet, on the surface, following the lines of the stories as they are presented by the three individuals, we find very clear Israeli images. In his first dream, David is concerned with missing the war. He goes through a chain of events in which he loses his way, his unit, his gun, and his driver; wanders through the desert; and finally arrives too late. His second dream describes a different military experience. Returning from a military operation, he is unharmed and equipped, somehow, with two guns instead of one. Ella describes another very Israeli picture: an Arab refugee with her old donkey trying to cross the Jordan River in no-man's land between Israel and Jordan, whose soldiers stand guard on both banks, watching. Finally, Chana tells a dream about an invasion by enemy soldiers on a peaceful beach; and a mother and daughter cruelly interrupted in the midst of their playful morning in the sand, driven in search of shelter in a deserted city.

On a certain level, therefore, these dreams and images are the personal expression of very specific components of the reality in Israel. They convey David's wish never to participate in another war and his relief that he has returned alive from former ones; Ella's guilt feelings concerning the Arab refugees who have had to abandon their homes; and Chana's fear of being surprised by the enemy and her need to protect her children from an assault. This surface meaning was especially evident in Chana's dream, which occurred a week after a deadly attack by Arab commandos on a beach hotel in Tel Aviv, a fact that was mentioned by Chana as she presented her dream.

Yet, in Chana's work on her dream, as well as in the other two cases, completely different circles were revealed and explored. Apparently, there are many paths which may be embarked upon by the individual confronting his dream, many messages to assimilate, many circles of which the dreamer may choose one to close. Following my beliefs, I have always made a conscious attempt to let the dreamer select his own circle to close. His nature and needs, the period with its outstanding events, the group with its dominant atmosphere, and probably myself as a factor in the immediate environment determine the actual path taken.

It is tempting to speculate what leads a person to choose one message rather than another, to focus on the inner struggle rather than on the external threat. For one, their individual needs to work out their internal conflicts may have been, at the moment, stronger than their fear of danger or their wish to share memories of war; or, perhaps, they were trying to escape from wars, to avoid dealing with their meaning, thus preferring to concentrate on personal dilemmas. Finally, the war contents of the dreams may have been so obvious and familiar that they seemed, to the dreamers, unnecessary to explore.

Whatever the correct explanation, we in Israel are indeed faced with war in these two different yet interlocking spheres: the "real" war outside and the personal wars within. Is one sphere more "important," more "central," more "true"? Obviously, there is no answer. Both deserve our attention. Periodically, I have thought that the war outside, and the mental energy it demands, frequently obscures internal struggles, reduces awareness of them, and decreases the chances of their solution. (This is one aspect of the psychology of heroism which will recur later in the book.) Yet, direct confrontation with the war out there and its personal implications is not easy either. This will become evident as we go forth.

Unknown Driver in the Desert

David was born and educated in Europe. Coming to Israel at the age of eighteen, he served in the army. He speaks a fluent Hebrew, yet he is not a sabra*; he did not receive the "toughening" Israeli education, and his military achievements somehow do not seem to correspond to his mild, slightly foreign-looking appearance.

DAVID   I had a dream about the war. I have dreamt it several times since the Yom Kippur War. It's a dream about how I missed the war.

---

*Israeli nickname for the Israeli-born

At this point people in the group interrupt with various comments like: "You wish you would miss the next war, that's clever of you!" and "Don't worry, you won't miss it. If you can't find the war, it will find you."

DAVID   Look, I am not stupid. I have been trying to analyze the dream by myself, as I do with dreams of my clients. So, of course, I know it must be my wish not to undergo another war. Don't we all have the same wish? Moreover, you will be pleased to hear that I dream about losing my gun.

Here David waits meaningfully for the reaction, and the group responds with laughter.

DAVID   Everybody knows what a gun stands for in psychoanalytic terms, so all right, it's a dream about my fear of becoming impotent. Now all this is wide open, but I feel the dream has another message for me.
I   It's funny. We haven't even heard the dream, and we're already arguing about its analysis.
DAVID   Since I am well acquainted with my dream—
I   You thought we might skip it? No. Tell me the dream in first person, present tense, as if you see the things now.

The group settles down for the serious business of sharing David's work. I think about the opening discussion, with its humorous tone, demonstrating our common reluctance to again face the war, with its threatening meaning for each one of us.

DAVID   In my dream I am standing in line with many soldiers, since we are supposed to start our march to the battlefield any minute. The order to start is announced, and I begin to put on my gear. As I try to assemble the various parts, I feel very clumsy and inadequate. It takes me a long time to get ready, and in the meantime the whole unit is gone. I am alone in the desert. I have a very strong sense of my obligation to join my unit in the battle, but I don't know the direction they have taken. I feel lost. Inexplicably, a command car with an unknown driver shows up and takes me through the desert to a camp where I find my unit. However, now I realize that my gun is missing. I go to search for one in the storage area and cannot find any. Finally I find a pistol, but as I try it I discover it does not work. All this takes a while, and in the meantime I hear that two thousand six hundred soldiers were killed in the first day of the war. I realize that my unit, for which I was searching, does not exist any more, and I missed the war.

I   What is the dominant feeling of this dream for you?

DAVID   My feelings of inadequacy, my clumsiness, and my anger at myself for being that way. This is a feeling with which I am very familiar. In the army, even in officers training course, I often felt clumsy, slow, and, in general, inadequate. I am the schlemiel type. I keep daydreaming or solving a problem in my head, and in the meantime I don't manage to accomplish what is demanded with the necessary speed—or, at least, I have to put lots of extra effort into being as efficient as necessary.

I   Be the unknown driver of the command car.

DAVID   I am a soldier like you, but I am completely adequate and can perform my tasks successfully. I never get lost. I am well acquainted with the desert, and have my bearings. I have all my necessary equipment with me, my firearms and a well-functioning car. In short, I am very competent, and I can save you.

I   Can you have the two, the unknown driver and the schlemiel, talk to each other?

DAVID   Yes, I'll start with the schlemiel.

—I have lost my unit. Can you help me find it?

—Sure I can, just hop into the car.

—Thank you. I don't know where you have come from exactly when I need you so, but I know you very well. You're this famous Israeli type who can function under all hazards and hardships. You don't think too much, but you act swiftly and effectively. You're one of those people whom I encounter in the reserves time and again. You can take the military service in your stride.

I   What does the competent driver say?

DAVID   He says: Don't be so clumsy. Don't stay behind. Come on, I'll give you a hand.

I   Two things stand out for me here. First, that you put your schlemiel part down, and the competent driver, high up. And yet, and this is the second point, there is a feeling of cooperation between the two.

DAVID   Yes, the cooperation exists once the unknown soldier shows up and finds me, the schlemiel, lost in the desert.

I   Is only the schlemiel you? You know, in Gestalt work we believe all the parts of the dream are aspects of oneself.

DAVID   I identify more easily with the weak and the incompetent part. Physically, I am not in great shape; and even if I am, I keep perceiving myself as incompetent.

I   What does that mean, "even if I am"?

DAVID   Well, outwardly, I have been functioning fairly well. Even though I keep feeling like a schlemiel inside, I finished my basic training and the officers training course with distinction. Yet, whenever I accomplish something with my body, my physical strength, I am the first to be surprised at my achievement. For instance, for years I convinced myself I was unable to dance, and especially not able to enjoy dancing.

I   And now?

David laughs gently and brushes his hair, somewhat shyly, away from his forehead.

DAVID   Well, I am OK now in this respect. One night I was very drunk at a party, and from my seat on the floor I watched everybody dancing. I was thinking that if I'd join the dance, I would certainly look ridiculous. Suddenly it occurred to me to join the dance nonetheless and to make myself look ridiculous on purpose. In this act I enjoyed myself tremendously, and gradually I felt more free and relaxed with my movements, so that I could dance without ridiculing myself. This was a case of one-trial learning. From then on I was fine at dancing.

I   You're not a schlemiel there.

DAVID   No, I am not.

I   Tell this to the driver.

DAVID   Look here, I am not a complete schlemiel. [*laughing*] I feel I am you more and more. Actually, I am not sure I even like it so much, being like you. Do you read poetry? Do you like classical music? Do you enjoy philosophical debates?

I   Does he?

DAVID   I guess not. These are the qualities of my schlemiel.

I   That's nice. So you have something to boast about in the schlemiel part.

DAVID   Yes, I realized that just now. Both roles are fine.

I   And it is not a matter of choice. You are both.

DAVID   Yes, I know. And I have to allow more space for my unknown driver.

I   Very well. Now I want you to be the desert.

David waits a moment as he reconstructs the image of the desert in his mind.

DAVID   I am the desert. I am big, enormous, yet there is no sense of form or direction in me; my landscape is very confusing to the people who try to orient themselves in me. I have these hills, and as you climb the hilltop, expecting to see the end of me, of the desert, you just see more and more of the same . . . no roads or direction . . . very confusing.

David stops here, reflecting on what he has just said.

DAVID   I know this part of me. Recently it has been very strong, and I am well acquainted with it.

I   Now be David and talk to the desert.

DAVID   You are enormous, and it isn't easy for me to orient myself within you. But I have the feeling that I'll find my way.

I   Repeat that to some of the people here.

David addresses several people: "I know that I'll find my way."

I   Finding the way has appeared in the dream before, too. When you identified with the unknown driver, who found the way for the schlemiel, there was the same message for you.

DAVID   Yes, that I can save myself and find my own way. This sentence has meaning for me on many different levels, which I don't feel I need to specify now.

We decide to stop at this point. As the people express their reactions, David adds:

DAVID   I have an afterthought. I am somewhat surprised at the things I said while working on the dream. I didn't realize that I am so well acquainted with my inner desert and my unknown driver.

At the beginning of the summer, several months after David's session, the group separated. Later, during that summer, David came to visit, telling me excitedly about his new dream, which he clearly perceived as a development of the former one, presented above. Indeed, his dream was his motivation to make that visit, since he saw it as symbolizing a certain improvement in his self-image, something he was glad to share with me after our year together in the group.

I asked David to report his dream in writing, and I received the following note, which he entitled "Two Rifles."

After we worked on the dream in the group, I had it once more, a couple of months later. At that time, the details of my dream were pretty much the same as in "Unknown Driver in the Desert." I got lost, I lost my rifle, and when I found it, it didn't work. The feeling was the same, too, of being that schlemiel, my well-known image.

A week later, however, the dream reappeared with a variation. I have the feeling it's the same dream, although many of the details have changed. Maybe it's Part Two of my old dream, which better presents where I'm at right now.

In my dream I've just completed a period of army service in which I participated in some sort of a military operation. I am going through the bureaucracy of getting released, returning all my military equipment. I already have civilian clothes on, but I'm still dirty and sweating. I stand in line, together with other soldiers of my unit, waiting for my turn.

A good friend, who is known to be a very good soldier, has also participated in the operation with me. I have returned all my stuff; and as I'm standing on that line, I suddenly discover that I have two machine guns to return, two rifles instead of one. One rifle belongs to me, and the other, to my friend. My friend has already left, and probably forgot his gun, or perhaps he left it with me so that I'd hand it in for him. I'm not quite sure.

I feel strange with two guns. I take one, my friend's rifle, and put it, for the time being, into my civilian handbag, which I have with me. I'm worrying whether they will agree to take back my friend's rifle without his being present. Yet I know that I'm the only one to worry about such matters or to get into that kind of trouble. My friend, I'm sure, always succeeds in being a good soldier without extra worries or complications.

When I woke up I realized I was much more satisfied with myself in this dream as compared to my reaction to the former dream. I don't get lost, and I end up having two rifles instead of none.

The Refugee in No-Man's Land

It is twenty minutes or so before the end of the session. Orit has finished working, and we are sharing reactions. One of the members, Ran, is talking to Orit: ". . . and I like the way you look today, the dress you have on." Orit is in a long black dress, and she says she had bought it in a refugee camp after the Six-Day War.

It seems as though we have finished with Orit's work, and then Ella speaks.

ELLA You know, I have a soft spot for refugees. The word refugee is enough to make me shiver. I think I grew up with this word: Jews being refugees in Europe, my parents searching for their families lost in the holocaust in the Second World War, and now the Arab refugees, and refugees somewhere very far away in Asia—all over the place. Do you think we have time for a story about a refugee I once saw? It is just a short story.

I   We have time, if you feel like telling your story. I am not sure, though, if we'll have time to work on it today.

ELLA   No, I just wanted to share the story with you.

Ella starts quite cheerfully, drawing a picture for us, as if it were some sort of an impersonal story. She becomes more and more serene and sad as she goes along, especially when describing the refugee woman.

ELLA   In June 1967, immediately after the Six-Day War, I was visiting my brother at his army post near one of the bridges of the Jordan River. Since I had never seen this area before, my brother offered to take me for a ride, to see the sights, especially the river. It was summer, the level of the water in the river was very low, and in certain places it could be crossed on foot. The bridge had been partly destroyed in the battle, I think. I don't quite remember. In this area, walking in the water was the only means of crossing from Israeli to Jordanian territory. My brother told me that many Arabs, new refugees, had crossed the water in the first days after the war. Soldiers watched from the two river banks—the Israeli post and the Jordanian post— those refugees crossing the Jordan in no-man's land.

As he was explaining this to me, an old woman approached with a little donkey carrying some bundles of clothing and blankets, probably all her possessions. She passed the check-point, showed some papers, and was motioned toward the other side. In her long black dress and head covering she looked like a peasant—she was barefoot and alone with her donkey. As the donkey smelled or saw the water, it protested, refusing to step into the stream. A long struggle developed, the woman trying soft words as well as her stick on the donkey's back, but the donkey was a real donkey, stubborn, standing firmly on the edge of the water, not moving an inch. Soldiers from both sides were shouting, advising, and cursing. No one would approach the place, since the narrow river with its two banks was in no-man's land. The woman looked so helpless, forlorn, with her useless donkey and those miserable bundles.

Here Ella, who had been swallowing her tears for some minutes now, bursts out crying in uncontrollable, violent sobs, during which she cannot talk or tell us the end of her story. A few minutes later, she resumes, still weeping.

ELLA   I never saw the end of the crossing. Did someone help her? My brother called me, we had to leave. She could only cross if she left her belongings behind.

As her crying subsides, Ella looks embarrassed. Our time is over, so I just say generally:

I   You are so touched because you yourself are probably the refugee. You carry these bundles, and somehow, you are stuck in no-man's land. Stay with it and feel it. Later you'll perhaps be able to go on and find your way out.

It is late, and some of the group members have to leave. Some are kind and affectionate, some are surprised by Ella's outburst. Ella looks pale and relieved, muttering that she is ashamed, she has never cried like this since she was a little girl, and in public, too. I close the session, promising Ella to work with her next week, if she wants to.

   Next week Ella starts at the beginning of the session.

ELLA   I am still puzzled by what happened last week. I did not expect it, I mean. I was completely surprised. When I started, I did not feel like crying, and in such a manner, too.

I   This story must have been very important for you.

ELLA   I guess so . . . and I tried all week to find out why or how, but I don't know.

I   How far have you gone? I mean, what did you discover about the meaning of this story for you?

ELLA   I tried to be the refugee. It went something like this: I am a refugee. I am my mother, I am my father, running away from Europe. I've left every

I   Do you feel it is your part, or are you telling us about your parents?

ELLA   That's it, you see. I don't feel it's me, therefore I've discovered very little indeed. Well, I am not special in this sense. To be Jewish in our generation is to be a refugee, in a way, or the child of one. If this is a part of me, it is a stranger. I don't know him or her.

I   Talk to this stranger.

ELLA   Hi, stranger, who are you? The stranger is veiled, I don't see his face. I don't know him. I am stuck.

I   Stay with it, don't rush.

ELLA   Stranger, are you a man or a woman? No answer. I am not getting anywhere by asking questions.

I   Try without questions, then. Make some statements.

ELLA   I don't know you. I don't see your face now. I am not sure you are the old woman under your veil. I only know that you make me very sad. I feel sad. I don't know where to go from here. I can't move.

I   Like—

ELLA   —the donkey? Yes, like the donkey. I'll be the donkey, then. I am a donkey. I am stubborn. I am not going to move anywhere. I will stay right here.

I   How do you feel as a donkey? [*laughter from the group*]

ELLA   Ugly . . . stupid, a stubborn idiot.

I   Good. Is this part of you?

ELLA   Why, sure. You don't know how stupid I can get.

I   Now, what is the other part, this side of you which is pushing the donkey to move?

ELLA   The other side. I am the woman, the refugee. Wait a minute. She is—

I   I am—

ELLA   I am without the veil now. I am not old. Actually, I am young, strong, and hopeful. I am going. I'll move, change, start all over again. Don't call me a refugee, I am not running away. I am a nomad. I am going to explore the world, to watch and see. I am not staying in one place for long. I have no connections, almost no possessions. Nothing is going to stop me.

Ella, in this role, sounds excited, full of life and energy. She looks around the room, then at me.

I   Where are you? What are you now?

ELLA   Now I recognize the parts. The donkey—the stable me, not risking anything, standing right on the spot—and the nomad—the wild, free me, unrestrained, camping wherever I please, following the winds and the seasons, free.

I   Let these two parts talk to each other.

ELLA   (as a donkey) I am not going anywhere. I am not entering the water, not crossing the river.

—Why? This is just a small river. There is no risk, I tell you. I want to go, come on. I don't want to stay forever in this no-man's land.

—Then go ahead without me. Leave me alone, I don't mind. What do you need me for?

—I don't, really.

—You don't sound convincing. If you don't need me, take off my burden and go away. You won't be so light and free with these bundles that I carry for you.

—Yes, you make my life easier, that's true. When I am tired, I ride on your back, and you carry my belongings so I can feel free. It would be better if you would come with me.

—Oh, yes? Then I have some conditions for you: Don't call me names, I am not so stupid and ugly. You don't treat me well, you despise me, yet I am your equal, you know. We are a team; we will cross this river together.

—My goodness, you are not so stupid after all. We are a team as you say. I think we are. OK, then, let's get out of here together. Find the way.

Silence and fascination.

I   This was fascinating—you are fascinating.

ELLA   I am surprised. Now I see so very clearly, they are crossing the river out of the no-man's land.

People in the group later ask Ella to clarify the symbols for them. I object. I feel that the message is loud and clear, and words of interpretation would only dissipate it. As I learn more about Ella, I perceive more and more meanings for her symbols —picking a new career, doubting her family role. She is always the stable donkey and the fleeing refugee, coexisting.

•   •   •   •

Tin Soldiers on Jerusalem Beach

CHANA   In my dream I am on Jerusalem Beach with my daughter and her friend. My daughter is pale and pretty; her friend, Miri, is robust and plain. Both of them are four years old. We are all alone on the beach, and the girls are playing in the sand. All of a sudden I see millions of soldiers coming from both north and south, marching on the sands. They look like ants from far away, but I know they are dangerous and we have to get away fast. I call the girls but they don't hear me, and later they hear but prefer to continue with their game. I get all upset, hurriedly explaining that we have to escape, or we'll be killed. They agree reluctantly, collecting their toys, and we start to march. We have to climb about a hundred steps up from the beach to the street, and then mount a very long, steep road up the hill. I am dragging the little girls after me, one on the right, one on the left. They complain they are tired and pull at my arms; it is becoming an extreme effort to move uphill, to progress, and danger is approaching from the rear. I am afraid I won't be able to make it. The streets are all empty, the shutters closed. These streets are unfamiliar under the bright sun. I knock on a door and ask for shelter. People give me water and indicate the direction to my home. There is just one more hill to climb. I wake up in a cold sweat, my arms aching.

I   What do you feel now?

CHANA   It was a nightmare. I feel as I felt while dreaming— my heart is pounding very fast, I am exhausted, tired from the effort, and I am afraid I won't make it.

I   What are you running away from?

CHANA   From the soldiers . . . these millions of tin soldiers, which in a moment will grow to become real, big ones as they come near me. They'll kill me and the little girls, or probably step on us, stamp us to death.

I   That's very frightening, but suppose these soldiers do not grow, that they remain tin soldiers or a troop of ants as you see them just now?

CHANA   I don't know. In my dream I was sure they'd grow to become millions of real enemy soldiers with rifles and all. You know, I had this dream about a week after those terrorist commandos came in their rubber boat from the sea to massacre the hotel guests in Tel Aviv. I guess that's the connection with reality. The funny thing is that here, in Jerusalem, we don't have an ocean or a beach, and the streets in my dream are unfamiliar, so maybe I was dreaming about the massacre in Tel Aviv.

I   Yes, maybe. Yet I am looking for the personal message, so try to forget reality and Tel Aviv, and let's return to the Jerusalem beach. All these soldiers are approaching. Can you be one of them?

CHANA   I am a very tiny soldier and have millions of other soldiers like me around me. I want to kill you and your girls.

I   Ask him how he can threaten you if he is so small.

CHANA   How can you kill me? You are as small as a toy tin soldier.

—I'll grow, you'll see.

—How can you grow? You exist just now, this very minute, in my dream. The way you are now cannot possibly kill me.

—But there are millions like me.

—So what? You'll only be a nuisance, like a troop of ants, no more.

Finishing her dialogue, Chana looks at me.

I   Are you still afraid?

CHANA   Not as much. I am not afraid, just nauseated, disgusted, as if expecting a whole troop of ants to start marching over my body.

I   So be the ants.

CHANA   I am an ant . . . a whole troop of ants. We can't kill you, but we can march all over you and cause you a lot of discomfort. Ugh, that's an unpleasant feeling.

I   What could these ants be? They are part of you, you know.

CHANA   I was thinking about it just now. It's me worrying too much about tiny, unimportant things, minor things which tend to appear over and over again. Did I pay for the electricity? Did I buy bread? If not, can I make it before the store closes? Did my daughter remember to take her gym shoes? Did I turn the heat off? And about the future, too. Worries about how different things will work out, great plans for minor events. These are the millions of trifles that bother me, crawl all over me like ants.

I   They prevent you from having a good time on the beach?

CHANA   Yes. They prevent me from relaxing and from paying attention to more important and joyful things in life.

I   Like what?

CHANA   Friends, sometimes, and books and playful activity. You know—the good life.

I   Tell the ants, the soldiers, whoever you see on the beach now.

CHANA   You are simply tin soldiers. You can't grow or harm me. You are ridiculous, you think you are so big and important. Go away, or even stay. I am not going to pay attention to you. I may take a broom and sweep you away, and the beach will be clean again.

I   So this is the message of your dream. You know, Chana, I don't feel completely at ease with that. I remember it was my suggestion that the soldiers may not grow to become real ones, and it is as if I have treated it as my own dream. I am not sure you would arrive at the same conclusion, which is certainly good for me.

CHANA   Oh, did you suggest that? I don't even remember now. I do feel these are my parts, completely so, and I really wish I could learn how to stop myself from worrying about trifles. I got this message. Yet, in the dream there was another aspect that impressed me very strongly. It was this painful sensation in my arms, my arms were so very tense, aching and trembling from the effort.

I   Can you feel that sensation in your arms right now?

CHANA   Yes. [*moves her arms around the chair*] It is not pain now, just tension and some tremor. Now that I said that,

I feel it even more. This trembling . . . almost showing, I am sure.

I   Let this trembling be and develop, even exaggerate, it.

CHANA   This is awkward, it is difficult.

I   Yes, I know. The difficult things are the most worthwhile to go through.

Chana moves her hands, lets them hang loosely from her shoulders, and starts to tremble slightly, then more visibly, until an exaggerated tremor is developed.

CHANA   Actually, I feel better that way, when I am not withholding the trembling. My arms are more capable of relaxing now. I feel the pain inside my arms. I am simply tired from pulling and dragging . . . the two girls are very heavy when they don't cooperate with me.

I   Talk to them.

CHANA   Listen to me, girls. If we want to get to the top of this hill, to get home at all, you have to put some effort, walk on your own, cooperate with me. Together we could make this steep hill. I myself, without your help, could never do it.

I   Whom are you talking to?

CHANA   These two little girls, the pretty and the plain. Wait a minute. It just occurred to me, I could get to the top of the hill myself if I get rid of the girls and leave them behind.

I   Could you do it?

CHANA   Mm . . . no, I don't think I could. I don't think I want to. This is my daughter, after all. I could leave her girlfriend, but I would not do that either. It would make me feel awful, worse than the pain in my arms now, I guess.

I   I'd like to hear this in a more convincing way.

CHANA   [*firmly*] These girls are with me; it's my responsibility to take care of them. I like them a lot, and we'll have to make it together.

I   OK. Now, whom are you talking to?

CHANA   Ah . . . you mean inside me? Yes, I know, the children within me, the pretty and the plain.

I   Can you be one of the girls? Which one would it be?

CHANA   Let me explain, they are both one and the same, that is, me. When I was small, I considered myself plain, I was heavy-set like this Miri of my dream. Later I grew up to be quite pretty. That does not sound too modest, I know.

I   So you are saying there is actually one little girl. How old?

CHANA   She is about six.

I   Be her for a minute.

CHANA   Very gladly.

She sounds very excited as she goes on.

CHANA   I am lovely. I am very creative, I invent all sorts of games and stories. I am wild, yet I get along with people. I am a happy child. I have the feeling everybody likes me, all is well, and there is nothing to worry about in life.

I   Do you notice what you have said just now?

CHANA   That I don't have to worry? Yes.

I   This little girl is the other end of the tin soldiers, or the ants, as you presented them before.

CHANA   You are saying they are both me, that I should integrate these parts?

I   Yes, you are acquainted with the theory all right. I suggest you talk to your girl as Chana, the grownup person.

CHANA   I'll talk to her: Don't be afraid, there is no real danger. And if we have to run away, we will stick together. I will help you, and you have to help me. You have to stand on your own feet, I know you can. I like you a lot, your smiles and faith, your absorption in your games on the beach. And your courage —you weren't afraid, only I, the grownup, was afraid. You can help me in all these, and I'll take care of the practical sides; we'll cooperate.

I   Do you think she'll accept this contract?

CHANA   I hope so. Right now I feel she may. I have a great sense of joy since I let myself be the little girl. I don't have to drag her along; she is inside me. And I am not afraid of the tin soldiers any more.

People of the group have several comments.

AMI   I watched your face as the girl, and you surely looked very young and free. I noticed how easily you can switch to the girl part, and that is what I like about you so much. Now that I think about it, this quality of the child is something I feel attracted to in many other people as well.

DAN   I have a different reaction, from an altogether different direction. As a soldier, I was somewhat disturbed by your image of the tin soldier on the nonexistent beach in Jerusalem. It is strange, but I felt insulted when you worked on that part of the dream, as if you were making fun of my serious role, depicting a small-sized futile soldier.

CHANA   Yes, I did find out how small and meaningless these soldiers are. But remember, they are my tin soldiers, the creatures of my dream, and have nothing to do with your real-life experience of being a soldier in the Israeli army.

DAN   I know you are right. It's my problem, certainly, yet I do feel somewhat insulted.

CHANA   Come on, Dan. We all see you are not a tin soldier.

DAN   I guess I am insulted because . . . because maybe sometimes I do feel like one. [*looks around somewhat puzzled*] Forget it. I don't feel insulted any more, and I don't know what made me say all this nonsense.

On Freedom and Country ____

Introduction

Israelis have a very special attachment to the State of Israel, an attachment formed by Jewish history and reinforced by war. Like all other attachments, it may become burdensome and oppressive, and in Israeli society, it is one of the unutterable subjects. In the group, with masks down, as we uncover more and more of our basic dilemmas, this subject is also examined. In the deepest sense, people are asking: Is life in Israel a moral commitment for me? Does it dictate a certain style of life? "On Freedom and Country" is a set of cases that centers around these issues.

Israel is a very small country, and its society is a tightly knit one. You grow up in a neighborhood and attend nursery school with the children who will be your permanent company through school and army service. There are no great distances within the country nor friendly neighboring states in which to attend college, so the "group" continues together. Very few emigrate—this is still considered an act of treason. Some get killed in this war or the other, and those remaining mourn for them together. Norms are very strong, and deviation from them is frowned upon and sometimes severely criticized.

Amit, Shlomit, and Reeny explore this feeling of siege, in which no easy ways out exist, heavy demands for conformity are made, and being closed in with the same group of people is a fact of life. The tight group provides security; yet, at the same time, it isolates one from the world outside and may even result in the feeling of suffocation.

Although Reeny refers mainly to the oppression of personal loyalties, she hints at the more general issue of the burden inherent in an attachment to Israel. In her words: "I need to break out from all these loyalties. I feel as if I am in a siege; if I plan to be myself, you always stand in my way. Some people say this whole country is too small for them to grow in, like a plant trying to develop in a miniature pot." Amit likens life in Israel to a caged existence, and Reeny compares it to a tiny room. Both women, however, express a deep love for the country, despite its tough, merciless desert, which Reeny considers to be the most beloved landscape of all.

For most of the people I know, it is quite obvious that the sense of attachment to the country is reinforced by the wars and imminent danger rather than weakened by them; and for those who decide to leave the country, conflict and guilt feelings are prominent and everlasting.

Within this normative context, Shlomit's work stands out for her unpopular opinions. She has chosen to live in Israel yet continues to be ambivalent about her choice—not only because of her sense of siege and fear of wars but because, both morally and politically, she objects to the accepted policy of the country vis-à-vis the Arabs. Her dream exposes her conflict—to be an Israeli, and therefore to fight and negate her principles, or to cling to the status of a foreigner, an uninvolved newcomer. A third possibility is to remain the child clutching her teddy bear, allowing adults to take the responsibility for politics and war.

The need to travel, to move around freely, is another product of this feeling of siege. Rachel expresses her yearning to be free; yet beyond this are the additional Israeli-specific realities; namely, that it is physically difficult to move without restraint in a small country surrounded by sealed borders, and it is psychologically impossible to be a traveling gypsy with two children serving in the Israeli army. But Rachel, who is the traveler craving for freedom, is also the person who expresses the clearest acceptance of her loyalty to this country, her simple belonging to Israel, her home. She is willing both to accept her emotional ties and national commitments and to look for her personal freedom within those limits.

Another member of the Israeli society is the Arab citizen, born in Israel and living here with all the problems imposed upon a minority group frequently identified with the enemy side. What are the feelings of Arab citizens toward this country? What place do they find here, among the Jewish majority? This is, indeed, an area into which this book provides just a very partial glimpse through the story of Nadim, an Arab professional living among Jews in Israel. Opening a crack into his complex personality, he admits that he is neither friend nor foe, yet neither is he indifferent to the conflict. He lacks a sense of belonging to either his Arab village or to the Jewish town, which is eternally suspicious of his intentions. He finds relief from his rootlessness in fantasies of becoming a mythical creature and of carnal fulfillment very remote from his daily reality. Whether this personal story of Nadim's can be extended to his minority group as a whole is unanswerable.

Pelican-Penguins

AMIT   I want to work on a dream I had the other night. In my dream I am in a bakery shop, examining some packages. Most of the packages are damaged, and some cookies are missing from them. The owner shows me a big barrel full of unpacked biscuits and suggests that I buy them by weight. I agree. My shopping done, I go out onto the street, which stretches straight uphill. The street is full of strange brown pelicans, standing quietly, staring at me. They cover practically the whole road all the way up the hill. I am surprised and wonder how to cross over. Suddenly I see Nurit at the top of the hill with a friend I don't know. They walk toward me. Nurit looks much heavier and older than she really is. I watch them walking down the street in between the birds. They walk softly and calmly, and the birds don't fly away.

This is the dream, but I have to add something that happened the next morning. When I woke up, I was very absorbed by the vivid picture of the brown birds on the road, seeing them clearly with white aprons on their necks, nodding their heads. I was quite sure of their name too, which was, in my mind, brown pelicans. I asked my husband if he had ever seen brown pelicans anywhere. He then reminded me of a trip we once took on a coastal road in California. While parked on the top of the cliffs, we saw brown pelicans resting on a rock near the beach. Then a very strange thing happened. As we recalled this scene together, I became aware that the brown pelicans of my dream did not look like the real ones we once saw but rather like brown penguins with wings. Real penguins can't fly, I know. This is a very strange combination, and it puzzles me.

I   Let us start then from this point. Be the creatures of your dream.

AMIT   What shall I call them?

I   You name them; they're your invention.

AMIT   Pelican-penguins, or P.P.'s.

I   Very well, now be one of these creatures.

AMIT   I am a brown pelican. I live on the coast of the Pacific Ocean. I hunt for fish, and I fly wherever I please. I live on the prettiest spot on earth. I am free and content.

I   This was the pelican?

AMIT   Well, yes. Now you probably want me to be the penguin. I am a brown penguin. I live in a zoo, maybe in London. I am in a glass cage with lots of ice to keep me comfortable. People look at me through the glass. I am passive and bored. That's all.

I   You have done two separate parts, the pelican and the penguin. In your dream, however, they were one creature.

AMIT   One creature with a mixed-up identity. One creature which is nonexistent, a fabrication of some sort.

As she is saying this she sounds desolate and rather angry.

I   Be this creature, the pelican-penguin, in the first person.

AMIT   I cannot feel it. I just feel how I am torn between the two separate parts. Well, let me try. I am a nonexistent creature. I have no identity. I am confused. Maybe I am a mistake of nature.I don't feel I can be the combination, really. I think it is a matter of choosing between the two alternatives.

I   Can you clarify these alternatives? What is their significance for you?

AMIT   Yes. When I was the pelican, remembering vividly that coastal road in California, where I lived before, it all became very clear to me. The dream is another manifestation of the basic conflict in my life now. The penguin part is my Israeli part. To stay in this country, to decide to really settle down here. I already feel too attached to this land, and I don't want to be. And I know that if I stay another couple of years, we'll have a baby and our baby will grow up to be an Israeli. He will always want to come back here and serve in the army. Wherever we take him later will not make a difference. It is not just the army, the wars. It is also the strong attachment that gradually grows until we feel we have no choice.

I   Who is "we"?

AMIT   Me, first of all. And all my friends, the *olim**, the transients, who did not make their final decision yet.

She looks around the room, then adds:

AMIT   You must be shocked; most of you are Israeli-born or were raised here. You condemn everyone who leaves the country, call him *yored.*** I want you to understand me. I am entitled to make my choice, as you made yours. Or maybe you're so attached to Israel you don't feel you have the choice any more. Like the poor penguins in the cage.

I   Who are you speaking to?

AMIT   To the people here. To you. I could say that to my husband as well.

I   Talk to him.

AMIT   Meir, you were born here; and although you studied in America, you don't have this conflict. I am alone with this. I know you hate to think about the possibility of leaving Israel

*Immigrants to Israel; literally, "those who go up"
**An Israeli who emigrates from the country; literally, "he who goes down"

to settle elsewhere. You'd never be able to face up to your friends as a *yored*. It would break your pride, the basis of your identity. So we don't talk about it, although you know it is on my mind.

I   What would you say if you were not concerned with his reaction?

Amit looks into the empty chair and smiles hesitantly.

AMIT   Remember, Meir, the years we studied in California? We were so happy there. We owned very little and didn't need more. We didn't have worries of any kind. We were the brown pelicans, unattached. We could pack our belongings together in two hours and drive out to Canada, to the East. These were happy times. Here, I sometimes feel as if I live in a siege. I want out. I am suffocating.

She is quiet now. She looks down and plays with her wedding ring.

I   What would he say?
AMIT   He would somehow comfort me physically, try to avoid the issue.
I   Be him.
AMIT   Come on, baby, did you have a rough day? Was it too hot for you? You go and rest, put on a record. I'll take care of everything.

She switches chairs and says angrily:

—No, I don't want to avoid the issue. Can we discuss where we are going to live?
—Right here, and you know it. There is nothing to discuss. Let's go to the movies or call on some friends. It will cheer you up a little.
I   So he avoids talking about it with you.
AMIT   Yes. He is very good to me, and I love him. I don't want to hurt him. It is my own conflict, and I have to live with it.
I   Is this like being a pelican-penguin?
AMIT   Yes. I am fluctuating. I have no clear identity.

I   Can you talk to Nurit now?

AMIT   Yes. Nurit, you look so much heavier and older than usual. Why is that so?

—It's just that I am already forty.

—And you lived all your life in Israel?

—Yes, I did. I travel sometimes, but this is my home.
    [*to me*] She is gone.

I   This is another part of you.

AMIT   I realize this, that I love Israel as Nurit does. She does not feel imprisoned in a cage here.

I   Try the first person.

AMIT   I do not feel imprisoned here. It is not completely right yet. Maybe it is my choice, to grow older here, to walk uphill here, but I don't accept it yet with my whole being.

I   That's good enough. On the road uphill you have all these pelican-penguins, the *olim* and the others, who have not yet determined their identity. And Nurit, the Israeli, walks among you. In your dream, she is not frightening you away.

AMIT   No, she is not. Actually, she is smiling.

After a few minutes of silence, Amit adds:

AMIT   I want to talk to you, Nurit. I like you; you're a very warm person. There is something you don't always realize. It was a difficult decision to settle in Israel. There is a price that I keep paying. The transition is not easy. I miss a lot of people. I have selected a new name for myself, and now even I don't recognize me too well. And you, you're sometimes impatient. You think of me as a rich, spoiled, American kid. I was neither rich nor spoiled. Try to understand me better.

I   Can you say that to some of the people in the group?

Amit goes around the room, repeating those sentences to several of the women and adding some facts about her past.

I   What do you feel now?

AMIT   They, the people here, do not condemn me for my conflict. They, I mean you, can understand.

I   And Meir?

AMIT He, too, perhaps. What I have to learn is how to share my confusion and doubts with him without threatening his deep-rooted attachment to Israel.

I This is a project for both of you. Take it as homework with you.

People in the group express their feelings toward Amit, reassuring her that they can accept her with her conflict, whatever its outcome might be.

AMIT You know, now I suddenly understand the meaning of the first part of the dream, too. The bakery-manager is telling me that there are no ready-made packages here, no ready-made mixes for your identity. Here is a barrel of all the necessary ingredients. Make your own package. He is a clever man.

I He is you, too.

AMIT I hope so.

Teddy Bear

Shlomit is a young woman who grew up in England and immigrated to Israel when she was twenty years old. In the group she frequently refers to her tendency to prolong her status as a newcomer, someone who does not yet belong completely to Israel. Although she wonders why, she does not work on it during the year.

Several months after the termination of our year-long group, she handed me the following paper, describing a dream and some thoughts about it.

A few months ago I had a dream that I was participating in some kind of a gathering—all men, and I'm the only woman present. Jonathan, my boyfriend, is talking, and I understand that the men are planning a military action—to occupy an Arab village—which Jonathan is to lead. As he is giving last-minute instructions, I hear myself say that I want to take part as well, that if such things have to be done, I also want to be involved.

The men object, with much joking and ridicule; but Jonathan overrides them, saying that he believes in equality of actions and decisions for women. If I want to prove myself in battle, that is my right.

I am given a uniform and a gun. I try on the uniform and put my hair up. The men tell me I look fine—"like one of us," they say. But I still have misgivings that people will see through me, that I'm really just a girl dressing up as a soldier.

Then we disperse with instructions to make our ways separately to the spot from which we will launch our attack. The path leads through a nature reserve, similar to one where I had once taken a group of Arab schoolchildren on a summer trip. A beautiful day, the sun sparkling on green fields, and glistening ponds, it seems to be some kind of a holiday. Families are picnicking by the lake; naked children are paddling and splashing and laughing; swim-suited parents are sleeping off their lunch in the sun. An idyllically peaceful scene.

As I pass them I am filled with an almost arrogant sense of importance. Here are these people, relaxed, enjoying themselves, with no idea of the important mission facing me. As I walk, my heart jumps from time to time as I notice members of the group looking strangely freaky, long-haired, bearded, and bare-chested, but wearing army trousers. We exchange quiet, brooding glances, then continue on our way.

I arrive at the appointed spot. We have decided to camouflage our intentions by making our gathering seem like a political picnic of the kind the Left sometimes organizes. People are sitting on the grass, listening to speeches. Jonathan's rising to speak is to be the signal for us to start the attack and for me to fire the first shot. Tension mounts. At last Jonathan rises, I jump to my feet, and suddenly I realize that I have left my gun behind and am clutching a teddy bear instead. Jonathan gapes, horrified, and I wake up.

At the time I had the dream I tried to work on its meaning for me. I found in it the themes then occupying the foreground of my struggle in reality: the internal battles over my femininity, and my difficulties with trust and feeling deserving of trust. I closed some circles and did not suspect that there were others still left open.

Then, the other day I read a truly touching war story in the newspaper, and the dream flashed before me again. I realized there were other layers that I hadn't grasped at first.

I am re-living the scene of my dream. I see myself volunteering to attack this Arab village. I'm again walking through the happy park. I think I have a gun, yet I'm clutching my teddy bear.

I am aware of my conflict over belonging and feeling bound to this country. One part, the volunteer soldier, wants to be a "real Israeli," "one of us."

—How can I become one of you?

—By fighting with us. Belonging here is possible only through unquestioning participation in military action, even in suddenly occupying an Arab village on a peaceful summer's day.

—But this is in complete contradiction to my moral-political world-view.

I'm stuck there. If I want to belong, I suspect that I'll have to negate my basic beliefs.

The other part, the child clutching the teddy bear, now pops up, renouncing responsibility and commitment, leaving the serious business of decisions, involvement, and action to grown-ups, to men. This part asks the world to leave her alone to do her own thing.

—What's your thing?

—Playing. Being a child. If we could only maintain our innocence, be more like children, not strive for much, would war still be necessary? War is an adult game. Children play with teddy bears.

(This, however, I feel is a different issue.)

Basically, then, I am ambivalent about Israel. That's why I keep my status as an outsider among you. I have tried to resolve my ambivalence toward Israel by becoming intimate with Jonathan, the real Israeli man. He can make me an Israeli, too. But in my dream, I am still ambivalent toward him. I make him the commander of an attack against peaceful Arabs; I make him plan an act that is the extreme negation of my principles—the principles of both of us, in fact. (In the morning after I dreamed this, I told Jonathan about it. Indeed he gaped, horrified, as in my dream—not because of my blunder, but because of the role I've assigned to *him* in my dream. He was really insulted.)

In reality, I further tried to resolve my ambivalence toward Israel by finding commitment in political action, by belief in a different way for Israel and her neighbors, a way by which Jonathan will not have to agonize over whether or not to fight, a way by which my children will not be called to war. But I never realized before how I see in this commitment a compromise, perhaps a "middle way," as we used to call it in the group, between my two parts: the one which strains to be like everyone else, to join the mainstream without doubts as to its fairness and correctness; and the other, which just wants to be left alone, to have no part in it all.

I want to be an Israeli in my own way.

Now that I have put it all down, reading it through again, I can't say that the circle is closed, but at least I am better able to see what is holding it open.

Closed-in

REENY   Next week I'll be twenty-six.

She sighs deeply and waits; then she continues.

REENY   On Friday I had a dream, which I remembered after a long time of not remembering any dreams at all. In my dream I was screaming: "I don't want to be twenty-six! I don't want to have a birthday at all, not any more!"

I   Try to remain in the present tense, please.

REENY   In my dream we are all there. I do not recollect all the faces, but I am convinced it is impossible that any of them would not be there, all of my group. There were Allen and Ted and Ester and Tanya, and even Eric, though he is not any more.

I   You are using the past tense again.

REENY   In my dream I am with my group. Not the group here, but my group of friends from school, from the army. We are all closed in in one room together. This reminds me of two recent occasions in which we all met again.

I   Are those occasions part of the dream?

REENY   No, indeed they are not. This dream is so real that it gets confused in my mind with scenes from my reality. Let me explain, and then, perhaps, I'll be able to go back and work on the dream. We are six friends. We grew up together, three boys and three girls. We were inseparable as kids. This closeness is somehow absurd today, and anyway, one of us, that is Eric, is gone.

I   Gone? How?

REENY   This is very hard to say. He committed suicide. A month ago. We all met then, at his funeral, and buried him in the soil of the white hills. That is the last time the six of us were together. And the time before last was three months ago, at Tanya's wedding. Again the six of us. This time we accompanied Tanya on her way to life with a stranger.

I   Her husband?

REENY   Yes. She was the first one to tear herself away from the group; then Eric did, in his own way. And I would like to be the next in line, only I don't know how.

I   Reeny, I am very confused. You say many different things, and I don't know where you want to lead.

REENY   Maybe I'll tell you the dream now. In my dream the whole group is there, closed in one room. I ask Tanya: "Why did you do this?" and I ask her again: "How is it to be twenty-six?" And Tanya says: "It isn't too bad." To which I answer proudly: "But I, I won't follow your steps. I won't do what you did." That is all I remember from the dream. This, and the notion that we were gathered in this tiny room to mourn for someone, and strangely enough, it is not for Eric, who is still among us, but for Tanya, I think.

I   OK, so now we have the dream, and you told us about the group. What do you feel now?

REENY   I feel confused, and I want to cry. I think I cried enough when I woke up from the dream on Saturday morning. I cried for Eric and for the group, but mostly I cried for myself. I felt very lonely. I think it's the first time I let myself go, crying in such a manner; and I thought this must be the end of a stage for me, the end of my youth and of my belonging to this group, which is falling apart. I want to tell you something. When I woke up it was very early on Saturday morning. I felt suffocated, boxed in. I had to go out, as if to escape from the tiny room of the dream. I walked out to the deserted streets. Only a few black-bearded men were hurrying to the synagogues. Everything was damp from the night's dew, and very quiet. I climbed the hill of Abu-Tor, I sat on a rock in a place from which the whole Judean Desert and the blue mountains spread out before me. The scenery was so lonesome, barren, and sad. That's where I cried.

I   Could you say the last sentence in the first person, what you have just said about the landscape?

REENY   I am sad. I feel barren like the desert.

She is quiet now for a while.

I   Please go on. Stay with your feelings and be the desert.

REENY   I am a desert. Nothing grows in me. I don't get any rain. But I have impressive mountains and the prettiest colors. And there are some Bedouins who live in me peacefully.

She opens her eyes and watches me, puzzled.

I   The desert part of you, do you recognize it?

REENY   Yes, I do. The desert is, I would say, my solitude. I very rarely let myself experience this part. I don't usually perceive myself as a lonely woman. Maybe that's what my group has prevented me from experiencing. You know, the surprising thing about being the desert a minute ago is that it was not so bad; actually, it wasn't bad at all. Suddenly I saw the blue of the sky, the bright, glorious sun, the brown-violet of the far mountains, the perfect roundness of some of the far magnificent peaks. And between these, the black-robed Bedouins. I am in love with this view—it has the lines and the colors that I like the best. This is a very peculiar discovery, since when I sat there on Saturday, actually facing the view, I was crying and longing for a magic way to get out of this country, to leave everything here and start all over again.

I   When you said that it wasn't so bad, being the desert, I was reminded of this sentence which appeared in your dream.

REENY   Yes, this is what Tanya said to me in the dream.

I   Talk to Tanya now.

Reeny looks at the empty chair, then starts:

REENY   Tanya, I always wanted to be like you. You are one month older than I. As a child, this made all the difference. When you had your birthday, I would look up at you and ask: "How do you feel to be ten?" I admired your looks, and I considered you to be a very strong person. We could talk about everything; and we were, both of us, part of the group. Then, in recent years, we went our different ways and grew apart. But for me, in my mind, you still remained my best friend until you got married. Why did you do it? I see you in white at your wedding, for which I arranged the flowers. Your parents, your new husband—a stranger to me and to the group. Why did you do it?

I   What does she answer?

REENY   She smiles and says: "Your time to grow up will also come one day." And I say: "I will not grow up the same way you did."

She is reflecting and then adds:

REENY   Actually, I need to talk to the whole group. That's what I would like to tell them: I see you here in front of me. As always you're my good friends, meeting on Fridays and holidays, singing our happy childhood songs. I understand how you have been my security, my guarantee for all the best. With you, I thought, I'll always be happy and together. But now, after the wedding, after the funeral, I want to tell you that all this togetherness was a big illusion, like a big beautiful soap bubble, and no more. Now it is all gone. This bubble, this togetherness, has managed to suffocate each one of us, like the way I felt in this tiny room of my dream. I need to break out from all these loyalties. I feel as if I am in a siege; if I plan to be myself, you always stand in my way. Some people say this whole country is too small for them to grow in, like a plant trying to develop in a miniature pot.

She stops and sits here, looking at her hands.

I   Do you feel finished with the group?
REENY   No, I am just confused. I think I have gone off the track. I don't think the country is too small for me, although I have entertained the fantasy of going abroad to make a fresh start. But I think this is the easy way out; I have to be alone in order to grow up.
I   Say that to the group.
REENY   I can face you now and tell you that I want to be alone and away from our tight room. I need to be alone and to see how I'll cope and what I will do with my life. Enough of our childhood games. Enough of one of you boys entering my room through the window, saying, "Hey, baby, I'm here." From now on I am going to grow my own space around me.

Her voice sounds very strong and convincing.

I   You sound convincing.
REENY   Yes. This was important. For the first time today my confusion is gone.
I   OK. This room image appears again and again. Would you like to be the room?
REENY   I'll try. I am a tiny room. I close you in with your childhood group of friends. I am whitewashed and barren. Like a prison, there is only one window, high up. Some people may come in, but you can't get out.

She looks at me and adds:

REENY   That's all.

I   Do you know this part of you?

REENY   Yes, I know. I am responsible for being enclosed in this room, in a sense. Besides, it is also the problem of this country—being closed in—but I don't think this is as important.

I   What is your fantasy of a different space to live in?

REENY   A big house . . . a big room with huge windows on all sides, a door that I can open when I want to, carpets on the floor, music, but mainly, lots of air and a beautiful view outside —and I can walk out easily if I choose to.

I   OK. You may want to talk to Eric, too.

REENY   This is more difficult. I am afraid to visualize him as sitting on the chair here, since I know he is deep down in the ground.

I   You can start by saying that to him.

Reeny hesitates for a minute.

REENY   It is extremely painful for me to see you there and to know you'll never sit across the room from me as I imagine you now. I have to talk to you, and the thing I have in mind to tell you is rather horrible. I feel some gratitude toward you and your deed. I ought to thank you for what you have shown me in a very clear fashion, something that I refused to see for many years. You showed me that our group was an illusion, a soap bubble. It did not provide real security, and it prevented us from growing up. I am going to be twenty-six; I am not a teenager any more. You showed me that no one can help, only I can help myself. If the group were the security blanket it pretended to be, you would not have been that desperate and killed yourself. I'm sad you did it, and I don't know why. I wish I could help you. Yet, right now, I thank you for the most important lesson in growing up. I have to be my own security. I am the only one I can rely upon.

Some people share their reactions with Reeny.

ELLA   Your stress of your need to be on your own sounds to me like an adolescent trying to break away from the family.

REENY   That's right. I broke away from the family into the group, and now it is like searching for my own identity for the first time.

ELLA   Also, right now you did not express any need to be together on another basis with someone, a more mature and intimate relationship of your own adult choice. Like Tanya found.

REENY   Yes, I guess you're right. But I don't feel this need yet. It may evolve out of my solitude if I manage to cut myself away from the group.

GABY   I want to react to the description of the group. I came to this country from France when I was fourteen. Everybody of my age was already well "grouped." They all knew all the words to the kindergarten songs. For years I felt out of it and envious of the central members of these groups. I always felt that something basic was missing from my life. Today I saw the other side of the group. It is some sort of a revelation. I don't feel as envious as before.

Travelers

Rachel was thirty-seven years old at the time we worked together, and training to become a psychotherapist. She was married and the mother of two children, a son just starting his army service and a daughter in high school. Both in looks and in her approach to life, Rachel seemed much younger than her age; actually, she looked like a sister to her two tall children. Her career as a clinical psychologist was her second one, after a few years of working in publishing and journalism.

I selected two episodes from the work with Rachel, taking place at an interval of half a year from each other. The following happened on a very cold winter afternoon.

RACHEL   I want to tell you about something strange. I want to understand what was really happening. I went to this movie the other night with my husband and two friends. It is about a rock musician and his band, their work and travel, with many songs. I guess the music is the part that attracts people to this film. Anyway, as we left the theater after the show, I was amazed to discover that neither of my friends nor my husband found the film outstanding or even touching, whereas I was completely overwhelmed and could not even explain by what or why. I feel this picture was very significant for me and had some message which I can't formulate.

I   Tell me, please, the scene or the picture that comes to your mind now as you think about the film.

RACHEL   I see the artist—the singer—and his musicians backstage after the show, or perhaps it is during intermission. They are all there, all dressed in white, decorated with beads and flowers, and all the technicians are moving around, and the women and children walk among the musicians like a huge family. They are all dressed in white. Some of them are busy, but the feeling is of being content and relaxed. And these children, they seem to be happy and gay, as if everyone in the band —all the adults—are their fathers and mothers.

I   Could you focus on anything in this picture?

RACHEL   The children, three of them, very pretty and free. The sense of togetherness and relaxation. The huge cases and boxes in the background, where everything will be packed later when they resume their traveling to go to the next place.

I   The children and the cases. Would you like to be one or talk to one?

RACHEL   I am very attracted to the children. I'd like to talk to them.

I   Go ahead.

RACHEL   Children, tell me, how do you go to school? Do you ever, if you travel all year round?

Several people in the group laugh when they hear this question. Rachel looks at them puzzled.

RACHEL   What is so funny?

PEOPLE   Right away you have to ask them something, and about school, of all things. Can't you accept that some people just don't live the way you do? Their children don't go to school, and nobody makes a fuss over it.

I   Well, these are your reactions. Let Rachel work her own way, though.

RACHEL   Now I don't know, you threw me off. I guess it may sound funny to ask the children about going to school, as if I came to visit from another planet.

I   Say that to the children.

RACHEL   Children, I feel as if you and I belong to different planets. You live with music and with those cases, which carry all your belongings, and with trains traveling from one stage to the next. You seem to be so happy, satisfied, free. I envy you. I'd like to join you.

I   Join the children of the troupe?

RACHEL   Yes, that's what I was thinking. I am not a musician, so I cannot join the adults. They take the children along, and they don't go to school, or sing or perform with the band. Maybe I, too, could find my place among them.

I   Ask them.

RACHEL   Ask whom?

I   Whom do you think should be asked about that? Ask, and then give the answer as well.

RACHEL   Children, could I join you?

(as children) Join? What for? You are big and don't belong. What can you do among us?

—I could play with you or teach you things.

—Go away. We don't need you, you don't belong.

I   Try with the grownups.

RACHEL   Hey, you guys of the band, can I stay with you?

(as band) Can you play? Can you sing?

—No, I can't now, but I want to learn.

—Sorry, you belong to the audience. Don't bother us.

I   Rachel, I want to be the band for a moment. As the band, I'm asking you: What do you want from us anyway?

RACHEL   I want to be free like you. I don't want to be tied down by obligations, school, family. I don't want to belong to one small country with sealed borders on all sides. I want to be a wanderer like you, to see new places, to have new opportunities every day, to be able to leave things behind and start all over again.

I   Be the band and answer.

RACHEL   I don't think I can. I think the band people are very busy. They have to pack for tomorrow, and the children are running around, distracting them.

I   I feel that you don't want to face them. You prefer to leave this issue unfinished.

RACHEL   What do you want me to do?

I   I don't want a thing. Let's stop if you wish.

RACHEL   OK. Hey band, you have to talk to me for a minute. Answer my question. Why are you laughing at me? I don't mean to be funny.

(as band) Rachel, you incurable romantic, you really don't understand what you're talking about. Yes, we go to places, we live without borders, but we are not as free as you imagine. There is a timetable to keep, rehearsals, concerts, lots of work. We have to be good to get the best reviews or else we're out of business. We have to keep on our toes all the time. Yes, it is fun, too; but if you knew of all the times we long to have a stable home, some simple loyalties like you have, and not be constantly on the run.

—But you look so happy.

—Sometimes it is our business to look happy. Often we really are. Aren't you? We are not happier than you are.

[*to me*] Wow, what an illusion! Another soap bubble . . . it's all gone.

I   What is gone?

RACHEL   It is as if there were an alternative, another kind of existence, that if I try very hard—like, if I learn to play music —I may find it, may join in. I feel confused, trapped.

I   And sad.

RACHEL   And still want to go with this band.

I   OK. If that is your choice.

At the end of summer, Rachel came back to the group after a three-week trip to New York with her husband.

At that time it became known that she had accepted a position as a clinical psychologist in a hospital in Jerusalem, a permanent job, a commitment she had hesitated to make for a long time. When she came to the meeting, we congratulated her on the job and asked her about the trip. She seemed very content, with a young, eager look on her face.

RACHEL I had a good trip and am happy to be back, back home, back to the hospital, and here with you. It's nice to come back home, where you belong, I mean. Where I belong. To speak the language in which I feel most natural, my own language.

I What is this? You really sound content to stop running for a while, to settle down. I don't hear your gypsy part yet, or did you leave that Rachel behind in New York?

RACHEL I don't know that I have. Perhaps I did, and perhaps my gypsy just lies dormant. I had a funny moment in a New York train station. I sat there for twenty minutes waiting for my train to be announced. I was alone and sat there looking at the crowds of people, waiting like me or rushing on their way. A lot of young people with backpacks and sleeping bags, probably going for a vacation, since it was during school break. And here I am, also traveling again. And, as usual, I say to myself: Suppose I were free? Suppose I did not have any stable place to go to? Suppose I could be on the go forever, would I be happier with that freedom? So I developed a silent dialogue with one of these young people. It went somewhat like this:
—Where are you going, Jim?
—I don't know. I am going to California to meet a friend, and then we'll see. Maybe we'll go together to Mexico.
—I'd like to go to Mexico myself. I have never been there.
—And where are you from? You are not an American, are you?
—No, I am an Israeli. I am here only for a short visit. I'll go back in two weeks, maybe visit some friends in Oxford on my way back.
—Now that sounds great. Israel must be such an exciting place to live in. I heard so much about your kibbutz and the Red Sea. Is it really red? I wish I could go there.

[*to me*] Here I stopped this imaginary dialogue and caught myself smiling. It is so ridiculous. I have these fantasies about the stranger's trips and he about mine. And why can't I stay happily in my own skin, my home?

I   Can you?

RACHEL   Don't rush, that's exactly what I want to share with you. I didn't let myself become depressed this time by all these travelers, did not invent romantic stories about their wonderful freedom. I am a traveler, too, in a sense, so I know better. I imagined myself saying to the stranger: "I go my way, and you go your way," paraphrasing the famous Gestalt prayer, "I do my thing, you do your thing."

I   Could you develop it? I'd like to hear you talk with that stranger.

RACHEL   Very well. Stranger, you go your way, and God bless you. I don't envy you, and I don't think you are freer than I am. Somewhere along the line I know you are pretty tied down to things, to people. So am I. I like my ties, they are part of me. And I have my freedom also, even though I carry a nice, respectable suitcase and not a backpack like yours. Maybe we both travel on paths that have heart. I feel good, and I cannot explain it completely or convey the feeling to you.

I   Don't try, just stay with this feeling.

RACHEL   I feel this young stranger would have liked me and accepted me. We could have had coffee together at the station and talked, then gone to our separate destinations.

I   I hope this stranger is your inner gypsy, the traveling musician, whatever you used to call him here.

RACHEL   It may very well be.

I   So you are sitting down together, finally, to talk—

RACHEL   About freedom and traveling, about our different paths—

I   And you enjoy each other a lot.

Rachel smiles at the composition we've created together.

I   That's good. I am very pleased and glad for you.

RACHEL   I feel very much at peace with myself today.

I   Yet the struggle may come back.
RACHEL   I know. It's me, after all.

Black Bird

Nadim is a young Arab social worker who participated in one of my workshops in 1976. He is tall and very slim, and the dreaminess of his black eyes is somewhat infectious. He is the first Arab to participate in a group of mine, and I feel strange about his presence, which is, for me, very unusual. It is not the language problem, I know, since he is very fluent in Hebrew. I start to feel more comfortable when I realize that the members of the group who have had some other group experiences together before our meeting accept him very well. Gradually I relax and see him as a person, not as a representative of his culture.

On the second night of our workshop, we have a fantasy trip. This is basically a suggestion to fly and to land at a preferred spot, to stay for a while in that chosen place, to take some souvenir, and to come back. We then share our fantasies, which are usually pleasant and revealing experiences.

Nadim remains in his relaxed position on the floor for a long time, while people are sharing their trips. He does not seem to be back in the group yet. Finally I ask him:

I   Where are you, Nadim?
NADIM   I am not here with you. I am trying to avoid listening to the fantasies you have been sharing and to remain in my own.
I   Tell me about your trip, in the present tense.

Nadim starts in a dreamy voice, his eyes closed, the words formed and pronounced very slowly in a monotonous sound.

NADIM   You say to walk out of the room, face the dark sky, and start to fly. I feel like a bird, a big, dark-winged bird with infinite possibilities. I am aware of my strength and wisdom. I am omnipotent. I can go anywhere, places that do not exist or have never existed. I breathe deeply. I start to fly. At one point I do not know if I am me, Nadim, or this mythical bird. It does not matter. I make up my mind I am both at the same time. This is very good. As I fly, I go beyond the night, through the darkness, and it is bright daylight now. I look down. I am above this country. I recognize the valley of Yizre'el, tiny squares of cultivated land, different shades of yellow, brown, and green. I see the white homes with their brick roofs, miniature red tractors, and I am even able to recognize the forms of little children playing with a dog. The sight is so pretty and calm I feel like descending there. I am moved as I start on my way down. Suddenly I feel tremendous forces pulling me up and away. This is not my personal, my very own place. It cannot be. I feel like crying, part of me refuses to be separated from the scene. And the bird flies on. As I keep flying, my longings change into hatred and despair.

I keep flying. Now I am above my hometown, where I was born, where my parents and brothers still live. This is my place, I think. Again I start to descend, with a sensation of heaviness, almost dropping like a stone. Suddenly the picture of my village comes into focus. Under the blazing sun I see my village completely ruined. All the houses are roofless, the walls stand uneven, like columns of ancient times. Furniture and clothing are scattered on the unpaved streets, and all is very quiet. There is nobody there. There is nothing to descend to, only a lonely dog barking desperately in the dead square. Time and again I circle the village from above, and I absorb the sights. I see my parents' house, which is wide open and not in better shape than the other ruins of the village. I circle the place like a bird of prey. For a second I contemplate landing and joining the lonely dog, but again I am pulled upward and far away. This is not my place either.

Now I fly over the Mediterranean, which is blue and sparkling. I feel exhausted from my search, my wings are very tired. Suddenly I see a white island; and without giving it any further thought, I land. I touch the ground, which is soft and pleasantly warm. It is of the whitest, purest sand, and I enjoy walking on it barefoot. I am me, Nadim. My wings wait patiently in the shade of a rock. I am naked and feel very free. In the center of the island I see this woman. She is blond, her long hair covers her white naked body, and she is beautiful. She greets me with outstretched arms and offers to share her drink with me. We drink wine; there are many bottles around. And then we slowly make love. We are alone on this island; we are happy and we lack nothing. This is the perfect existence.

Here Nadim stops his narrative; and with his arms covering his face, he bends over his knees, very remote from us all.

I   Is this the end of your trip?
NADIM   Yes. I did not want to go any further, nor to come back here. I feel completely satisfied there.
I   You speak in the past tense now, do you notice?
NADIM   Yes. I am not on my island any more. As much as I try, I am unable to stay there now.
I   Then look up at us here.

Nadim straightens up slowly and opens his eyes, looking around vaguely.

NADIM   OK. Don't rush me, I will come back all right. For me, this fantasy trip covers very familiar territory. I used to take such trips frequently on my own, I don't need the suggestion. When I feel bored or out of contact with the people present, I just withdraw and take off on a fantasy trip.
I   Were all the landscapes and experiences you told us about, the ones you encountered in today's trip, completely familiar from previous fantasies you have had?
NADIM   The island is a very familiar scene, with the wine and the woman. Only today I had a very intense experience of it, almost as if it were real, and I was very unwilling to depart. This is an image I frequently put myself to sleep with. The beginning of my trip—no, the scenes of the valley and the village—were new today. I never had this fantasy before.
I   One more question. Did you bring anything back from there?

NADIM   I hesitated whether to tell you about it. I don't understand this part too well. When you said to look for a souvenir
to bring back and say good-bye, I was very upset and unwilling
to obey. I wanted to stay, yet I felt compelled to follow your
suggestion. I then took one empty wine bottle and broke it on
a rock, so I had in my hand the neck of the bottle with its sharp
edges. With this in hand I put on my black wings and flew back
in.

I   I feel very clearly your message here—I am angry, I am
dangerous, I am able to hurt or to wound you.

NADIM   I see how you can get this message. But in my fantasy
this happened very automatically. I did not have a sense of
aggression. I am a very mild person; and when other people get
angry, I usually withdraw and just pull myself out of contact.
But, perhaps, yes, I was angry at you for commanding me to
come back here.

I   OK, if it felt like a command to you. Let me tell you something. The trip you have just described has been a deeply moving experience for me. I think you can draw a lot, in terms of
self-understanding, from the various parts of your trip. Basically, there were three scenes: the Israeli valley, the Arab village, and the fantasy island. And perhaps a fourth one—the
powerful black bird with the sharply pointed piece of glass. Can
you identify with each part in turn?

NADIM   Yes, I can. Let me start with the Arab village. This
is really my place of origin. It is a Moslem village and quite well
off now. I am the first-born son in my family. I have been taught
to be totally respectful and obedient of my father, who is the
postmaster of the village. At the same time I go to school and
learn about the world outside the village. To make a long story
short, I go to high school, I study well, and I become more and
more alienated from my own family. I never show open disrespect for my father, I just withdraw from him and his ways.
They build a private room for me, with a side entrance of my
own, so that I can have peace and quiet for my studies. But, in
fact, they drive me away and reinforce my alienation. I bring
wine to my room. At first I take care to throw the empty bottles

away. Later, I keep it all openly. My mother enters to clean up, so she knows. My father never refers to this fact. I am drinking, something which is strictly forbidden for Moslems. I am accepted as different as long as I show outward respect for the village and its ways.

I   In your fantasy the village is all ruined.

NADIM   Yes, I am not surprised by this image, although I have never had it before. The village is ruined and dead for me. Since my years at the university, I have found myself more and more a stranger to my own family and village. I come for a weekend or a holiday, eat with the family. My younger brothers are already married and have children, we are a big family. I sit and talk to them politely, while inside I feel nothing. The village is dead for me. I cannot find there any single thing to satisfy my recent needs. And the young generation, my classmates who still live there, just follow in their fathers' footsteps. Maybe it's all for the best for them, but I can't help it if I see them all stagnating, already dead. The traditional way of life is dead for me.

I   What is the next part you want to describe?

NADIM   Well, the valley part is not easy to express, especially here among you. I don't think you'll be able to understand me.

I   Do try, please.

NADIM   It is the Israeli-Jewish part, what I have absorbed of it. I live and work among you, I speak your language, study in your university. When I travel I see your villages, the kibbutzim, the white houses, and I feel a strange longing to belong. It is very difficult to admit. I sometimes feel like saying: Take me in, I am more familiar with you than with my own people. I am, however, very different from you. I don't think you could absorb me the way you absorb all the Jewish immigrants. No, and I don't think I even honestly want to be absorbed by you.

I   You were talking to the Israeli-Jewish inhabitants of this country. What is their answer to you?

NADIM   The first answer that comes into my mind is quite unpleasant. They say: Forget it. You're an Arab, you're the enemy. From time to time I had a period of harmony and felt accepted by my Jewish friends. I thought my adolescence, so to speak, was over. This harmony was shattered again and again by some tactless remark or, more seriously, by the occurrence of some terrorist act that would immediately mark me as a suspect.

I   Were you confronted like this in reality?

NADIM   Once, yes. I was put in the police station with all the Arab students when a bomb exploded in the school cafeteria. I was interrogated and then sent home to the village. This was the only time it actually happened. But in looks, frowns, more thorough searching at gates than any other person walking in, the message is conveyed to me every time. It cannot be denied.

I   I am not denying. And with all that, I like you and appreciate you as a person.

NADIM   Thank you.

I   So the Jewish part—

NADIM   It is important. It is my professional life, my education, my entrance ticket to Western literature and culture. I am a product of all this more than of my village. Yet it does not penetrate my inner being, which is a stranger here, too, and sometimes afraid. I do not belong here either. So there is my fantasy island.

I   Be this part.

NADIM   I am free and unattached. I have no religion, nationality, or even clothes. I am just me. I tend to my body, my needs —sun, ocean, sex, and drinking. All is there to satisfy me. I am happy and carefree. That's the only place I really belong to.

I   And your remaining needs?

NADIM   I don't think they really exist now. If I had my island, I would forget all about them.

I   The village and the valley?

NADIM   No doubt. I escape from my village to the valley, and from both of them to my secret island. The only trouble is that whereas the village and valley really exist, the island is the bubble of my dreams.

I   They are all parts of you and make you the special person, Nadim.

NADIM   I knew you'd say that, and I know it, too, in my head. Yet I can't see the way to be these different parts together. We keep fighting.

I   Maybe that's what you need your weapon for, the broken glass you brought back with you.

NADIM   You mean, for my different parts to fight with each other? Well, if that is true, I am relieved. Then you don't suspect me of trying to kill you with it?

I   No, I don't. This war is inside you. You may solve it someday and achieve some peaceful arrangement. You'll need to work on it.

NADIM   Well, yes. Right now I would rather fly back to my island.

Reminders of the Holocaust ____

Introduction

One of the most outstanding sets of cases and, for me, most moving and awe-inspiring is concerned with the holocaust and the way we young Israelis, who did not experience its horrors first-hand, deal with its memory. Several of the people who worked in my groups are children of concentration-camp survivors; but they are not the only ones haunted by holocaust recollections, which come to mind readily when the threat of war comes to the foreground.

Two recent periods in the history of Israel were specifically mentioned in relation to the holocaust. One was the waiting period before the 1967 war. For long weeks before the outbreak of this war, the impression was that the Arabs were mobilizing their forces from all directions, threatening war, while our then small country fortified itself against this forthcoming attack. Besides building trenches and preparing bomb shelters, people at home felt rather helpless, and many remember this period as one during which memories of the holocaust were brought to mind. Yet, this waiting period ended with a tremendous victory for us, reinforcing the feeling that the holocaust could not be repeated.

On a different note, the holocaust was again mentioned six years later, with the growing awareness of our horrible losses in human life during the Yom Kippur War. As an army commander said at one of the mass funerals: "A whole generation of warriors has been wiped out in three weeks." And, of course, in between these acute crises, some forget, some remember . . . some days more, some days less.

The close association between the perils of the former generation and the dangers of the present one has many faces. In Yoav's case, he is horrified by any signs of weakness: "If I'll be powerless, I'll be sent again to the gas chambers." He is compelled to be strong and, at the same time, deeply resents the image of the powerful Gestapo officer persecuting the helpless Jew. His choice, as he finds out working on a recurrent nightmare, is to be both strong and virtuous, a slogan closely related to the Israeli army's claim that it is built on its "moral strength." This theme is central also in Gal's letter, when she expresses her strong desire to be victorious in war so that her mother, a frail holocaust survivor, "will be safe this time and never suffer any more." Her letter has the flavor of a continuous need to escape. It also represents the dilemmas of a guilt-ridden generation, a guilt which may be the motivating factor behind many of our actions and decisions. In the same context, Mory raises another issue—the fear of being flooded by feelings that he has inherited, so to speak, from his mother, another holocaust survivor. His tough exterior, as well as his difficulty experiencing emotions and expressing them, he has adopted from his mother, who coped with her impossible existence in the concentration camps by blocking her own fear and despair. And now, he asks himself: If I let myself loosen up, will I have to feel all the horrors of the holocaust in retrospect? And, if so, would I be better off as an efficient robot without any emotions?

It is therefore apparent that the compulsion to be powerful, coupled with a certain insensitivity on the emotional level, has its deeper roots in the Jewish history of our century, with its focus on anti-Semitism, persecution, fear, and helplessness. The mentality of the Israeli soldier, his wife, and certainly his parents does not begin with the establishment of the State of Israel; it has far-reaching sources.

•   •   •   •

Today I had an American visitor, a psychotherapist from New York. It is her first visit to Israel.

—Would you like to hear one of my strangest experiences here in Israel? I am a survivor of the holocaust. As a girl, I lived through this trauma in Poland. I was forced, as were all other Jews, to wear the yellow Star of David on my arm. As an adult in the States, I have always resented this Jewish identification symbol and felt that I wouldn't be willing to wear another Star of David on me—whether gold or silver, as a pendant or whatever. My son wears one; he got it as a present from his grandmother. But I, I couldn't. Well, imagine, the other day I walked by a jewelry store; and without giving it any thought, I walked in and bought a Star of David for myself. Here it is, you see. I put it right on. That's what Israel does for me.

I watch her large, golden pendant in fascination. It stands out conspicuously on her black sweater. I ask her:

—How is it that we all talk about the holocaust so much recently? Where has it all been before? And why? Here, in Israel, I feel this growing awareness has to do with our wars. But for you?

Here she looks at me quite indignantly.

—What do you mean "your" wars? Why, it works the same way for us in the States. It all started with the Six-Day War. In the waiting period, and then during the first few days of the war, before the outcome was known, people in New York City cried in the streets. We feared it was the Jewish destiny to die once again. And then, with the victory, in one day our whole psychological world was changed. Our heads were lifted; it became possible to be Jewish yet not ashamed. So, you see, once the shame was gone, we were suddenly able to confront the shameful experience of the holocaust. Since, basically, it's a memory of tremendous shame—rightly so or not—it doesn't matter. With the shame gone, part of the repression was lifted as well.

—You mean, like a corrective experience, which helps one cope with previous bad memories?

—Yes, indeed.

•   •   •   •

And so we see that the revival of interest in the holocaust may be accounted for by either the experience of extreme danger or the relief of victory. What remains quite clear is the apparent association between it and the Arab-Israeli wars.

Whatever the correct theory, when people in the groups dared to express our proximity to the holocaust, they were also aware of the inevitability of our dilemmas, which can be neither solved nor absolved within such a short period of time. As Chana comments at the end of Yoav's session: "Personally, I do not believe we can overcome the psychological effects of the holocaust in our generation. Some unfinished business can never be finished, so let's not delude ourselves. It seems to me immodest, in a certain way, to pretend that psychological techniques can solve historical grievances. It isn't so."

Strong and Virtuous

Yoav is a young counselor whom I met at a weekend workshop. A skullcap on his head, he is the only observant Jew in the group. It is wintertime, and we are meeting between meals in a wooden cabin near the beach. We have been working continuously for about three hours. It starts to rain, and water is leaking into the cabin, while stormy winds are wailing, slamming the shutters with a bang.

YOAV   I have a recurrent dream. Usually I do not remember my dreams, but this one I remember, as it appears again and again, with very few variations.
I   Tell me in the present tense, as if you were dreaming now.
YOAV   Well, it is a very disturbing dream. In my dream I am in the Jewish ghetto in my parents' town in Poland. I see my father, only he looks very old with a white beard, like pictures I saw of Jews from the old times. My mother is also there, but I don't see her face. It is nighttime, and I wake up to the sound of violent knocking at our door.

He stops at this point and covers his face with his hands.

I   Please continue.

YOAV   The knocking is the most frightening sound I have ever heard. You have to kick the door with your nailed boots and rap it with the butt of your gun to get the right blend. I know very well how it feels to be outside the door: when I was on a patrol searching for terrorists in an Arab village, I was the one to knock like that on doors in the middle of the night.

I   Is this a part of your dream?

YOAV   No. I just saw myself on the other side of the door for a moment.

I   In the dream you are inside this door?

YOAV   Yes, and it certainly feels better to be on the strong side, the side that is active, outside the door.

I   While inside—

YOAV   —inside they are all so helpless.

I   Who are "they"?

YOAV   Us, of course. Me and my parents, in the dream.

I   Can you shuttle between the two positions, that of being outside versus being on the inside?

YOAV   I did not finish my dream yet.

I   Just the same.

YOAV   OK. Outside the door I am a man. I have on a sparkling uniform, I have a rifle and lots of ammunition. I am with my unit, we are together, we are the victors.

He then stops still and swallows several times, tense and pale.

I   What has just happened?

YOAV   I cannot continue. I cannot utter the things that came to my mind.

I   So think them out quietly for yourself.

After some minutes in which Yoav sits in obvious agony, he continues:

YOAV   This uniform, it is, of course, the Gestapo uniform which I saw. I can see the insignia quite clearly. I had this wild train of associations—you want me to identify with the people outside the door, so I should have said I am a member of the Gestapo. But my whole being revolts against this, and I cannot say it even for a second. And then my memory of the search in the Arab village came back; and putting one and one together . . . it is impossible . . . I refuse to continue with this.

I   Very well. So switch over, and be those who are on the inside.

Yoav gives a deep sigh and wipes his sweating face with his hand.

YOAV   This is not easier. Inside it's me and my parents. I am a young boy, the only child. We hear the knocking. I scream with alarm, and my father tells me to quiet down. I am very frightened. My father talks loudly to the Gestapo, telling them he is opening for them immediately. I feel so helpless. I want to hide, but the tiny room does not have any place to hide in. I want to tell him—

I   Tell him now.

YOAV   Father, don't open. Think of something to do, a way to resist. Fight back, for heaven's sake.

I   And he—

YOAV   He does not listen, of course. In the dream I don't even say anything. I just see him opening for the Gestapo. I myself feel helpless, and I see my father as an old, weak good-for-nothing.

I   Let me ask you a question. Which of the two roles do you prefer, inside or outside the door?

YOAV   Some question. That's the whole point. I hate the role of the Gestapo as much as that of the helpless victims.

I   The way I hear it, when you are strong and victorious, you feel at the same time cruel and immoral. When you are weak, however, you yourself become the victim of the cruelty.

YOAV   That's right. Precisely. There is no compromise possible.

I   You said the dream has another part.

YOAV   Yes. Sometimes it does. Lots of times I wake up as I hear the knocking. The next episode is in the morning. There is a huge square in town, and we are all gathered there. All the Jews. There are thousands of us, maybe more, and it is unnaturally quiet. I have a clear picture of the pavement of this square. The stones are beautiful and very old. So many people have walked on them, smoothed them over, that they are almost alive. Right now you don't see the stones. Every inch is occupied by feet, by the standing people. And the way they stand there somehow looks as if they were in a synagogue for prayers. The older, most respected members of the community stand up front. The women are all in the back. At the edge of the square, and on the roofs and windows of the neighboring houses, stand German soldiers, their machine guns aimed at the crowd. I know we are going to be killed in a moment and am struck by the complete silence, the serenity of the scene. No one moves. Now the inevitable happens. Shots from all directions, and all these Jews fall in silence, as if they were made of rags. I fall, too, but I know I am not dead. I push my head through these very light bodies, maybe rags, and I peep out carefully. That's how far my dream goes. All I know is that I am the sole survivor of this huge crowd.

Yoav is silent for a while, and then he looks up at me as he continues:

YOAV   This is my nightmare. I feel relieved just sharing it with you. But I ask myself why I have to re-experience the holocaust in my dreams.
I   I don't know why, but perhaps you'll find out.

I ask Yoav some questions regarding his background. He tells me both his parents survived the Nazi concentration camps in Europe and came to Israel in the forties. He was born in Israel in 1950.

YOAV   I know they spent some years in concentration camps, they have numbers on their arms. But they never told me about their experiences or about the remaining members of the family who were exterminated. As a child, when I started hearing about the events of the Second World War, in school, I made the connection. These horrors, I told myself, were experienced by my father and mother. I never brought the subject up at home, though, and neither did they. I am twenty-five years old, and to this very day I don't know about their experiences or how they managed to survive.

I   Would you like to find out?

YOAV   Well, I did, indirectly. In high school I started to read about the holocaust—any book I could lay my hand on. So I know enough, and I don't want to upset them with my questions.

I   Is there anything you want to tell them right now?

YOAV   Very little, I guess. I feel estranged from them. I would just say: "Mom, Dad, I know a little bit about the agony you lived through during the war. I don't know how you deal with your memories, and I certainly don't want to cause you any more pain. I hope you can have a secure life from now on." Yes, I think this is something which always existed in the back of my mind; namely, that I am their oldest child, and it is my duty in life to bring my parents some *nachat** after all their sufferings. This is OK, however; I can live with this minor demand.

I   Very well, then. So you have the holocaust experience somewhere in your background, and the pictures are probably from your readings. Now let us work on the dream. What is the part that stands out in your mind?

YOAV   The square, its stones, how big it is.

I   Do this in the first person.

YOAV   I am a huge square, paved with beautiful, smooth stones. I am very big, enormous. Thousands, millions, of feet have stepped over me. I am passive. I cannot do a thing. I cannot warn these people who are crowded now on top of me. What's the use of being so big and perfect if I am unable to comfort, to hide someone in me, to protect, or to scream, at least, to break this damned silence?

I   How do you experience yourself as the square, then?

*Pleasure and pride; a Hebrew-Yiddish term mostly used for parents' satisfaction from their offspring

YOAV   I am big and useless like the people above me who are small and useless. Being big or small does not matter; the feeling is the same.

I   What is missing, so that you'd feel different?

YOAV   Power, of course. Power to do things. Activity. Strength.

As I listen carefully, I again make the connection with the Gestapo image mentioned previously and wait to find out if Yoav will also return to the combination of strength and immorality. I decide not to mention my own train of thought at the moment.

I   Suppose I could infuse you with strength right now, you as the square or perhaps as the child in the square among the crowd. What would you do?

YOAV   My whole being craves for this strength. As in children's cartoons, suddenly I grow muscles and I am omnipotent.

I   Well, what would you do? Try it in the present tense.

YOAV   I am strong. If I were powerful, I would like to say to the old Jews standing up front—

I   Talk to them.

YOAV   You are the leaders of the community. The people look up to you, you have to tell them what to do. And, I say, the Torah, our religion, is against our standing here quietly like sheep, waiting passively for our destiny. Do something. Organize. Show some resistance. In the confusion of the fight maybe some of us will escape.

He stops, looking despondent.

I   There was no conviction in your voice. It was not the voice of a powerful person, or square, whatever.

YOAV   [*very sad*] I know. I feel I am not strong enough. I cannot mobilize the power to change anything. These old men will never listen to me.

I   Be the old men.

YOAV   This is easy. We are here together, with the whole community. I hear two voices representing these old leaders.

One says: "Don't worry. If we do not resist, nothing will happen to us. It is just another humiliating formality, and we Jews have survived many of those." This is the voice of stupidity, I am sad to say.

He sounds very scornful as he says that.

I   And the second voice?

YOAV   Some of the old men are not that stupid. They say: "We have no chance against the Gestapo. We have to bear our fate with honor. It is God's wish, and He will compensate us somehow. Maybe this is the last war on earth, and soon the Messiah will come to redeem our people."

His voice is very low, almost crying. And then he looks up and adds:

YOAV   I am not condemning them.

After some time I ask Yoav about his feelings.

YOAV   I think I got in touch with my weakness, my helplessness. It is a part of me I don't show very easily. I guess that I am afraid that if I'll be powerless, I'll be sent again to the gas chambers. Only they do not exist any more, I know.

I   Then maybe you can allow yourself to feel weak sometimes. And what about the other extreme, being very strong?

YOAV   Just now, I feel I failed in that, too. I was not powerful enough to bring about any meaningful change in the scene of my dream.

I   Repeat that sentence to several people here in the group.

YOAV   I was—

I   I am—

YOAV   I am not strong enough. I am not powerful enough.

He goes around the room, repeating these sentences about six times, and then stops abruptly and turns to me.

YOAV   No, I *am* strong enough now. I am not in the holocaust. I am strong enough, here and now, for an Israeli, for what is demanded of me now. And I am going to take care that we will never be shoved into a square and be shot at again.

He goes on repeating these ideas and becomes very alive and convincing.

I   That's how you stayed alive in your dream. You survived.
YOAV   Yes. I feel my head is very clear now. And there is this overwhelming feeling of being rescued, liberated. I want to hug you all. I felt like this when I met my friends in the Sinai after the battle, you know. We survived this crisis together, and here we are, back to life again.

People share the excitement of Yoav's work. They comment on the fact that he looks and sounds more alive than ever before in this workshop. And, as if by agreement, the wind has suddenly opened the door of the cabin, and the sun shines in. When all the feelings are shared, Chana intervenes.

CHANA   I do not want to disturb the happy-ending atmosphere, if that's what it is. Perhaps we are just happy to be able to change the subject and to take a break after so many hours of sharing Yoav's nightmare. Personally, I do not believe we can overcome the psychological effects of the holocaust in our generation. Some unfinished business can never be finished, so let's not delude ourselves. It seems to me immodest, in a certain way, to pretend that psychological techniques can resolve historical grievances. It isn't so. Anyway, this is not what I intended to say to you, Yoav. There was one thing that stood out for me, in your work. Your dilemma is to be strong or helpless, and if you can be both, arrive at some integration. Now I noticed one time when you conveyed strength very clearly. This was at the beginning, when you identified with the Gestapo knocking on the door. Strong and aggressive, strong and immoral. While the weak ones, they had God, religion, and all the human morality on their side, and thus accompanied, they walked into the gas chambers. And I grasped something while you worked, which is true for me and maybe for you, too: I am afraid of our becoming really powerful because then we may also become immoral. I know this is the keynote of the Arab propaganda. I wish you could, I could, be convinced that there exists a combination of being strong and virtuous at the same time.

Yoav thinks for a few minutes, then turns to Chana.

YOAV Chana, I want to tell you I accept a lot of what you have said. I feel you have sobered me up, out of my euphoria of ten minutes ago. And my feelings now are more balanced, more realistic. Yet I feel that a few minutes ago, when I suddenly realized that I am an Israeli and not a holocaust victim —not a Gestapo officer, either—I sensed that I am getting closer to that combination you mentioned before. How did you put it?

CHANA Being strong and virtuous. Very well, but that's not easy, mind you.

To Feel or Not to Feel

Mory is a student. In our ongoing group he misses several sessions, as he is frequently called to reserve duty. He returns from these service periods, trying to bridge the gaps of the missing time. Naturally, we know very little of his army life out there in the desert or in the training camp.

On Monday the newspapers have, on the front page, an item concerning a famous, high-ranking Zahal* officer who got killed as his jeep hit a land mine. In the corridors of the department, someone tells me that this officer was the direct commander of several of my students, deeply loved by them. People plan to attend the funeral.

On Tuesday our group gets together. Mory is pale, with dark rings under his eyes. He sits, very tense, listening absent-mindedly to some of the interactions going on in the group concerning last week's work. Then he speaks up.

MORY I hesitate . . . I don't know if I want to start on this at all, or if I am even able to. There were things I wanted to

*The Israeli defense army

tell some of the people here, and I feel I can't bring myself to start.

I We'll wait awhile. I see you look very upset today.

MORY Yesterday, you know, I found out that my commander was killed. Another one in the chain. And today . . . I didn't go to the funeral. I am, how would you say, "functioning" . . . I really can't imagine who am I punishing by blocking myself like that or not letting myself speak now.

All this is said with immense difficulty, with long pauses between the short sentences, between every word, as if the words are being forced out very slowly. I do not want to press Mory into working. Maybe I am afraid. Another member of the group is taking my place.

BEN Do go on, Mory. I know that it's terribly hard, but I feel you need to share this. Maybe we can help. You can just try to tell us about it, about your commander, if you wish. This may make you feel better.

I add that he can tell his story, and we'll not press him into "working." These remarks help Mory continue.

MORY My reaction to the news yesterday was very familiar, sort of typical of me. It reinforced my sense of being different from everybody else, a feeling I have always had. Something is wrong with me. I have always been ashamed, have always been trying to hide something from the world.

I Ashamed of what?

MORY Lots and lots of things. Ashamed of not having a father, for one. This always made me feel different from the other children. I tried to hide it from the children, tried to cheat them sometimes.

I When did he die?

MORY When I was thirteen, and from a heart attack, too. Such a stupid cause. He wasn't a hero or anything. I am angry at him for dying this way.

I Was his death very sudden?

MORY No. I saw his decline for two years before the final stroke. Actually, I was the one who came home and found him

fainting, unconscious. I was alone. I found him in the bathroom. And then, too, as today, I was "functioning." I called the
doctor, called the ambulance service, I don't remember exactly.
I remember, however, being very angry at him for collapsing
like that. And then another scene that I recall—the stretcher-
bearers are taking him down to the ambulance, and I stand at
the window, watching from above as he is being taken away. I
didn't cry then, just as I didn't cry yesterday. It was very
strange. The world outside my window looked the same as
always—children were playing outdoors—and my father was
being driven away. I didn't feel afraid, either. Just some anger
and blankness.

I   When you visualize this moment in the present, what do you
feel?

MORY   First of all, I feel a tremendous force preventing me
from going into the scene. I do not wish to. And inside is a
mixture of pain and anger. The pain is stronger than the anger.
I want to cry. I want to cry very badly, as I did at my father's
funeral. But I cannot cry. I never can cry when I am being
watched.

I   And when you are not watched?

MORY   All the same, I don't cry even then.

I   Who is watching you when you are alone?

Mory answers right away, with no hesitation.

MORY   My mother. She is watching.

I   Talk to her.

MORY   Mother, you do not let me cry. You stand in my way,
preventing me from crying.

I   What does she say?

MORY   Nothing. She does not answer. She gets up from her
chair and walks out of the room. She cannot stand my sorrow,
my weeping.

I   You have to be strong for her sake?

MORY   More or less, yes. She, she does not feel anything any
more. She cannot stand emotions. She cannot stand my emotions either.

He is quiet for a long time, crying a little and obviously with-holding.

I   Where are you now?

MORY   I was remembering many of the things I used to hide.

I   Like what?

MORY   More things I was always ashamed of. Mostly the fact that my parents lived through the holocaust in Europe, the horrible things that happened to them in the concentration camps. My mother keeps talking and talking about that period, telling me all the details of her terrible experience. And I, I don't even listen any more. The way she talks, I know she does not feel anything. Once, during the war, she told me that when the alarm sounded all the neighbors rushed down to the shelter, while she stayed in our apartment, which is on the top floor. I asked her why, and she said she has lost the ability to be afraid, so whatever happens, happens.

I   She does not feel any more, and you are afraid you're like her.

MORY   Yes. My father, he did. He was able to feel.

I   Talk to your mother and tell her in what way you differ from her.

MORY   Mother, I am different. I want to be different now. I am different in that I want to feel. It is very difficult. There are some events people never even talk about, so how can we start to experience the feelings attached to them? Like, only the other month I grasped the fact that in the camp you survived from, there were cases of cannibalism. I forced myself to think about it, and what the conditions must be to make human beings act this way. Yes. We are different. You do not want to feel, and I do.

I   You may be different in another respect. You have the strength to feel, and she, perhaps, does not have much strength left.

MORY   I don't quite believe you when you mentioned my strength. I don't believe in myself. I am not completely sure that I am capable of feeling.

He is silent for a long time, sniffling and rubbing his eyes. Suddenly his tears come freely, as if the barrier is gone; and he lets them fall down his cheeks, on his shirt, very quiet and immobile.

I   Are you with someone?
MORY   No, I am alone. I felt how I am actively trying to ignore you, to shut you out, to isolate myself, as if saying: Get out, I want to be alone.
I   This reminds me of your mother leaving the room. Maybe it's your responsibility, too, that you somehow tell her to get out.

Mory is silent, still crying.

I   Can you tell her you accept her, with the way she has chosen to cope, although it's different from yours?
MORY   Yes, I can. Mother, lately I feel that I accept you more —not totally, though. Sometimes I am still angry with you. Now I recall an event that happened a month ago. You suddenly reacted like everybody else. I sensed this intensity in you, as if you did feel something.
I   And you, you are afraid that if you let yourself feel, you'll have to feel it all, the holocaust, all the horrors and the atrocities. But, perhaps, it does not have to be like that. You do not have to undertake to feel *everything*.
MORY   That's strange. I have never seen it that way. This is something I have to remember.
I   As if feelings were "all or nothing."

Mory looks around at the people in the room. Somebody hands him tissues, while one of the men mutters: "I can't stand men crying. This is sheer agony for me."

A Letter to My Mother

At the end of a year's work in a group, Gal, a twenty-five-year-old woman, handed me the following paper, which I record in full:

Twice, in the group, people worked on their relationships with their mothers, and on both of these occasions I burst out crying and was unable to think or to talk about my feelings. Now I feel unfinished about this. I owe it to me, to you, to clarify those feelings.

Let me start with a recurrent scene of my childhood, which went something like this: My father announces, as he comes back from his factory in the evening, that next week, or sometime in the near future, he will go abroad on a business trip. My mother listens, swallowing with difficulty, her face as pale as a sheet; then she starts to implore him—beg, really—that he not go, since she cannot stay without him, will certainly collapse, and she is afraid that something awful will happen to him on the trip—he'll never come back alive—and she'll die or take her own life, and I'll remain alone in the world, with nobody to take care of me. She cries and trembles, and Dad talks to her gently, explaining that he must go, reassuring her that he will be back as soon as possible, that nothing can happen to him.

As I listen to all this, I am terribly afraid, and later also angry. Afraid that something may really happen to Dad, and then I'll be alone with Mother, a terrible situation for me. And will I be able to handle her if she really collapses as she says? Afraid to see how fragile she is, how weak and dependent. Angry at my father for doing this to her, although as I grew up I identified with him more and more, saying to him in my heart: "Go on, don't be afraid of her threats. You are entitled to your freedom. When I grow up, I'll leave, too." My fear of my mother, of her fragility and out-bursts, was also mingled with anger; and in my heart I'd say to her: "Why can't you be stronger? Why are you so worthless?"

It took me years to find out the answer, to understand the meaning of the tattooed number on her arm.

As I grew up under the impact of such scenes—and many more "secret" ones that were going on out of my view—with a chronic tension in the air, the presence of tragedy, I was mostly afraid and wanted to run away. I was a girl of many fears, and now I think they were transferred to me by my mother. Was I trying to escape from her—or for her? Or was I trying to run away from the things she stood for? One of my clearest memories is of returning home after a carefree afternoon with friends and immediately feeling the contrast, a home haunted by fears and tensions. The curtains were drawn, and electric lights burned even during the daytime —my mother could not stand exposed windows or very bright light. This was only one of her "symptoms." She did not read any newspapers or listen to the news broadcasts. She always had some soft music on her record player to dampen the noises of the world outside. "The tension is not good for her nerves," I was told. "The world outside may harm her delicate constitution."

In school some years later, I learned about the holocaust; and like all the other children, I was horrified. I knew better than to try to share my fears at home. Only much later did I find the missing link of this puzzle: Mother is from over there. Is that why there are lots of things left unsaid between us?

So, after the second session in our group when I cried and was unable to talk, I went home to my own apartment and sat down at the typewriter. With one hundred miles between me and my mother, I felt quite safe, and I wanted to write her a letter in which I'd say everything. No diplomacy this time or fear of the results, since I'll not mail this letter anyway. Like talking to the empty chair, this is all for me.

Here is my letter, done all in one night.

Dear Mother,

As I am thinking what I'd like to tell you, I feel this familiar fear, that I will hurt you, that I may lose you. I see you so weak and helpless.

The main thing I want to tell you is how guilty you made me feel from the day I found out about your childhood. I am pretty sure this heavy feeling of guilt existed in me even before I really knew. I was guilty of being alive while so many of your original family had died in the holocaust. I was guilty of being happy and normal, while you continued to live under the burden of your adolescence in the concentration camps. I was guilty of hating you, yes, hating you for being so different from the mothers of my friends, for not wanting to give me a brother or a sister, for being so immersed in your own self.

I am writing this in the past tense, but sometimes I am not sure whether my feelings have changed much. Indeed, I do feel guilty even now, and I resent you for making me feel that way.

I remember one episode now. I am in high school, about fifteen. It is springtime, and you offer to buy me some clothes, new sandals. I say I don't need any. I would like to tell you now the thoughts I had in mind at that time. I wanted to say: "I do not want any gifts. If you could only love me, talk to me, play with me, relax." I also wanted to say: "I know you did not have any new dresses when you were my age. I saw pictures of children from over there. I won't have anything for myself either." I identified with you, and I was afraid of this identification and was trying to squeeze out of the bind. And you, you gave in so easily, then as always. You did not insist on giving me these things, and I imagined you saying: "How ungrateful of her." You never said that to me, though. We hardly ever talked. I kept all these endless dialogues in my head; and throughout my childhood, I learned that I had to be strong for you.

In the army I put some safe distance between you and me, and life seemed more bearable. Gradually, I realized you are you—while I am me. You had your past to deal with, and it is not *my* past. You are all shattered inside, hence your fragility. I am going to be different. I have no reason to be like you. Talking with Father about it helped a lot. He was part of my world more than of yours. I started to forgive you.

If war had not broken out . . . I was mobilized in the spring of 1967, when tension started to build up. In the long weeks of waiting and suspense, the Arabs gathered tremendous forces against us from down south and up north. In my army position, I had all the information, and I was numb with fear. The Arabs are preparing a second holocaust, somebody said. I felt it was my destiny to live through your experiences. It seemed to me as natural as the closing of the circle.

I remember now two distinct feelings. The panic, the defeatism, were like being drawn to you, becoming you, Mother, in actuality. I felt as if the forces pulling me down, to give up, to surrender, were stronger than life. On the other hand, there was my desire to win, to mobilize my energies to the utmost extent, so that there wouldn't be a second holocaust, never again; so that you, Mother, would be safe this time and not suffer any more. I don't know if that was the driving force for every single fighter in this country, but it certainly was mine. I realize I am me, Gal. I am different from you, yet I cannot grow too far apart.

I feel exhausted now. It is very late, and I have had my say. Did you ever imagine, Mother, that I had all these thoughts and emotions pent up inside me? Did you ever realize how important you are to me, despite our estrangement?

Now that I have expressed myself, I wish you could know these things, and we could talk about them. I don't know if we're strong enough, though, and whether we'll ever try.

In the morning I found all these pages near the typewriter. I read this letter and was amazed and bewildered. I know I will never send it to my mother. I'll share it with you, with a copy for myself.

War and the Family _____

Introduction

In Israel the roles and relationships of mother, father, husband, wife, son, and daughter are deeply affected by the continuous strain of the tensions and dangers of our life here and by the sudden crisis of war when it breaks out. People have been talking a lot about this indirect consequence of the war. Because it would be impossible to survey all the different manifestations of our problems in this area, I will present just a few cases of individuals facing their family members, with the threat of war as a third side of the triangle.

One example concerns parents' relationships with their children. Parents worry about the safety of their children, who grow up in the shadow of war. Will my son have to fight for this country when he grows up? Will we manage to achieve a peaceful solution before his time to be mobilized comes? These questions obsess parents, even when their children are mere infants. Such an infant is Ud's boy, and the father's frantic attempt to save him is the focus of the dream that opens this section. Ud handed "One Man's War" to me in writing after a year of work in the group. This is a dream with a minimal amount of augmentation, in its raw state—a parable in which we may find many meanings. Yet its message is rather straightforward: people are endangering the child's life, and the father (Ud) wanders back to his military training camp in the desert in search of a weapon with which to ward them off.

Significantly, this dream dates from 1971, a relatively peaceful period before the Yom Kippur War. Yet, in his search, Ud encounters an abandoned radio, which goes on broadcasting the screams of a tank crew hit a long time ago. War, its demands and its dangers, is an ongoing process, for us as well as for our children. This idea is formulated by Ud at the conclusion of his dream when he says: "I realized . . . [this is] my private war in which I have to keep my son alive, and this war is sort of unconfined by time. It exists within me and will be with me continuously. I have to learn to live with it and to keep my gun ready at all times."

As the mother of a thirteen-year-old boy, Sara tends to see her son as a future soldier. She confesses her anxiety about him, which sometimes overcomes the normal considerations involved in upbringing. Thinking about his future, she tends to forgive him for the mess in his room, which, in perspective, becomes meaningless; and sometimes she unnecessarily indulges him in material objects. With all the other common dilemmas of parenthood, Israelis have this additional one: Am I raising my son to become a soldier? And if so, what are the values I would like to pass on to him? And, in the back of our mind, there is, perhaps, the faint tendency to provide our children with the best possible conditions *now,* since who knows what might lie in store for them in the future. Regarding these points, an American visitor once asked me two questions: At what age do you start seeing your son as a candidate for the war? With all this in mind, why are your youngsters not terribly spoiled? To the first question, the answer is clear: from the first year, the first day, even before they are born, we see these boys as future soldiers. The answer to the second question is much harder to give. Perhaps our youngsters are not spoiled because though their mothers may be tender and merciful, the country is not. Sara just touches upon this point; we do not attempt to solve it for her.

For a different viewpoint, one can listen to the story of Maty, the father of three boys. He asks himself if it was fair to immigrate to Israel, thus preventing his sons from making a free choice—a choice he himself made by coming here. He is worried about his frequent separation from his sons, due to his army duties. He would like to reassure them that he will always come back safely to them so that he will not be haunted by the fantasy of his youngest son "waiting for your daddy, who'll never come back," a fantasy that is firmly based on his own childhood memories. On another level, the anxiety-ridden behavior of Maty's four-year-old son may result from that frequent separation and from his concern about his father. Thus, we may find a father worrying about his child and a child worrying about his father in an ongoing cycle that encourages each other's anxiety.

• • • •

It is a clear summer morning in 1974 when the idea that my son will become an Israeli soldier materializes in full color for me. At that time, he is ten years old. It is the last day of school, before the summer vacation. My son has volunteered to bring a cake to school to celebrate the end of the fourth grade, to make this last day a special one. I bake a big cake, put fancy frosting on top to please the children, and walk to school to hand it to the teacher. I arrive in the deserted schoolyard, which seems so vast when all the children are in their classrooms. In the center of this yard a new metal sculpture has been erected. It is a large, brown structure on which the children can climb and play.

I walk around it and find an inscription, a sentence from the Bible about children playing in the streets. I like the sculpture, yet it makes me sad. I don't know why. I enter the building slowly, waiting for the bell to ring for the break, and automatically my eyes fall on a stone plate. Engraved on it are the names of all the school graduates who were killed in the wars. Brightly colored drawings of students are hanging all over the wall around the plate. From one room I hear children's voices singing a song, "Jerusalem, City of Peace." Suddenly I know I am going to cry, and I rush outside, back to the sculpture. This time, through the tears, I know why it makes me sad. Now it looks like a monument. For whom?

The cake in my hands, I take stock of my feelings. Yes, it is not easy to be an Israeli; it is rough on the mothers of soldiers and future soldiers. I am frightened by it all. At the same time, there is a sense of value and significance to my life here rather than somewhere else.

The bell rings, interrupting my thoughts, piercing the silence. Children burst into the schoolyard, shouting; the scene is totally changed. It is the world of children, nothing else. I walk into the teachers' room, careful with the cake, and I hand it in. Somehow, I am extremely pleased that I made it such a fancy one.

•   •   •   •

There are other family relationships affected by the war. One appears in the story of Miri and her estranged husband, which is, perhaps, an unusual story. The experience of war, even when relatively short, may produce some deep and long-range personality changes. People lose interest in former areas of accomplishment and search for new ones after the war, and some of their relationships completely lose their meaning and value. And thus, a man may return from war and find his young wife unattractive, uninteresting, or perhaps a mere stranger. He may claim his freedom, run away. This is the story of Miri, I believe. Her husband's motives are unknown to us; we can only speculate. Miri raises the question that occupied many individuals who were personally hurt by war. Can one prepare for tragedy in life? Should one? The pride of those invulnerable before the disaster is one of the things to look back at and wonder: Why didn't I see it coming?

Other aspects of family relationships will appear in the cases of other sections, as well as in the interviews in Part III.

One Man's War

Toward the end of our year in the 1971 group, I received some written reports from the students who participated. Ud is a very quiet young man. He rarely talks in the group. Frequently he draws, recording impressions of the people or the room while listening. He has been with us for a year, and we know next to nothing about his life outside. The following is a dream of Ud's that he reported in writing.

Recently I had a dream that touched me very deeply. In the sessions following this dream, I thought of working on it in the group. At the beginning of every meeting I would decide to present the dream; and when there was silence, I would make up my mind to work. As the silence continued, my wish to work on the dream would become stronger; yet, I was pleased with the silence in the group. I always felt it was a very constructive period, when the small moments of silence grew together into a great quietude and calm. I hated to break it, and finally there was always someone else who did—and there I remained, nursing my untold dream.

In my dream I am suddenly awakened from my sleep by a large group of people in our bedroom, and I see something very strange: lots of people are standing around the cradle of my baby boy; and my son, who usually is constantly smiling and playing with his tiny legs and hands, lies there quietly, all blue and frozen. He has this strange expression on his face . . . very strange.

I want to find out what the problem is, but the crowd of people won't let me approach him. From what I hear, I understand that he is doomed to be sent to an orphanage; and somebody, probably a psychologist, stands there and lectures loudly on how destructive an orphanage is for babies. In the meantime, I see my wife hurrying away, telling me she is busy now and does not know when she will be back. I desperately try to reach my son and save him from these people, but they push me away. They all wear black suits and white shirts. They are sweating horribly, talking loudly, and flinging their arms around. I simply cannot pass through.

I search for something to hit them with, but all I find are pieces of white paper. Suddenly I realize I have to get a weapon, and I drive as fast as possible to an army camp in Sinai, where I used to serve in the reserves. I remember that half a year ago

I hung my machine gun near the bed, and I am determined to find it. When I arrive, I find the camp totally deserted, and only the radio continues to produce some noise, which I know to be messages that nobody is there to take. I am surprised to find the radio thus abandoned and run to take the message. I hear that it is the desperate cries of a tank crew whose tank was hit by the enemy. I don't know what to do, since nobody is there. I try to answer them with the radio, only to discover nobody is at the other end either. Suddenly I understand that the sounds are the screams of the crew hit half a year ago, and they go on, captured by the radio, all the time.

I find my machine gun and drive quickly back. The sky is as red as blood, and the horizon is black with smoke. Then I am standing in my bedroom and shoot all those people, and they all fall down, crumbling. Only the psychologist remains, staring at me sadly, continuously lecturing. Finally he, too, falls down, and it is quiet again.

I look at my son, and he is calmly asleep, his face clear and happy as usual. I realize I have saved him. At the same time I know I have to clean my gun so it won't rust and will be ready for the next time I may need it. Outside the sky is clearing, it is a blue night, and the sky is full of fantastic fireworks. I know the police may come for me any minute now, and I want to sleep.

I was walking around with this dream in my head for days, until finally I was not sure if this was the dream I had, reflecting all these parts hidden within me, or perhaps I invented it all to please my self-image. I remembered the story about the Zen monk who dreamt he was a butterfly and did not know whether he was a monk becoming a butterfly in his sleep or a butterfly turning into a Zen monk upon awakening.

One evening, as I drove the four-hour drive to Jerusalem, I saw a girl hitchhiking at the side of the road, and I gave her a ride. She was a tourist on her way out of the country, and she had marvelous eyes and a face amazingly similar to the girl's face I used to draw, and still draw from time to time. I felt I could tell her my dream.

I told her the dream and sort of worked on it as we used to do in the group. I realized how the dream represented my private war, in which I have to keep my son alive, and this war is sort of unconfined by time. It exists within me and will be with me continuously. I have to learn to live with it and to keep my gun ready at all times.

The girl watched me with her big eyes. Sometimes she smiled and attempted to understand my Hebrew. I don't think she understood much—or perhaps she did, since words are not that important. Two soldiers dozing off in the back seat and the other cars on the road were the group, the audience. I don't know if I closed the Gestalt of the dream, but I am not bothered by it any more.

The Corner of Waiting

Maty has a very heavy South American accent, and his Hebrew sometimes sounds like an old-time melody. A kibbutz member and a psychology student, he is a very warm and candid person, and extremely easy to work with in the group.

MATY I want to work on my relationship with my youngest son. He is four years old now.
I What's his name?
MATY Ofer.

He looks very sad and gentle as he pronounces the name, then adds:

MATY I guess I'll cry. I want to cry. I have been wanting to since we started to work in this group. I have the feeling of a deep buried pain, which is here [*pointing to his lower abdomen*] and needs to come out.

As he says that the tears start to roll down his cheeks, onto his open brown shirt.

I Talk to Ofer.
MATY Ofer, I can see you in that chair. It is too big for you.

His weeping increases, yet he goes on speaking, with short pauses between the sentences.

MATY   Actually, all I want to tell you is . . . Come over here, my boy. My small one . . . I want to hug you. Let's just be together.

He cries for a while, then talks to me.

MATY   I don't know why I have all these problems with Ofer. He is our youngest. We have two older boys, seven and six, and they did not give us any trouble. But Ofer, he has something like a tantrum every evening as we put him to sleep in the children's house.* He just cries his little heart out. He does not want us to leave him there. And I don't know what to do, how to help him.

I   Talk to Ofer about it.

MATY   [*crying*] Ofer, I feel so helpless, unable to help you enough, to give you enough. It's as if your needs for love and attention are infinite. I feel so incompetent as a parent with you.

Maty goes on crying and mutters: "Don't worry about my crying. It's OK. I am pleased to be crying."

I   I would like you now to be the little boy yourself. Not Ofer, but Maty as a four-year-old boy, and talk to your father about your needs.

I do not know, at this stage, anything about Maty's background or his father. His crying at the moment is, however, so childlike that I can actually visualize him as a child and make the transition of one generation back.

Maty looks at me, amazed for a minute, and then starts:

MATY   As a little boy, I am, of course, in Buenos Aires. We live on a Jewish street and are rather poor. My father died when I was fourteen. He was a salesman and traveled around most of the year, while we stayed with Mama.

*In most kibbutzim, the children do not sleep in their parents' home but with the other children of their age group in a children's house.

I   Talk to him, talk about your needs.

MATY   I am trying to go back in time. I have not given my childhood any thought for such a long time. I live in completely different circumstances now. Israel, the kibbutz—it takes time to go back.

I   Start and see what happens.

MATY   Father, I see you walking out of the house with your black leather bags. A small man, so completely worthless. I see you walking out and then vanishing around the corner at the end of our street. And I want to ask you—

Here he starts to cry again, more violently than before, and can hardly talk.

MATY   I want to ask you, when will you be back? I need you.

After a pause he adds:

I need you with me, though I would like you to be different— stronger, somebody to look up to. I love you just the same, you could not be somebody else. You know, for years and years we used to go to this corner every afternoon, me and my sister, and look up and down the main street. Maybe you'll be back to-night, maybe it will be our lucky day. You'll be back, bring something for us, sit at the head of the dinner table. This corner has become for me the corner of waiting, the corner of longing, of being different and alone. For years, as I stood there waiting, you usually did not show up. And I was thinking, all to myself and never sharing it with anyone, that perhaps, perhaps, this time you'd not be back, never again. And this is what finally happened. You went away around this corner and never came back with your black leather bags. You walked out of my life. Just like that.

Maty cries, and the group shares his expressions of pain and grief. Later he quiets down and says:

MATY   Oh, I never believed I had so much crying to do! I feel very relieved now, and not as heavy as when I started. I am pleased I let myself cry. The pain in my abdomen is gone.

I   I am pleased, too. Now all this started with Ofer.

MATY   Yes, I want to make the connection. You're hinting—

I   No, you do your own script.

MATY   OK. So we have me and my father, on the one hand. His frequent separations from us, my needs, and finally his sudden death in a lonely hotel room somewhere. And, on the other, me and Ofer, my son. His needs, are they like mine?

I   I don't know. If you identify with him, you become extra sensitive to his needs, and this starts a circle going. But you have to find your own message.

MATY   I leave him quite frequently, too, to go to the university. And sometimes, for longer periods of time, when I go to the reserves.

He is silent for some time, very absorbed in his thoughts.

I   Where are you now?

MATY   Going off to the army for thirty days, and again for forty-five days. I am called a lot. We all are. And during the war, of course.

I   Whom do you want to speak to about this?

MATY   To Ofer, naturally. Ofer, you are a big boy now, and you know that I am called to the army quite often, as all daddies are. I want to make a promise to you that I'll always come back to you, so you don't have to worry.

I   Your voice is so soft, I can hardly hear it.

MATY   Because I am cheating, and I know it. I wish I could say what I just did honestly. But you all know I can't.

I   And if you'd speak truthfully, what would you say?

MATY   I cannot speak truthfully to a four-year-old.

I   Maybe not for real, but just try here.

MATY   Look, Ofer. You were born here, you didn't make the choice yourself, and you'll grow up to be an Israeli kibbutznik. I made the choice when I was eighteen, I came here, went right into the army and later to the kibbutz. I married a kibbutz girl, and now this is my only home, our home. I very rarely think about my home in Buenos Aires; and when I do, I don't long for it. I know that, for me, I made the right choice. I take this responsibility.

I   You say "for me, I made the right choice." And for the others?

MATY   That's the root of the problem, or one of the roots. I have three sons, and the year is 1976, and peace is not yet at our gate. I sometimes wonder if it was my right to determine the fate of other people when I made my own choice. Do you see what I mean? My son didn't make the choice to live in a country which has to fight for its survival.

I   Neither did my son and daughter.

MATY   So . . . maybe you are not bothered by this guilt, since you yourself were born here anyway.

I   It never occurred to me to be angry at my parents for making the decision to leave Poland for Israel. On the contrary, I am very thankful for that, for otherwise, who knows? We probably would have never made it through the period of the Second World War in Europe.

MATY   I know. You are very rational. You're telling me that maybe I, too, saved my children from an even worse kind of life. It is partly true. As a Jew, I would not like to raise a family in Argentina today. But the guilt is there, just the same.

I   Talk to Ofer again.

MATY   Ofer, I hope it will be more peaceful here when you grow up and your turn to serve in the army comes around. Sometimes I feel guilty for having made the choice for you, for the fact is I am afraid it will still be wartime when you're eighteen, or when Ran and Guy are. I pray to God you'll all survive.

I   And how about yourself?

MATY   Yes, you're right, that is also true. I pray to God, whatever it may be, that I'll survive. Not for me so much, but for you, Ofer. So that I'll always come back to you as I promised, so that you won't have to be as anxious and needy as I was in my miserable childhood, so that you'll never be the child standing on the corner waiting for his daddy, who'll never come back.

He sits there with his eyes closed and gives a deep, moving sigh. Then he looks around the room, slowly returning to us.

MATY   I feel finished. I think that I finally told Ofer what I needed to tell him. And I cried for my father and finished. Do you think Ofer will finish his crying, too?
I   With a father like you, I am sure one day he will.
MATY   Thank you for saying that.

People in the group are exhilarated. There is a great deal of emotional exchange, and Maty looks on, still very much with himself. One of the girls asks him whether he got from his work any ideas about how to deal with Ofer's problem. He answers curtly: "To love him as much as he needs, that's all."

Thirteen-Year-Old Future Soldier

Sara is a social worker who attends a short training workshop at the university. She is older than most of my group members and somehow looks out of place in the room. She is the mother of three daughters and a son, now thirteen years old.

SARA   I want to work on my problems with my son. Actually, my whole relationship with him is problematic.
I   Talk to him directly, as if he were here with you.

Sara is smiling forgivingly, as if I have just shown my ignorance.

SARA   If only we *could* talk. Talking is so difficult. I always see him in motion—on his way to search for something in the refrigerator (he is always hungry) or jumping to answer the phone or rushing down the steps, three at a time. He is as tall as I am.
I   Is he always in motion?
SARA   Yes, or else he is very busy, absorbed in his own work, reading, woodcarving. I don't know what exactly.
I   So, he is always in motion or very busy. Could you say that in the first person?

SARA   Me? I am very busy. Mostly, that's true. I am always in motion, rushing to make it on time. Yes, the tempo is similar. Dan to the refrigerator and I to the grocery store [*laughs*].

I   Tell him how you are similar.

SARA   Danny, did you ever realize that we are somewhat alike? We both have many interests, we care about things, we try to change things we don't like. But we are so different in relating to each other.

I   "But" is a very bad word here. Try "and" instead.

SARA   . . . and we are also different. This sounds as if we can get closer . . . maybe.

I   And how are you different? Talk to Dan about your differences.

Sara takes my instructions with no delay, as if these words were here all the time, waiting to be said.

SARA   You are young, and I am old. Well, not old but much older than you.

She stops. Her breathing is faster, and her face takes on a frightened expression.

I   What is happening?

Sara does not answer right away, and then continues with her dialogue.

SARA   You are rejecting me, while I try to get closer to you.

Now her words flow breathlessly, as if she is escaping.

SARA   I am very well organized. I try to be clean, our house is well taken care of. You, you are so filthy. Your room is such a mess, your clothes, books, schoolwork. You make me feel so disgusted.

I   Would you like to be him and talk to you?

SARA   No, I don't think I can. You see, actually I cannot imagine myself talking to Dan like that. He shuts me off—finds an excuse and runs away, or closes the door to his room, with all the mess inside.

I   Say that to Sara, as Dan.
SARA   Mother, leave me alone. It is no use. He is locking his door.
I   What do you feel right now?
SARA   Sadness. I am sad, of course, as if I lost him already.
I   Please repeat that.
SARA   What? What did I say just now?

Her eyes fill with tears as she continues.

SARA   You see, now I am making a fool of myself.
I   Crying?
SARA   Yes. I know I don't make sense, and I can't talk.
I   We'll wait for you to be able to talk. And for now, I just want you to pay attention to where you started to weep and what you stopped yourself from saying.

Sara keeps on crying. Someone offers tissues, and we all sit quietly.

I   Where are you now?
SARA   I am here. Just a few minutes ago, I felt this loss, when his door was locked in front of me, as if he were taken away, and I lost him.

Her voice becomes very soft and difficult to follow.

SARA   I am ashamed, ashamed to have these thoughts, yet how can I drive them away?
I   Maybe you can, if you stay with them first for sometime, now, and if you can share them with us here.
SARA   It is so frightening. The thought of raising a boy in the family, here, with all the wars, or even the accidents during training. And Dan is my only son. My daughters are older, and one is going to be drafted soon for her service. And I look at the mothers of her boyfriends and admire their courage. I can't understand. They must be so brave. When Dan is in the army, I don't know how I will live through that period.

Rachel, who is another member of the group, interrupts:

RACHEL Oh, no, you'll live through it all right. There is simply no choice, and everybody does. When you spoke, I was thinking of when I was pregnant. I was so afraid of childbirth and watched every woman who went through this event with total admiration. Then, some months later, when my time came, I just behaved normally, I knew what to do, what to expect, and simply lived through the events. I have the feeling that your case is similar. As long as you rehearse for a frightening future, you are much more afraid than when it is part of your daily reality, part of your present.

Sara is quiet while Rachel talks, but she does not seem to be listening. As she continues, we realize she is still very much with her own experience, almost ignoring Rachel's intervention.

SARA I can't help it. I sometimes have this nightmare of—you understand, it's a daytime fantasy, not a dream—of me losing him.
I How?
SARA In the war. I am afraid he will be killed somehow.

There is a deep silence in the room as Sara sits with her eyes closed, motionless.

I Stay with it, with this feeling.
SARA I feel awful. I am in a dark pit. There is no life. I guess if Dan is killed in the war, then I will die, too. Not my body, you know, but in all other respects.

We remain silent for a while longer.

I And now?

Sara opens her eyes and looks at me in wonder, as if uncertain about her surroundings. She breathes deeply.

I You are not in a black pit, you are with us.
SARA Yes, that's right. I am alive, and so is Dan. Thank God.

She sighs deeply and rubs her eyes.

I   As long as you stay in the now.

SARA   You know, I am very pleased that we talked about all this. I never uttered this fear to anybody. I was afraid it would come true. Before, when I said here that he was young, I was asking myself: Will he live to be my age, to have children of his own? Will he be lucky enough to be a father to his own children with all the pleasures and difficulties that parenthood involves? As I ask that, I feel that the actual reality of the mess in his room is so meaningless. The idea occurred to me the other day. Now I think that this is what caused my outburst today.

I   Tell us about the other day and make it in the present tense.

SARA   Well, we are going to shop for gym clothes, you know, for gym training. Dan is never fancy in his dress, does not have expensive tastes. Actually, he has minimal needs in this area. He wants some things from the sporting-goods store, and I am glad we have the chance to walk downtown together, he and I. In the store, he suddenly picks out the most expensive outfit, some imported goods of very high quality. This is so out of character for him. He insists on having just this one, and I feel very displeased. No, even worse, I feel angry. And I say: "Why, the Israeli brand is just as good, it looks just the same, and it costs half the price!" I feel embarrassed; I am not usually tight-fisted, not at all. He likes this one better, he says; he will be able to use it for a much longer time. I feel awkward arguing with him in the store, in front of all the people. This encounter, this episode, takes about a minute, and Dan does not even insist too strongly. And then, out of the blue, I have this terrible thought, which I told you about before.

I   Continue, try to live through this episode again.

SARA   Well, this inner voice of mine says something like: "How dare you? He is becoming a young man, and pretty soon he will be a soldier, and then what? If the worse happens . . . You have to compensate him now. There is no time, you have to make him happy, give him the best possible childhood, since as a young man in Israel, who knows?" I am ashamed of this voice.

I   It is one of your parts.

SARA   It is part of our reality, sadly enough.

I   Are you ashamed of this reality?

SARA   No, not really. It is tough but not shameful. Yes, I think I may be able to accept the fact that I worry about Danny. It does not sound so weird and out of place now.

I   And if you stay more in the actual present, then you must admit that you are both well and alive.

RACHEL   And you may even resist buying him imported gym clothes.

This time Sara listens to Rachel and smilingly turns toward her.

SARA   I know I might have. He is not a spoiled brat, far from it. But because of this thought, I did not resist him, not this time. He got his outfit all right, and he looks great in it. We are both pleased.

A Silent Gap

Miri came for therapy in 1976. Divorced in 1974, she was worried about her difficulty to separate herself from her husband and her inability to form new relationships with men.

MIRI   I think that, in fact, I lost my husband in the war. Not in the sense of becoming a widow. Everybody takes care of the widows. We all try to compensate them somehow for their loss. But me, who helps me? And I am sure there are other women like me. We might get organized and get some rights.

I   I prefer that you would talk about yourself more than about a group of women.

MIRI   OK. I am willing to talk about myself. My story is very short. So many details are missing. I can only tell you my side of it, since my ex-husband, Gil, has never told me his story.

I   Very well. I am interested only in your side of the story now.

Miri finds it difficult to start.

MIRI   Well, it will sound stupid. Gil was one of the soldiers who fought very far to the south in the 1973 war. He was away from home for a very long time, half a year or so; and when he came home for his rare vacations, we were hardly ever alone. His parents came over, our friends invited us out, and so on. If I felt him withdrawing from me into himself, I thought it was natural for the situation. I was disappointed.

I   I suggest you say all these things to him, as if he were sitting here. Tell him your side of the story.

MIRI   This is very difficult and artificial. He refused to talk to me or to listen to me when I tried to start a conversation.

I   Just the same, suppose he were sitting here on the chair.

MIRI   I'll try. Gil, at the beginning, I was quite unaware of how you got further and further away from me during the war and the months which followed.

I   And you, did you create any distance between you two?

MIRI   No, I am sure I didn't. I longed for him.

I   For you.

MIRI   Gil, I longed for you. When you came home I tried to please you so much. We were married just one year when the war broke out, and I thought we could resume our love, our intimacy, at the point where we left off our relationship when you were mobilized. I was disappointed when you came home a stranger, so aloof. And I attempted to get closer, to break the barrier that stood between us. Maybe I tried too hard. I should have let you return in your own time.

I   You blame yourself?

MIRI   Yes, in a way. I did not hide my disappointment too well when our encounters became so cold, when you, Gil, started to avoid me. Maybe I should have kept my disillusionment to myself. You needed support from me, you needed someone to talk to, and I was only aware of my own needs, my loneliness, my longing for you.

I   Whom or what do you resent about it?

MIRI   I resent myself for not being independent and more mature at the time Gil needed me. I failed as a wife.

I   You are very harsh with yourself.

MIRI   Yes, I know. And it's all for nothing, since our relationship cannot be reconstructed. I am harsh with Gil, too.

I   Tell him.

MIRI   I am mad at you. I am angry at you for being so egoistic, for not paying attention to my needs, only to your own. And most of all, I am mad that you refuse, to this day, to talk to me and explain in what ways I failed you, or how we failed each other, from your point of view.

She really looks angry, her face red, her eyes sparkling. Gradually her expression changes to deep sorrow.

MIRI   I feel like crying.

I   Now that you've expressed some anger we arrive at the grief.

MIRI   You see, Gil was such a sweet guy before the war. We had such a harmonious life together. We were both students, we lived in the dorms, our apartment was a center for all our friends, we were very popular. I know people envied us, envied me. We were the perfect couple.

I   I got the impression of something very childlike about your description and the way you talk now, as when people remember their happy childhood with nostalgia.

MIRI   Yes, it's true, though I never thought so before. We were like two happy children. We were not mature enough to face war and separation. You see, we had no training for that. We had absolutely no trouble before, and then . . .

I   Tell me in the present tense, as if it's happening now.

MIRI   He comes home finally, discharged. It is February 1974, a new year. I hope that now we'll overcome our difficulties. We have all the time for it, not just a short weekend. The first night we make love, but it's so mechanical, no spirit in it, no joy. I try to revive your spirits, and you are so tired, I let go. After midnight I wake up to find you very pale, sweating, sitting up in bed, your bare feet on the cold floor.

—"What's the matter?" I ask.

—"I don't know. I woke up not knowing where I was. And now I don't know where I was before. I am confused."

I get you a cup of tea and wait for you to fall asleep. You look so anxious in your sleep. I don't know if I can help. I am sure it is the war.

Next morning we ignore the episode. We go to school together. You look so disoriented. You have to register for
classes. It seems too much to accomplish. I go to my courses
alone.

Night after night we go through similar scenes. I am afraid
of nightfall. The coldness, your attacks of blankness, my helplessness. Days, you drift around the campus, sometimes I meet
you with a girl. Nights, I imagine you suffer from war nightmares, which then you forget or refuse to share with me.

I suggest we get some help, counseling for you or for both
of us. And then I realize how wide the gap between us is. "I
don't need any help," you say, "but you might profit from it."
I ask, startled: "How so?" You refuse to talk. This is the first
of a long list of refusals. No clarification at all.

We go through the motions of living, with a silent gap between us. I am anxious, you are hostile, we don't talk about it
to each other or to anybody else. And then a few weeks later
you say, one day, that you'll move out. You pack your clothes
and walk out. For two weeks I am crazy with pain, but I
survive. And then I hear you went abroad, to Greece, to take
shelter on a peaceful island. Sometime in June I get a postcard,
asking for a divorce.

I   This is very sad, and frustrating, too.

MIRI   I don't feel all that just now. I feel empty.

I   Is there anything else you'd like to tell Gil?

MIRI   Yes, I think so. Gil, I wish you would tell me how I
failed you. What do you think has happened between us?

I   Be him and answer.

MIRI   It's impossible. He has no voice, he would not talk to
me.

She is silent for a long time, and I don't see any point in pressing
her.

I   And suppose he tells you the following: "I came back from
the war and found out that many of the old things I used to like
to do, lost their meaning completely. There was no sense in
continuing just out of habit. I have matured, or maybe I have

regressed—I don't know which. But I feel I have to start all over again, to discover my worth, my values, and I needed to open a new page, without you, without my studies, even without this country."

Miri listens with tears in her eyes.

MIRI   You mean he does not blame me for anything?
I   In my fantasy he does not. It's just his own thing. It's only a fantasy, you know.
MIRI   I like your idea. It is more like the Gil I knew from before the war.

After Miri went home I felt very strange. I didn't know whether I had helped her with my fantasy, but I certainly had helped myself.

Early Effects of the War_____

Introduction

We have claimed that war is always with us, that war night-mares and fantasies do not obey the time-and-space rules of the real world of political events. Yet, when I follow the record of my work from 1970 onward, transcripts of sessions that deal with the experiences of war and their immediate outcomes, these records seem to be drastically divided by a time line—before and after the sudden alarm sounded on the quiet noon of Saturday, Yom Kippur 1973. Before, war and its effects occupied the minds of a few people, mostly as a symbol of their own inner struggle; after, war became one of the dominant themes in the groups—war as expressed in the threat of injury, death, and mourning.

The remaining sections of this part of the book will be presented chronologically, thus underlining the profound effects of time and external events on the issues preoccupying the members of the groups.

This section begins in the spring of 1972. The year has been a relatively calm one. We all live in the atmosphere of victory and security gained by the Six-Day War. There is no mention of war in the groups. People come and go; some miss sessions due to reserve duty, but this is regarded as part of the normal rhythm of our life. In this atmosphere, Natan describes the stretching time, the blank state of mind of being continuously half-asleep while on a long period of reserve duty in the desert. He vividly presents the group with the antithesis of the alert soldier. Michal reacts, saying: "To think of you as you just

described—and being our outpost guard against the enemy—
well, it frightens me, that's all." But there is nothing to be
frightened of, we then thought, slowly feeding the false sense of
invulnerability that characterized us at that time.

The sense of foreboding we now find in Natan's story, the
hints of war-before-war, may be just a case of hindsight, reading
danger into his then tranquil mood. It is, however, clearly a
succinct description of the state of mind of an entire nation
from which only a shock could awaken us.

•   •   •   •

The shock of the war has been mysteriously connected for me
with the visit of my teacher, Jim Simkin, to Israel for the first
time. An unfinished visit.

It is Wednesday in October 1973 between the Jewish New
Year and the Day of Atonement. Jerusalem is sliding into fall.
We decide to set the Simkins up in the American Colony, an
old geranium-covered hotel in the Old City. At night we go on
the traditional tour around the illuminated wall of the Old City.
We stand on a deserted hill, facing the luminous Tower of
David, and we talk about Jerusalem. "It is different from what
it was before the war," we say, referring to the war of 1967.
"The city is not divided; the partitions are down; the walls, the
mosques, and the churches are lighted up." Jim says there are
too many armed soldiers around. We do not notice them. The
Simkins lovingly describe their new home in California. We
know the place, and we say that Jerusalem is the best.

Thursday morning we meet at the Notre Dame monastery in
picturesque Ein Karem, where Jim holds a workshop. In the
midst of olive trees, orchards of unearthly tranquility, the
kitchen helpers whisper in Arabic and French. No one suspects.
We decide to meet with the Simkins again on Saturday night,
after the fast.

Friday. The city is empty. Thousands of people gather at the
Wailing Wall on the eve of the Day of Atonement, praying.

Saturday night. Jerusalem is dark; the lights of the synagogues, mosques, and walls are extinguished. Many people

have died already. At the American Colony, the Arab work-ers whisper. We look suspiciously. The city is divided again, friends and foes. And mysteriously, we do not see any sol-diers in Jerusalem that night. All is unnaturally dark and quiet, in suspense.

It took us several days to get information about the events of those days on the borders, and many months to really grasp them. For me, life has not been the same since the war. The confidence, the security, the sense of superiority, are gone.

I vividly remember a bizarre morning during the second week of the war. The university, though open, is not func-tioning; the men are at the front; the children are safe in school. There is nothing for me to do. There must be a lot to do somewhere, but I lack the connections. I can't find that "somewhere." I feel useless. On an impulse of surpris-ing intensity, I wander into an elegant dress store, where the salesgirls listen to the radio and exchange neighborhood tales—so and so is wounded, missing, killed. I make them work; my entrance forces them to turn down the radio, stop their chattering. I buy an expensive suit and a dress—com-pletely out of character—and kill the morning. An attempt to move time backward, to force an appearance of normality on our shaky existence. An outcry of "life must go on." Some sort of self-indulgence: don't be unhappy; I'll buy you a present. An outlet, another outlet.

As soon as work in the clinic started again, I found my release in helping others, the little I did assuming tremendous personal meaning. And, with work and involvement, the inner compulsion to write down everything, to record it, so that we won't forget.

For the first few weeks after the war, I did only individual work. Zoe, an ex-soldier, was referred to me in November after being released from active service in the war. He talked openly about the war and his reactions to it, and introduced me to the traumas of war, as well as to the healing process of recovering from them. Sol and David were soldiers, too. They participated in a weekend workshop, which I held in the early winter follow-ing the war. David was still in uniform and Sol was still carrying his rifle.* Most of the others were women. This was still wartime, so to speak, although the direct fighting was over. Many men were still mobilized. People could not bury their heads in the sand. They shared their war experiences, and their feelings—hesitantly, searching for the appropriate expression, yet without denying.

The work of Sol and Zoe, which is presented in this section, deals directly with war traumas, each of a significantly different intensity. While Sol experienced fear—even panic—in combat, he found his own way of coping with this reaction and managed to function as required and end up unharmed. Zoe, who perhaps fought under more disastrous circumstances, was incapacitated, diagnosed as shell-shocked, and discharged. The total meaning of this label does not concern us here; we will have, however, an intimate view of the nightmares accompanying this condition and a case to demonstrate the principle that fears which are completely experienced frequently cease haunting us.

A very different kind of war trauma is to be a man in Israel and *not* to fight. This is, to say the least, an awkward position to be in. When there is a general army mobilization, most of the men eighteen to fifty are called to their units. The homes and the cities become the territory of women, children, old men, and a very small number of men who, due to physical limitations or foreign nationality, are ineligible to serve. These men try to cope with their feelings of incompetence as they remain behind the lines on the home front, and to form an identity as a loyal Israeli who did not fight for his country. Moreover, they ask: "If I did not fight, how can I send my son, when his time comes, to endanger himself?"

Ron is one of the men who did not fight. Working through these feelings in the group sessions, he realizes that the members of the group who were fighters were willing to accept him; they did not condemn him. It is his own inner demand with which he had to deal. [Actually, the specific session recorded dated June 1973, before the Yom Kippur War; yet I find it a

*It is common practice in Israel for soldiers on leave to carry their rifles with them

good example of the dilemmas of those who stayed at home when others, like Sol and Zoe, were at the front.]

Bedouinism (April 1972)

Natan comes to the group after a long absence. He has been serving in the reserves for a period of forty days. The long stay outdoors has left its traces in his deep tan, his bloodshot eyes, and his white-bleached hair.

The group greets him warmly.

NATAN   It is so strange, to be back here, to see you all. I drove in last night; and today, as I walked out of the house, I had a color shock, you know. The flowers in the garden, the clothes women wear—all the reds and the greens. I think my eyes have to get adjusted. Down there in the Sinai it is blue sky over white sands, black rocks, and the remote black figures of a wandering Bedouin.

DANA   Sounds very pretty, your description.

NATAN   Oh, yes, it's very pretty. If you like sand in your eyes, nose, ears, under your skin.

MATY   And in your food, don't forget.

NATAN   That's right. I see you know the place.

MATY   Or a similar one. They are pretty much alike.

NATAN   Actually, it is a very beautiful landscape, and I would like to go there on a trip. But forty days . . .

He sits there pondering.

I   Where are you?

NATAN   Nowhere . . . nowhere, that's the whole trouble. I am so much nowhere that I don't even know if I am worried about it.

I   What is "it"?

NATAN   The void which enfolds me, which is me.

I   Be the void.

NATAN   I am white and foggy. I am warm and comfortable. Come into me. Don't act, don't think. Just be. I'll keep you in a trancelike sleep, and you won't feel the time passing.

His voice gets softer and softer, and he closes his eyes, as if he has gone into a trance.

I   Stay with what is happening to you, and when something changes, please tell us.

Several minutes pass. Natan looks asleep. Some people in the group seem worried, and Michal is whispering: "Do something." Finally, I become somewhat apprehensive, too.

I   Natan, where are you? Did anything change?

From far away, after a long pause, Natan answers faintly: "No," and goes back to his rest.

MICHAL   You must be very tired.

No reaction.

I   Natan, I would like you to open your eyes now and come back to us.

Natan stirs in his seat and looks quite unwilling. He opens his eyes very slowly, as if his eyelids were too heavy to lift. Without moving his face, with a blank sort of a look, he scans the room, distracted.

I   Where are you?
NATAN   I came back, as you told me to.
I   OK. Get up and move around.

He does, and even manages a few smiles. When he sits back, I ask:

I   What has just happened?
NATAN   Bedouinism.
I   Pardon me?
NATAN   Bedouinism. You had a demonstration of a medical phenomenon, so to speak. Didn't you hear about it before?

He goes on to elaborate.

NATAN   This is exactly what I have been doing for the last forty days, or at least for the last thirty-eight days, since I caught the trick. The flies wake you up very early, and the sun is too hot for sleep. You eat your breakfast at five o'clock, and the whole day stretches out before you. By seven you feel as if it were the middle of the day, hot and hazy. Lunch at noon, dinner at six—what else can break the monotony of your day? I brought books with me, and I had some papers to write. I planned to keep up with my studies. But believe me, I didn't take the books and papers out of my pack even once. And the problem is that I don't see how I can return to my work even now.

I   Wait a day or so. Let yourself go through the transition. Don't rush so.

NATAN   But you saw what just happened. You saw how easily I can slip back into my Bedouinism. It is a feeling of blending with nature, with your surroundings. You—

I   Try "I."

NATAN   I am not required to do anything, just let the time pass, completely passive. I even forget to move out of the sun into the shade. I don't care about dirt, flies, or personal appearance. I forget about politics and my family in the city. The expression we use comes from *Bedouin,* the natural inhabitant of the desert. A Bedouin walks alone in Sinai, with minimal baggage except the several layers of his personal clothing. He goes from one site of his tribe to another, sometimes a walk of several weeks, with no obvious plan in mind. If it's too hot, he dozes off. Like a most adaptable animal, he does not think, has no ambition, no duty.

I   And you?

NATAN   I am like that, too, or I was all these days. You saw just now how I trained myself to enter into the void. I could be a perfect Bedouin.

I   And your duty?

NATAN   What duty? Who's the enemy now, and where? Sorry, but I did not feel I was given any specific task to carry out. Just to be present in the area. So I was present.

I   And blank?

NATAN   Well . . . it may sound irresponsible to you, but if you were in my position there, you'd change your mind.

MICHAL   I want to tell you several things, Natan. First, that I got scared when I saw you blank out in the beginning of the session. And later, when I realized you were on guard duty in this condition—well, I don't want to give you a lecture. I just want to say that I became even more scared than before. To think of you as you just described—and being our outpost guard against the enemy—well, it frightens me, that's all. Perhaps it is my problem, not yours. Another matter: I don't think you have grasped the Bedouin mentality correctly. He seems to you as if he is walking aimlessly, but actually he is most aware. He knows every inch of the territory, the sources of water, and the location of the places where, maybe the year before, he had left some provisions. He is very perceptive, notices every minor change in the desert, can detect sounds miles and miles away. He is not blanked out the way you described your condition in the desert, not at all.

Natan thinks quietly over these things, and later he comments:

NATAN   All I have to say is thank you. Now I think I am finally wide awake.

With an Intact Body (November 1973)

Zoe was a twenty-six-year-old graduate student in agriculture when the October War broke out. He had just submitted a proposal for his doctoral dissertation, which was considered brilliant by his professors and which provided him with a research grant and an invitation to a well-known university in the United States. He planned to go in the spring term and to prepare for his trip in the fall. However, at the very beginning of the fall, the war unexpectedly broke out.

Zoe, as a tankist, was mobilized immediately; and for various reasons, he was assigned to a tank crew in a new unit, with soldiers he had never met before. For three days he fought in the north, in one of the hardest, most miserable battles of the war. On the third day his tank suffered a direct hit, and miraculously Zoe managed to escape unharmed from the burning tank. He hid in a ditch for ten hours, witnessing more heavy combat before he was evacuated. The medical crew found him physically intact; however, he was exhausted, amnesic of his whereabouts, and almost completely unresponsive to his situation. He was diagnosed as shell-shocked and sent to the psychiatric ward of a military hospital.

Two weeks later the psychiatrists decided to release him; however, Zoe preferred to remain hospitalized for another week before he would agree to confront his wife and parents and return to civilian life. Since he did not feel sure of his ability to face his former life again, the psychiatrists suggested that he maintain, for some time, a therapeutic contact in the city, and he was referred to me.

He showed up in my office the first day he was released, as if afraid to be on his own. As he presented himself, he made it very clear that he had worked through his traumatic experience in the hospital and did not want to go through this ordeal again. He told me: "I want you to help me to be my old self again—to sleep at night, to get up in the morning, to go back to work on my thesis, to be able to concentrate. I want you to help me discover again that my work is interesting or significant. I want you to help me to be a husband again, to relate to my wife. I want to talk about these things, not about the war, not again."

I explained that we'd work on whatever he brought up, and this pleased him. I did not promise to help him avoid the war in our sessions; and he knew, I am sure, that to become his old self he would have to go, again and again, through this painful territory. For the first week he wanted to come every day, in the morning. "This will give me a good reason to be out of bed, to get up and go out to the university. Maybe I'll be able to enter the library after the session."

I saw him every morning for two weeks, for an hour and sometimes more. Then he gradually reduced the frequency of the sessions until it was once a week and once every two weeks. At the end of the fall term he went to the U. S. as he had planned before *the war. He was, at that time, without any symptoms, but I don't think he could ever be his old self again.*

I want to present a few episodes from the work Zoe and I did together. The following happened during the second week of treatment.

ZOE   The other day I passed by a swimming pool and felt like swimming. I told myself: Zoe, you'll have to get a long-sleeved leotard for yourself to go swimming. You know, something black or brown, with long sleeves and long pants, something that would cover my body completely, with only my face and the palms of my hands showing. I wonder why. I don't think I have ever seen anybody swimming in such an outfit. It is a dancing outfit, isn't it? And I am not a dancer. [*smiles faintly*] All I need to swim is a small, regular bathing suit.

He is quiet for a minute, then looks at me piercingly.

ZOE   Didn't I tell you I am going crazy? I think I should go back to the hospital right away.
I   Be this leotard suit.
ZOE   Come on, you really want me to go nuts! No, I know that's a silly thing to say. I'll see if I can do what you want.

This was not the first time we had worked using Gestalt techniques, so he already knew that it could be helpful.

ZOE   I am a long, brown leotard. Now I am in a box, a nice new transparent box. It says something on the box . . . let me see . . . hey, you want me to be the box?

He is pale now and very tense, wearing the look he has on whenever he approaches a danger zone. I am reminded of the time he ran out of the office to throw up in the bathroom. I know we are again in a mine field and must be very careful.

I   I imagine it must be very frightening for you to be a brown leotard.
ZOE   No, but I am attracted to the box. The box says: "Hun-

dred . . . percent . . . nonflammable . . ." Oh, my God, could you leave me alone? Leave me alone, please.

He is hiding his face in his hands now. I feel my tears rushing to my eyes, so I imagine he must be crying silently. I compose myself and ask:

I   "Could you leave me alone?" To whom are you speaking, Zoe?

ZOE   I want to talk to Gadi. No, I don't want to talk to Gadi, but I guess I have to.

I   Go on.

ZOE   Gadi, I wish I had a nonflammable suit for you. I wish I had something to protect you, to save you. I wish it were not too late. If I had been stronger, if I hadn't run away from the tank, maybe you wouldn't have burned to death, there. Oh, now I have a funny vision about coming with a truck full of these boxes full of nonflammable, magic suits—whatever—giving them away to everybody . . . me, Zoe the almighty, saving everybody. Ha, ha.

I   How do you feel now?

ZOE   The panic is gone. I felt it a little while ago. I was afraid to face these brown leotards and to talk to Gadi.

I   And now?

ZOE   I am still afraid.

I   Stay with it. What is it now?

ZOE   I don't know. I guess I'll always be afraid, anyway.

I   Try to go back to the swimming pool.

ZOE   [*very quietly*] No, I want to go to bed, under the blankets, that's where I want to be.

I   Maybe it's enough right now. You have done a lot. Let's have coffee.

Zoe goes out to the bathroom while I make coffee for both of us in the office. He comes back, takes his cup, and looks out of the window. We have developed this coffee break, since I felt we both needed some transitional period after the stormy sessions before we could face the world outside or, sometimes, continue our work. As I sip my coffee, I watch Zoe from above my cup. His hands are trembling. When he catches my eyes he smiles, as if saying: Don't worry, I am OK. He puts his cup down, looks at me matter-of-factly, and says:

ZOE You have more time?

I Yes. We can go on, if you wish.

ZOE I am not finished with the swimming pool craziness.

I Yes?

ZOE It is this bathing thing, all over again.

I Bathing thing?

ZOE Oh, I thought I told you about it. Something bothers me about bathing, being naked. It is something else I brought back with me from the war. I must be completely dressed all the time. I almost feel like taking a shower with a leotard on. I would rather do that than be naked.

I Let's build this scene now. So you are in the bathroom, at home or back in the camp? Where?

ZOE At home.

I And alone?

ZOE Sure, I am alone.

I OK. And you want to get undressed to take a shower? Is that the situation?

ZOE Yes, no . . . wait a minute. We need a mirror, a big wall mirror. By the way, the dressing room at the swimming pool has many mirrors like this.

I Good, so maybe this is the connection. But go on with the bathroom scene. You take it from here, with every detail, and tell it in the present tense.

ZOE Well, I want to take a shower, I need to, I'll feel fresh and clean. I turn the water on. No, I have to undress first. But I do not want to undress.

I What is stopping you?

ZOE The mirror. The mirror says: "Ha, ha, I'll see you. I'll show you something."

I Talk to the mirror.

ZOE Mirror, I am afraid of you. I am afraid to take my clothes off, for I may catch a glimpse . . . I am afraid of a thing I may see . . . I don't want to see. I don't know what. [*He is silent for some time.*]

I　Can you live through this fantasy? Imagine undressing in front of the big mirror and see what happens then.

ZOE　No, I can't.

I　You mean you won't.

ZOE　I won't. It's too horrible. What's the use?

I　You want to stop now? I feel it's a very bad point to stop. I'll feel very bad if you go home like this.

ZOE　That's ridiculous! *You'll* feel bad! You sleep at night all right, don't you? You haven't got these nightmares. You do your work as usual. I am part of your work, too. Oh, poor soul, you'll feel bad . . .

I am silent for a while, watching his animated face, his fists clenched in anger. I feel hurt and confused and, for a minute, quite lost as to where to go next.

I　OK, I am sorry. I know it has been very bad for you, these last few weeks. And it's true, I did not live through the same experience, so you feel it is unfair, and you think I cannot really understand you.

Zoe looks at me very intensely, then his eyes become softer and he says in a subdued voice:

ZOE　I was unfair. I think part of what I just said is meant for Sharon, my wife, not so much for you here.

I feel much relieved and glad of his discovery. One part of me says: "If you were a good therapist, you would have asked him to whom he was really talking, to whom he felt like saying those things, instead of apologizing." "OK," I answer my clever part, "but he discovered the truth all by himself, while I just acted like a human being. Is that so bad, after all?" At the same time I say out loud:

I　We could talk to her, here. But perhaps you prefer to talk to her at home, about how you feel. I think you can handle this.

ZOE   I certainly can. Anyway it is very late. I'll go now and see you tomorrow, same time.

He leaves in a hurry, and I remain with all my thoughts. Basically, I think—as I have during the last few weeks—he is a healthy young man, and the mind has many ways of healing itself. So, I comfort myself, even if we don't manage to heal the wounds in therapy, time and basic health and Zoe's wish to get better are all on my side—or on his side, to be more accurate.

Zoe must have been thinking, too, since the next day, as he sits himself down, he says:

ZOE   You know, I am a coward. I know that for sure. And I have learned in this past month that I can live with it, with this knowledge. So what? So I am a coward who wants to live . . . survival, you know.

I   Yes, I know. Fear is very normal, but "coward" is not a nice word.

ZOE   I don't think I care. Words are not that important when we're dealing with survival. But to be afraid to take a medicine, that's something else.

I   What medicine?

ZOE   Talking, the talking medicine, therapy.

I   You say you are afraid of therapy. Can you tell me more about it?

ZOE   Yesterday, I don't know if you felt it, I ran away from here because I did not want to face what was coming, the mirror. So I got angry with you, and then we talked about my wife, but all this was simply to escape from the mirror.

I   You really trapped me there. I didn't notice. I thought that the need to talk with your wife was really important.

ZOE   I know, but there is nothing new there. Sharon and I talked about it ten times already, almost since the first time she came to visit me at the hospital.

I   That's very good. And you are saying that the mirror thing is a new issue, and you felt it is significant to work on—

ZOE   —And, somehow, it scares me to death. That's the medicine I was referring to before.

As he says this his face once again becomes pale and strained, as it has many times before. Now there is nowhere to escape from the fear and danger inside.

I   Where are you?

ZOE   I don't know. Maybe I was thinking of the fantasy I had as I tried to fall asleep last night.

I   OK. Tell me, in the present tense.

ZOE   It's very simple. This mirror has short legs and a grin, a sadistic grin, all over its front, and it is running, chasing me. I am escaping, running as fast as I can, and the mirror is following me always at the same short distance, with this grin. I jump over some rocks so that it might break, but nothing happens, it is unbreakable. It runs just the same all the time, after me. I am tired, and I lie down on the earth, hide my face in the sands with my hands over my head, like this. I don't hear, I don't see, I don't move. And I know the mirror is out there, waiting.

I   I want you to lift your face up and look at the mirror now.

ZOE   I know I have to. OK. I remove my hands from my eyes and give a short glance at you.

I   What do you see?

ZOE   I am in this uniform, as I was lying there in the ditch. All soiled with dirt, sweat, and blood. All soiled. And my face is black with smoke, and I have a blank, crazy stare. I've got to hide.

I   No, not this time.

ZOE   I want to take my uniform off. I see it all in the mirror. I open the buttons, tear my shirt away. It's sticking. And then I see it.

I   What do you see?

ZOE   The most horrible thing . . . it is all torn, wide open, my stomach! It is all one big wound, all the internal parts showing and bleeding. I actually see my wound even now, in that mirror.

I   Tell the mirror it is cheating you, you have not been wounded.

ZOE   Mirror, you are awful, leave me alone. This is not my reflection. I was not wounded in the war. (as mirror) Yes, you were, and you don't even know it. To look you have to take your clothes off, your uniform.

—No, that is not true. [*shouting*] You are lying!

—No, I am not.

—I'll get another mirror. You are all screwed up!

—But I'll still be there, just the same.

[*to me*] You see? Where do I go from here?

I   Just a minute. Can you finish the fantasy as if the mirror were right?

ZOE   And I am badly wounded?

I   Yes.

ZOE   OK. I am wounded, my abdomen is torn apart, I am bleeding, and I feel like fainting. I may even die.

I   Zoe, I watched your face and your body, and when you talked now about being wounded, all the tension left you, you looked more relaxed than I have seen you in a long time, almost at peace.

ZOE   Because I don't have to fight with the mirror any more. I would have felt better if I were wounded, you know that, don't you? It would have been so much easier. I'd be safe in the hospital, taken care of. Everybody could understand what had happened to me, they wouldn't ask me all these questions. I wouldn't be the weakling, the failure, the misfit, the crazy impotent. Oh, boy, that's what I thought out there in the hospital all the time! If I'd have broken my arm instead of falling apart, shell-shocked . . .

I   Yes, it would have been easier, I am sure.

ZOE   I thought I had solved this problem, the guilt, the shame.

I   You did, Zoe, but you'll have to go through this again and again, until it vanishes.

ZOE   Mm.

I   Is there anything else you'd like to tell the mirror?

ZOE   Yes. Mirror, I don't need you to remind me, I know very well. You wish I were wounded, and so do I. We are the same, so I don't think you have to stick around me as an added reminder.

I   I think it will go away now and not bother you any more.
ZOE   I hope so, and anyway, I am not frightened by it any more. You know, in the first days, when I took a shower, I used to check all my limbs and organs to see if they were all there. I used to look in wonder at my hands, legs, everything, saying: So you're all there. But I did not feel glad. I felt strange going through this ritual, as if I expected something to be missing.
I   Perhaps you felt guilty.
ZOE   Yes, I know I did. I did then.

Zoe gets up from the chair, stretches his arms, shakes his legs, turns around the room, stops at the window, then faces me with a smile:

ZOE   I cried here like a baby, and threw up, and sat there shaking. I might as well tell you something good, too. I am glad I am whole and intact. I have my body. I am glad to be alive, and I think now, for the first time, that I'll be OK.

The Secret Stick (January 1974)

Sol is a dark-haired, skinny young man, with a pair of rimless eyeglasses that keep sliding down his nose. Dressed in denim pants and a T-shirt, he impressed me as younger than his twenty-two years. In the long workshop we were having, I caught his troubled gaze as he kept peering at me from above his glasses with his soft, brown eyes. In the afternoon, following a period of silence, he took the hot seat and, for a while, just sat there, fidgeting restlessly, looking around the room as if searching for words. It was evident he was having a difficult time starting to work.

SOL   [*hesitantly*] This is something having to do with the war. I mean, with what I have gone through during the last war and after. In the equipment we have in the tank, we also get . . . what shall I call it? I don't want to disclose any secrets . . . it's some simple escape tool, planned to make, to help to make, an opening through which to exit from the front of the tank, if the main opening is blocked. The technical details are not important really, so I'll call it a stick just for the story, OK? Well, I don't know . . .

I I don't know either. What are you trying to say?

SOL I'll start again. My greatest fear was of being caught inside the tank, of not being able to escape after it was hit or had started to burn.

I Did this ever happen to you?

SOL No, not really, but I saw how it could happen very easily. It had happened to me before that, while trying to get out, I had a few moments of panic, and for some seconds, I was not sure if I could make it. This is the greatest fear I've ever experienced in my life, of being trapped down there.

I Go on.

SOL I developed this fixed idea—I don't know how good it is, anyway—to cling to this stick I told you about. It was as if my life depended on it, as if it were my fate, my fortune. I kept it on my knees all the time, ready for use, during five days of continuous battle. And when the firing was really bad, and I, inside the tank, did not know what was going on and feared the worst, all I had to do was catch a glimpse of my stick or give it a pat. It gave me the feeling that I was protected and would be fine. It sounds stupid now, but they were crazy days. And, you know, like some of the religious boys keeping a small Bible with them all the time, well, does it really protect them? But I am not religious. And a stick . . .

I Well, it worked out all right for you.

SOL Yes, I am here. I could have been elsewhere.

I Sol, I still don't know what it is you want to work on. I have the feeling that all this is an introduction, or am I mistaken?

SOL No. This is the difficult part. I am afraid you'll all laugh at me.

I Is it funny? I mean, are you funny?

SOL No, I am tense. I feel embarrassed.

I Nobody would laugh, if that's how you feel.

SOL OK. [*hesitates, looks around the room*] You, David, would probably laugh; you are such a great fighter. Have you ever been in a panic or been really afraid?

DAVID   Yes, I have. I never thought I'd bring it up in a group, though, or share my experience here. I don't like to think about those moments. In that sense, I am perhaps the great fighter, as you said, but you are braver than I am.

SOL   I cannot believe you mean what you said. You just said that to make me feel better.

I   You know, Sol, now we can work at this point, I can feel you. I don't think you'll believe David or me because you have inside you a part that laughs at you and causes you embarrassment.

SOL   Yes, I know.

I   Could you be this part?

SOL   Yes, that's easy.

He stands up in front of his empty chair and starts, pointing with his hand:

SOL   You coward, you little boy, go hide, baby, run to your mama! Don't look away, I am talking to you. You ought to be ashamed of yourself for acting this way! Oh, what a great outstanding hero you are, my boy!

I   Could you answer?

SOL   [*sits down*] What do you want? I do my best, I am not a hero and don't want to be one. You have no right to talk to me that way. In the war I did feel afraid, but I am sure not more than the others, and I acted like a man, like a good soldier. No one could complain. My fears and fantasies are my own thing anyway and no concern of yours.

I   Good, that was very good! I am absolutely impressed with your answer.

Other members of the group express similar reactions.

I   Now, this part, this nagging top dog, that you seem to know so well, where did you get it from?

SOL   I don't know. Just this country, I guess, being born in Israel and educated this way. We are all born to be heroes, to fulfill all the expectations of generations and generations of Jews out there. I don't know. This is, perhaps, this is only part of the whole story.

I   Where else could you get it?

SOL   Maybe my father gave it to me. He is a tall man, bigger than me, and stronger, too. He fought in the War of Independence, was an officer. I am not, you know. I am doing fine, but my ambitions are not in that direction. I now remember being five or six years old. Father took me to the amusement park, where they had installed this new giant slide. I went up there, and then I chickened out and had to force my way down the ladder, against the direction of all the children mounting to the top. I did not want to try again. I was afraid of the height, terribly afraid. Father waited for me down there. He teased me, calling me his great hero, pointing to smaller children who could do it and enjoyed themselves tremendously. I think he was disappointed in me. You see, he was always very physically fit and could do things I was afraid, or too clumsy, to even try.

I   Maybe it is connected, yet the way you tell your story and your father's reaction—why, your father sounds quite sensible. He is not mad or demanding, he does not seem half as strong in his stand against you, in rejecting you, as your inner topdog, the way you presented this part of you before, when you stood up and actually barked at poor Sol. I mean, your father didn't call you names, for instance.

SOL   I know, I know. My father is actually a very kind man. Still, I am his only son, and I would like to find out if he really is disappointed in me.

I   Why don't you ask him now?

SOL   Father, I see you as bigger than me, stronger than me, in spite of your age. And me, always sort of awkward, with my eyeglasses falling off and all, I wonder if you are not disappointed to have me for a son.

I   Now be your father, and answer.

(as father) Whatever gave you this idea? So, you're smaller than I am, is that important? Is that how you think I evaluate a person? You know better. You know that Mother and I are very pleased with you, with the kind of person you've become. You are doing very well, and the main thing is that you are back alive and in good health. You know how we worried about you during the war, and we thank God every day for bringing you

back. I am not disappointed. I would not want to be the father
of a dead hero.

[*to me*] That was him, all right. You are right. My folks are
OK, and so are you. Nobody demands of me more that I did
or am doing. It is all in my sick head.

I   Go on, call yourself some more names like that.

SOL   Ha? You sick, coward, baby, no-good. No, it does not
sound real now. I don't feel like doing it any more.

I   You don't feel like putting yourself down any more? That's
good. Maybe you'll like yourself better now.

SOL   I don't know. There is still something I am ashamed to
tell you all about. And this is what I really wanted to do, to
begin with.

I   You cling to your secret, don't you? I have a game for you.
Tell each one of us, around the room: "I have a horrible secret.
If you knew my secret, you would so and so."

SOL   I'll start with David. David, I have a terrible secret. It is
so shameful. If you knew my secret, you would think I were out
of my mind.

I   Go on.

SOL   I'll try the girls. Mary, I have a secret. I am not sure I
want to hide it from you, you look so understanding. Susan, I
have a secret. It's pretty bad, but now I feel that you may be
thinking it is even worse than it really is. Hey, I think I'll feel
better if I got rid of my secret after all.

I   Then what are you waiting for?

SOL   This . . . stick, about which I told you before, remember?
Well, how should I say . . . I . . . I stole it from my unit room.
I did not report taking it home or anything, and for the last few
weeks it has been with me, there, under my bed. I felt I needed
it with me, you know? I could not return it.

After a minute of silence, everybody is talking, excitedly, together. I hear such exclamations as:

—Is that all?
—Heavens, does it mean stealing? Everybody took some souve-
nirs.

—You're sure it is still there? Somebody probably cleared it away.

Gradually, it sounds as if everybody is relieved, after expecting something much worse—and Sol is more relieved than anyone else.

I   Congratulations, Sol, you have done it.

SOL   Done what?

I   I don't know. I feel like congratulating you. Maybe I feel that now that you've finished your prolonged stay in this tank, you've completed your own private war.

As Sol turns to go back to his seat, he is stopped by David, who says:

DAVID   This may sound like an anticlimax, but I want to ask you, Sol, now what? You have told us your big secret, and what will you do with this stick under your bed? Keep it against thieves or as a souvenir or what?

SOL   I don't really know. I feel so relieved now that I told you all about it that I have almost convinced myself that the stick is not there any more. Come to think of it, what do you suggest?

DAVID   If I were you—

SOL   You wouldn't have taken it in the first place.

DAVID   Good guess, so what? I was saying, we could pack it and send it back to the army supplies, that's all. No need to apologize or even to sign your name on the parcel.

SOL   Hey, that's neat.

We are silent for some time, then Mary asks:

MARY   Well, Sol, will you do it? What do you need the stick for? I know you don't. If you send the stick back to where it belongs, I believe it would make you feel better, really finished with that bad experience.

SOL   I guess you're right. I don't think it makes any difference now. I feel I can give the stick away. I think I will.

As he is rising from the hot seat, he says to David:

SOL   You know what? Let's go to my place and do it right away, after the group, OK?

David answers with the song "With a Little Help from My Friends," which makes us all laugh. In the evening, when the session is over, I notice Sol and David leaving the building together.

Ron: The Man Who Did Not Fight (June 1973)

Men in Israel who do not fight feel different.

   Ron is one of those men. An American who currently lives in Israel, he spent several years of his childhood here as well. In one of my group sessions, Ron talked about his dilemma, even before the Yom Kippur War had broken out.

RON   I had a dream about Joel, an Israeli friend of mine. In my dream, I finally come to see Joel, and I find him terribly deformed. His arms are thin and twisted, as if he has been suffering from cerebral palsy. He is crawling on the ground like a worm. I, on the other hand, am healthy and upright. Yet, standing in front of Joel, I feel weak and ashamed.

I   Talk to Joel about your feelings.

RON   Joel, I finally came to see you, and I found you prone on your stomach. Yet you are strong and confident, while I feel weak and ashamed. I feel like a young Jacob kneeling before his blind old father. I am somehow cheating, and you are morally superior. I feel guilty. Why is it that I feel ashamed and weak in front of you? It is guilt over my life being easy, while you faced hardships silently and proudly. I see you as a man, and I feel that you see me as a boy, still awkward, still immature.

He stops at that point and looks blankly at the other end of the room.

I   What is happening?

RON   I feel an impasse.

I   Stay with it.

RON   I have no desire to disturb our past relationship, Joel. Today our worlds are far apart. I just wonder about my guilt. We were childhood friends, best of friends. Then you went off into the army, and I started college in the United States. I returned to Israel and saw you once or twice. I realized that although we were still fond of each other, there was not much which could hold us together. Each of us had lived through events which had pushed one a step further from the other. You, Joel, seem to know very well the road you're traveling on; you are firmly anchored in your identity as an Israeli. In relation to you I have always been the "foreigner." During the last six years, I have been acutely aware of our contrasting roles, you as the soldier and I as the student. You had been in two wars and in other battles; your closest friend had been killed, and you had been wounded. During that same time I lived a relatively sheltered life as a student.

He remains silent for a long time, facing the empty chair.

I   What do you feel?
RON   Guilt, shame, the feeling—in contrast to Joel—of being a pampered child.
I   What does Joel say to you?

Ron starts in a very severe, authoritative voice:

RON   You are a pampered child, you're immature. You are obliged to justify the nature of your existence, your several identities, your being transient here in Israel.
I   He sounds very strict.
RON   Well, no, he isn't, not in reality. Joel my friend is kind and warm, although he rarely shows it.
I   So where does this strict demand come from?
RON   It is me, I am making the demands. I fear my own self-judgment more than that of Joel or others.
I   Judge yourself.
RON   Ron, you are a half-baked dreamer. Get out into the world and do something.
I   And now?

RON   I want to answer my inner judge.

I   Go on.

RON   So what if I'm a dreamer? I am happy to be one. I couldn't exist in any other manner. I made my choice to live as a transient; it fits me best, at least for the time being.

He is quiet, looking calmer.

I   What has just happened?

RON   I don't feel so guilty. I don't feel as if I'm being judged right now. At least, I'm sure Joel doesn't judge me. I might go and visit him, that's what occurred to me just now.

I   This feeling of being judged, perhaps condemned, for not belonging more tightly to Israel and its army, do you feel it here in the group, too?

RON   At the beginning, yes, I did. It is a general feeling which I have with young Israelis who have all served in the army. Being self-conscious. The group, especially Gidon, has balanced the scale.

I   Talk to Gidon about it.

RON   In the beginning I felt, Gidon, that you were arrogant and aggressive, and you told us about your experiences as an army officer, calling for our admiration. Appropriately, you told me that I was passive—so we had each other well pigeonholed. The scales were in your favor, and I felt again, in front of the group, like the "young" one. You were, Gidon, the prototype of the Israeli, and now I see that you were also a great deal of what Joel has always been to me. Then, as the group evolved and you let me see your warmth and, sometimes, your weakness, I started to like you. You are as human as I am, and I am no longer afraid of your judgment. I perceive myself as an equal to you and to the rest of the group.

I   Can you now say that to Joel, too,?

RON   Yes. You know, Joel, you and I both have the right to stand upright. Neither of us has to crawl on the ground like a worm.

People of the group express acceptance of Ron. Some mention that he'll be called to serve in the army if he stays longer as a resident in Israel, a fact which naturally is known to Ron. Oded's part of the conversation is of special interest.

ODED   While I listened to you, Ron, I was reminded of my father, who immigrated to Israel from Canada when he was thirty-eight. I was about ten at the time. My father, like you, is a very gentle person, and we have a close relationship. As he arrived here rather old and had some problems with his sight, he was never drafted. When I was seventeen and started my army examinations, my father used to drive me out there in the car. This was rather unlike him; he had never before played chauffeur to me. So once I asked him about this peculiar behavior, and I think you, Ron, would like to hear what he said. It went somewhat as follows: "Son, your going into the army makes me very uneasy. I know all parents feel worry and concern, but here, between us, there is something more to it. You see," he said to me, "I never served in the Israeli army. This experience of yours is completely alien to me. And since I did not serve, I feel you are going to do it for both of us. This identification scares me and also puzzles me from a moral point of view. I ask myself what right do I have to send you out there to endanger your life when I myself didn't go."

RON   At first, it sounds odd, but, to think of it, I might really think like your father if I had a son to send into the army.

ODED   Yes, but here is your fallacy, too, the same one my father committed in our conversation at the time. I told him: "Father, you are not giving me away to the army. I would go if I were an orphan, or whether or not I had your consent. You should not feel responsible for my being drafted."

RON   And did he agree?

ODED   Well, no. He argued with me, trying to distinguish between the rational-legal step and the emotional one. He even mentioned the binding of Isaac in this context. I laughed at him at the time; but actually, I have never forgotten this interaction. And today, when you called yourself a dreamer, I was struck by the similarity between you and my father.

RON   What does he do?

ODED   He is an English teacher, and a good painter besides.

RON   So, what you're saying is that this issue, of not serving in the army, keeps bothering one even years later and is passed on to one's children.

ODED   I didn't say that—that is your summary of my story. And, as a matter of fact, you may get rid of your conflict when you're drafted.

RON   I may, yet I'll never catch up with all the years of service you have given to this country.

I   A few minutes ago you said you feel equal to the others in the group.

RON   Yes, I did not lose that feeling. Let's say I am equal and different, OK? And I still have a lot to catch up with.

The Wheelchair Group of 1974 *___

Introduction

In contradistinction to the openness of Zoe, Sol, and Ron, the following account may be taken as a lesson in denial and disguise. One of the members of my 1974 group named whatever it was we were doing "the great denial game." Its basic rule: pretend that life is back to normal. None of the players is fully aware of the game; and I, too, discovered it only at the end of the year, when it was almost over. At that time, the fighting of the Yom Kippur War had been over about six months. People had tired of discussing the war and, perhaps, were trying to recover from its effects by simply avoiding the subject. Fundamentally, though, the emotions surrounding this war—the fear, pain, and shame—were, at that time, too dangerous to stir up.

It was February 1974, and I started working with a year-long group of students, a group I later named The Wheelchair Group of 1974. Thirteen psychology students participated in it: six young men, all of whom had served the previous three to five months in the army and took part in the Yom Kippur War; one woman who was serving in the army as a group dynamics expert and a trainer of personnel; one woman whose husband was a combat pilot in active service most of the year; and five unmarried women.

As I organized the group, I was somewhat apprehensive. I feared it would develop into a discussion group in which people

*An abbreviated form of this section appeared as a paper in *Voices,* Summer 1975, pp. 54–56, under the title "The Motif of Mutilated Legs in a Gestalt Group: One Year After a War."

would tell stories about the war—sometimes their own experiences but mostly hearsay. I knew such use of the time might be profitable to some, and this kind of activity had, indeed, been going on in most social gatherings in Israel before that period. However, I thought that a Gestalt group could offer more than a social gathering and looked forward to what might develop.

I organized and led the group in the same manner as I did my student groups in previous years, yet fairly soon I discovered that the content of the themes in the group was vastly different from that before the war. Most surprisingly, the threat of war as such, or direct war experiences, were very rarely brought up in this group and *never as a main problem to be worked on.* Yet, the subject of war, hovering behind the scenes, dramatically affected the contents and symbols which prevailed in this group throughout the year. Starting with a dream about a wheelchair, themes of mutilation, especially leg wounds and amputations, and the image of the invalid repeatedly occurred in dreams and fantasies of the members of the group. These themes appeared as main topics in five out of twenty-five sessions and many more times in group feedback and discussions. In this group, we were all physically intact; yet everyone of us had known and witnessed death and people who had been injured. It all came out in fantasy: in "real" life we were all heroes.

One of the typical heroes, or rather heroines, of this group is Edna, who presented what emerged as the common theme of the group in her wheelchair dream. She herself was almost completely unable to work on her dream and use its message; yet Orna, who just listened, developed it as if it were her own. Much later I found out that Edna had had a very rough time during the Yom Kippur War. She was posted way out in Sinai as an enlisted field psychologist; but when the war broke out, she was put in charge of listing the names of soldiers who were killed on the southern front and recording some basic information about each. As the list kept growing, after four days she had the feeling that everybody was slowly moving onto it.

She had to quit. Yet this recent experience of hers was never brought up in the group.

Another outstanding case in this series is that of Amos, who talked about a pleasant fantasy of injuring his leg. As we develop this fantasy, I realize that his fear of injury is never expressed; it is, perhaps, turned into pleasure. Amos is made to admit his fear during the session, and several of the other men share their own fears. Several weeks later, when Amos volunteered to work again, we found out, to our mutual dismay, that Amos had only vague and foggy recollections of his "moments of truth" during his former session. He is unable to bring these moments back to his awareness. It is, apparently, too dangerous to let go of the defenses, and this had been true for the whole group.

At the end of the year, Edith presented a dream about a young man with whom she had been very close. In her dream, she knew he was dead; she had heard people talking about him, mentioning his death. She saw a framed picture of his full body as an invalid, his two legs missing from the knees down. It was, indeed, when Edith presented her dream that the strange similarity in the contents worked on in this group became apparent to me. I remember saying: "I see this long line of people. Each one has some sort of a serious problem in walking freely, in moving around. Some just limp; some are in pain; some are wounded, broken, dead; and some wheel around in their wheelchairs. What a horrible picture to exist in the minds of young, healthy people!" I then thought that our whole group—normal people who had emerged physically intact from the war—was temporarily confined to wheelchairs, handicapped. The nature of these handicaps was something that gradually became evident in talking, writing, listening, and observing.

We find it hard to admit fear, to stand up and say clearly: I am frightened that I may be killed or wounded. We do not know how to express grief. We feel threatened by weakness, dependence, or vulnerability. We believe that it is wrong even to think about ourselves; it is, somehow, egoistic.

Therein lies the significance of the missing limbs and the wheelchairs. And the way out, the way to walk freely again, is, I believe, by talking and thinking about it, by experiencing the obstacles to feeling, by sensing the fear and pain and working through them. This can be done in silence or while talking in symbols. As Yuval put it: "I maintained my silence about the war stubbornly. I learned, however, that problems could be solved and feelings expressed without focusing on their cause or origin and without spelling out the contents of the trauma."

This was, indeed, what some of the group members were intent on doing, either directly or indirectly, using the symbols that evolved during the year. In written papers submitted to me at the end of the year, a few people continued to develop the mutilation fantasy and its meanings for them. These later products were open and direct, explicating the significance of the war without the foggy symbolism that had prevailed during the year. I combined the records of the group's work with some of the written papers to tell the story of the Wheelchair Group.

The Great Denial Game

Some months after the beginning of the group, Yuval put down in writing recollections of his moods and impressions upon returning to town, to the university, and to the group after six months of mobilization. This is a document of the atmosphere of the transition from war to work, our point of departure.

The group started a few days after I was released from half a year of reserve service in the army. I came back to Jerusalem feeling totally alienated, in the streets as much as in classes at the university. I hoped to find in the group a good way of returning to a feeling of involvement, of direct contact with people.

I can recall my feelings then: I felt detached from my surroundings, from the activities I had been participating in, and from people, even those who had been close friends before the war. I could not find any satisfaction in intellectual work. In

particular, I found it ridiculous that people still occupied themselves with small daily matters, as if they were of any significance and were glad or sad because of such trifles.

I felt that everybody was denying all the important things—
the war, the dead, the missing, the changes in all of us. At the
same time, I felt a need to join the great denial game. To be open
to my being and my memories could produce only pain and
fear. For the first time in several years I consciously, intentionally, tried to repress things—not to be in touch with myself.

As I tried to relate to the people around me, I discovered I
was seeing them through glasses recently acquired. They were
not human beings; they were categories. First, I looked at the
soldiers, those who had actually fought on the battlefield, with
appreciation, from a distance, as if saying: "You and I know
what it is really all about, we know the truth. And we know we
cannot share this knowledge with anyone, so we stay engulfed
in our silence and solitude. Each of us will maintain his own
seclusion."

For the men who did not fight, I felt contempt, sympathy,
and a willingness to relate, to demonstrate my superiority. I
wanted to tell them: "You don't know the truth about life and
death. But I know you feel guilty for not fighting, so I sympa-
thize with you."

My feelings toward women were mixed. Sometimes I felt
hostile and accusatory: "You don't even realize what men are
living through and how they are dying, so that you can sit nicely
at home and talk about *your* fears and rough experiences during
the war." Sometimes I felt protective: "Whatever happened
happened so that you could sit at home calmly. This is your
role; the other is ours." I did not see human beings, only types,
and I wanted to change.

A few days after the cease-fire, I had a dream in which I was
an astronaut flying through space. As I left my spaceship to
check something from the outside, the door slammed shut and
I could not get back in. I had an oxygen tube and a radio, from
which I heard that I would never be allowed to return to the
spacecraft but would remain alive, getting oxygen from the tube

and being able to communicate through the radio. I could talk with people through my radio, but I would feel completely alone. This feeling of loneliness scared me, and I woke up.

I know there are two of me: one inside the spacecraft and the other outside. They are both quite alone. The one inside the ship feels more secure, more in touch with the world. But isn't that an illusion, since he is in a spaceship, very far away from the rest of the world? The me outside feels lonely, yet he is proud of his separateness.

When I returned from the war, I was the me outside the spaceship. Gradually I am becoming more the me inside. It is better, but I am still far away out in the spacecraft. As to outer space, that is my war experiences, which I try to keep at a distance. I may come down to earth, but I will not invite anyone to come out to space with me.

I maintained my silence about the war stubbornly. I learned, however, that problems could be solved and feelings expressed without focusing on their cause or origin, and without spelling out the contents of the traumas. And, you know, to this day I feel that you were the first person who was there to welcome me back from the war, from my spaceship, and the people of the group were the first real people I saw.

The Wheelchair Dream (March 1974)

Edna, who is in active service in the army during that winter, comes to the sessions in uniform. This gives her a severe appearance, sometimes hiding her true personality. In the fifth meeting of the group, she wants to work on a dream.

EDNA   In my dream I am invited to lead a group in a private home. The group consists of a family whose son has recently lost both his legs in the war and is now confined to a wheelchair. I am to lead this group with a co-leader, a young man who has much more experience than I have. We start this group as we usually do in the training groups we lead in the army. However, nothing seems to work. My co-leader takes all the initiative, and

I am completely paralyzed and helpless. The whole time I feel a strong aversion to the invalid son, who is naturally part of the group, and I cannot relate to him. I am totally helpless and inadequate.

I ask Edna to be an invalid, legless, in a wheelchair.

EDNA   I try . . . but I really can't.

I   Or won't?

EDNA   What is the difference? Yes, I won't. I feel so disgusting when I am an invalid, and completely dependent on other people.

I   Well, this is the total feeling I get from your dream: as the leader of this group, you feel helpless and inadequate, like the young man in the wheelchair in your dream.

EDNA   That's true. I feel the same feelings, yet the invalid is also disgusting, so it seems to me. I can't . . .

I   You don't want to be in touch with this part, to discover the weak, the totally helpless, Edna within you.

EDNA   I think you are right. It is very important for me to feel strong, to maintain my strength all the time. I remember my husband said that to me, too, recently.

I   What would he say, supposing he were here?

EDNA   (as husband) Why do you have to be such a heroine? You don't have to work with people on the battlefield, on the front line. Nobody asks it of you. You could do a good job in the city as well. I am worried about your going all over the place in your jeep.

I   How do you answer when he says that?

EDNA   I never think that something bad, an accident or who knows what, might happen to me. As if I'm invulnerable, that these things can't happen to *me*. So your worries are unjustified. That's what I answer him. And, you know, I never imagine any harm coming my way. Sometimes I worry about my husband, though; he's in the army, too.

I   So you never thought, even for a moment: I may be killed, I may end my life in a wheelchair?

EDNA   [*very decisively*] No, and anyway I would much prefer to be dead than to end up in a wheelchair.

Later in the session, I ask Edna to be the wheelchair. I feel that if she were able to identify with the wheelchair, which takes her incapacitated, weak self around, she might also be willing and more able to face her helplessness and fear.

I   Suppose you be the wheelchair now.

Edna laughs nervously and does not react.

I   What kind of wheelchair will you be?
EDNA   I don't know . . . a simple hospital wheelchair, I guess.
I   Try it in the first person.
EDNA   I am a hospital wheelchair. I am ugly, heavy. Oh, I can't do it, I'm sorry.

People in the group interrupt and offer suggestions:
—Have you got a motor?
—Can you do a lot of tricks?
—Why don't you try being a bright-red wheelchair, with a nice horn, too? Edna withdraws and does not respond to any of these ideas. She looks helpless and dejected, yet claims to be able to feel and identify with only her strong, competent self. I feel, though, that she is somewhat closer to her vulnerability, and I decide not to push any further. Maybe I, too, am afraid of facing my vulnerability and am aware of this fear in myself. At the same time I know we have a lot more work to do to resolve the issue, to integrate the parts. "We'll return to this," I say, "some other time."

My main reason for discontinuing my work with Edna, however, is a violent reaction by Orna, the pilot's wife. She starts to cry, sobbing loudly, and says that she could do what Edna refused to do.

ORNA   As you worked I imagined myself as an invalid, without legs in a wheelchair. I felt such despair, everything was gone forever, no more joy in life . . . never to have intercourse, never to have children.

As her crying calms down somewhat, Orna smiles and says she feels relieved. Several members of the group express their support and concern, while Edna remains silent, looking depressed. We end the session at this point.

In the next group session, Yuval starts the meeting in a very emotional, angry manner:

YUVAL I still have some unfinished business from our work last week. I could hardly stand it when you girls talked about being wounded in the war. It makes me mad when women talk about the war. What do you *know?* What is your chance of finishing your young life in a wheelchair?

He seems very upset, and I suggest that perhaps he would like to talk about his war experiences or his own fears of mutilation. He declines, however, implying that these would be too painful for us all.

A Pleasant Fantasy of a Wounded Leg (May 1974)

During a long evening session toward the fourth month of the group's existence, Amos requests to work. A soldier in the reserves as well as a part-time policeman, Amos is usually a very shy person. He says that for the last few months, he's been having a pleasant fantasy, almost a wish, in which he has been wounded in his leg during a battle.

AMOS I have this fantasy, and it occurs again and again. I can't figure out, however, why it is that I feel this pleasure and relief when wounded. It's weird. I don't know what it means.
I Have you been wounded before?
AMOS Yes, in my arm. See the scar? This time it's different, though. I mean, in my fantasy, it's the left leg.
I I want you to close your eyes and imagine that you've got this leg wound. Tell us exactly what happens and how you feel.
AMOS I am out there in the field, fighting with my unit. Suddenly there is the sound of a shell exploding and a sharp

pain in my leg. Here. [*He clutches his left leg.*] I know I am wounded, the pain is very bad. Maybe I pass out. Some time later I am being put on a stretcher and carried out of the place. The pain is awful now. I pass out. Later, I wake up in the hospital. My leg is in a cast, the pain is dulled, almost gone. That's all.

I   Are there people around you, attending to you there?

AMOS   No, I am alone. I hear people outside my room, but they are not with me. Somebody is in the next bed. My wife and friends are not with me. I am thinking about my unit and wondering whether the fighting continues.

I   Do you feel satisfaction that you are out of the battlefield?

AMOS   No, that's not what I feel.

I   What do you feel, then?

AMOS   I . . . I feel pain. The pain was much worse before; now I am weak from the pain. I feel strange, not being used to lying in bed like that.

I   Listen to me, Amos. I do not hear any mention of the pleasure you derive from the wound or from being removed from the battlefield.

AMOS   That's right. It's very strange. I didn't feel the pleasure or gratification about which I told you before, but I never went through my fantasy in detail, as I did today. This, you know, feels more normal, so to speak, than what I used to feel; I mean, to be glad I was hit, that's ridiculous. Now I wasn't.

I   For me, something is missing from your story.

AMOS   Missing? What? I don't know.

I   Maybe I am projecting. Anyway, when you talked about this scene of battle, the sounds, a shell hitting you, I felt tension, yet I don't think you mentioned it. And you never mentioned that you were afraid.

AMOS   I guess I felt fear. I don't know.

I   You don't know?

AMOS   OK, you're right, I have blocked it out for years. I never admitted I could feel fear. It's simply something one does not say, does not feel. I have seen people killed, people blown to pieces, things I won't tell you about. There is no time for me to feel afraid, nor do I have the right.

I Now, I don't know. I myself have not fought; yet fear, to me, is a very natural response under these circumstances.

AMOS In my head, I know that's true.

I Can you try something now? Look around you, at the people here. Pick one you can start with, and tell him or her that you are afraid, afraid to be wounded, afraid to die.

AMOS Oh, no, I can't. It is too difficult to say. I have never done it before.

I Now, you didn't say you don't *feel* fear, just that you hate to tell us or to tell yourself. It's high time to start. Try.

After some moments of hesitation in which the inner struggle is very close to the surface, Amos looks at Yuval and starts to talk to him.

AMOS Yuval, it is very hard for me . . . I am not used to talking about myself, my feelings, at all . . . especially about my fears. I see, though, there is nothing to be ashamed of in feeling fear. I am afraid. I am scared that I may get killed or seriously wounded. I was afraid for my life.

YUVAL I was, too; you don't know how much.

AMOS Perhaps I know . . . now.

I ask Amos to continue around the room, and he talks to several other members, men and women, about his fear, his face becoming more alive and less ashamed as he goes along. All the same, it is a very difficult process for Amos. He stops himself frequently, then continues as if forcing himself.

In their reactions, two other male participants report how they have witnessed injuries, mutilation, and death during the war. They tell Amos that at the time, they were apathetic, otherwise, they would have been swamped by fear and grief. "You feel these fears and sorrows later," they comment, "when the shock is over, when you are out of the situation." Their message to Amos later in the conversation is that their apathy, like Amos's pleasure, was a defense used against the disastrous experience and the feelings it evoked.

The work with Amos does not, however, end at this point,

although during this session we seemed to achieve some closure and Amos felt he had finished.

Six weeks later, Amos bashfully tells the group about a continuous pain he has had in his leg, the same leg that had been wounded in his fantasy. Although he is not bothered by his fantasy any more, he feels the pain is connected to the former fantasy and that it is "psychological." He has postponed seeing a physician about his leg, saying: "Perhaps I should go." I encourage him to check with a doctor but add that whatever the result of the examination, he seems to still have a lot of emotion involved in that area. As I inquire about his feelings during the six weeks since he worked on his fantasy, we both discover that Amos remembers surprisingly little about the long session of his work. He says the conclusion of it was, for him, that he may, and perhaps should, pay more attention to his feelings; but he is very vague on the details. He says: "As I try to bring that night back in my mind, the time I worked, I feel as if I'm wandering in the midst of a heavy fog. I see everything in general, ambiguous shapes; nothing has proper contours, something I could grasp. Or sometimes I feel as if there were a wall all around me and no way out. I don't know. It is all so vague and unclear."

I   Could you be the fog?
AMOS   The fog? I mean, how? I am a fog. I am white and heavy, almost like a cotton ball. I . . . I just exist.
I   What, as a fog, do you want, do you say, to Amos?
AMOS   (as fog) I am here all around you. I prevent you from seeing.
I   What do you feel now?
AMOS   Nothing. Everything is vague and foggy.
I   Could you walk through this fog?
AMOS   I wish I could. I'll try.

He is quiet for a long time. Nobody says a word.

I   What is happening?
AMOS   It is no good. I am walking and walking, and the fog

is still all around me, or maybe walls, white walls. I don't know.
I   Yes, it must be a very bad feeling. You sound sad and lost.

At the same time I ask myself: Is there an instant way out of
this fog, or deeper into this fog, perhaps? Amos seems stuck in
his fog, and I myself can't see the way out of it either.

I   You know, I feel lost with you. I don't feel we can get it
resolved now. Maybe you have to live with this fog for some
time yet. There is just one thing I want you to realize: the fog
is not around you—you are the fog; it is inside you.
AMOS   I know that.
I   And it probably serves some purpose for you. You make
yourself foggy so as not to see, or perhaps not to feel.
AMOS   Yes, I know.
I   OK. You've worked a lot for today. Look around at the
people here, in the room.
AMOS   [*looks from person to person*] I can see. I see you. You
seem to listen to me, you seem to care. That's a good feeling.
I can see you very clearly. There is no fog here.

I don't think Amos recaptured completely what had happened
in the first session. He submitted a paper in September, which
included the following paragraphs:

I learned to listen. I always listened well to others, but the
group taught me to listen to myself. I became much more
attuned to myself, one may say egoistic, but who cares? I just
realized how I was always attuned to the outside, to other
people and to things and values, and very insensitive to myself,
to the world within me. That is the fog inside me, as we said.
The problem I worked on was a thing I had never talked
about or thought much about. It was always in dreams, fantasies—like being half asleep—and never in verbal form. I realized I wanted to work on it only after Edna presented her
wheelchair dream; since then, it never left my mind, and I
looked for an occasion to bring it up in the group sessions. I
was, however, so unused to focusing on myself that I didn't
think I would have ever dared to take the initiative if you hadn't
asked me. I never exposed myself before and was very anxious

about doing so. This learning to look inward, to search inside myself for echoes of what others said, and to expose myself as well, was for me a discovery. And, finally, reading this paper, I wonder: I never wrote anything like this before, so spontaneous and unstructured, never before. So I feel I have changed a great deal.

Living Through the Fear* (October 1974)

I wrote my first version of the mutilation paper, which included "The Wheelchair Dream," in October 1974, a year after the war. I gave the first draft to several of the members of the group to read in order to have their reactions and impressions, and, mainly, any corrections if my notes were inaccurate. Orna was one of the people who read the manuscript and spontaneously wrote the following account for me. I present Orna's work here, since I see it as a direct evolvement of "The Wheelchair Dream."

I started to write the following immediately after reading the article. I was interrupted twice by guests, but it was easy for me to return to my work. Throughout the writing I felt every single thing I was expressing, and the thoughts and feelings developed as I wrote. I found myself crying sometimes; you know I cry quite easily.

I read the paper, and it made me feel vaguely anxious—some kind of uncomfortable feeling and excitement—right from the start, where people were mentioned as E. and O.—but that's us! And it's moving, and I felt tears in my eyes. Actually, only when I finished reading was I aware of this anxiety. Everything was written so simply and accurately. I asked myself: Is it because strangers will read about us? and answered: No.

My feelings revolved only around us, the group and Amia. As if in these simple words, our inner beings were touched. I asked myself: Am I angry with Amia for writing about us? and answered: No, I love Amia.

(I am trying very hard to write what I feel, and I am afraid

*Following the article that appeared in *Voices,* Summer 1975.

that writing about my feelings may distort them, like letters that come out prettier than reality. I am afraid this may happen to me.)

As I ask myself such questions, attempting to understand the source of my anxiety, the image of the wheelchair comes back to my mind. But today it is Uri, my husband, who is in the wheelchair.

I felt great resistance to staying with this fantasy, as if I did not want to touch the things deep inside me. My picture of Uri in a wheelchair is vaguely idyllic. I am with him in the sun, and springtime and flowers are all around us. But this image was part of the I-don't-want-to-go-into-this bit, as if the idyllic picture were my hideaway from the reality of the wheelchair.

Then I started to go into the technical details of living with Uri the invalid (exactly as I did that time in the group when I imagined myself in a wheelchair): how we will have to move out of the flat and look for a new one; how difficult this is going to be for Uri. Perhaps I'll screen the available places first and only then bring Uri to choose, since he is the one who makes such decisions. We will come to this flat for the last time, to say good-bye and part with it. We are so sad. (When I, in the group, had imagined myself in this situation, Uri and I were on the roof. It was at this point that I felt I would rather die.) I'm not sure whether Uri wants to die. I wonder why the saddest moment is when we are at our home for the last time and we have to depart, since with all its stairs to climb, it would be unsuitable for an invalid. It does not matter who the invalid is, Uri or me. I think that my love for Uri and my love for our home are one and the same. Everything here is his style. (When I imagined Uri being killed, one of the things I could not figure out was the flat, as if the flat were a barrier that might stop me from being with somebody else forever. Alone, I am all right.) Again I am crying.

I imagine more: how difficult it will be, if at all possible, to walk through the Old City, through the flea market, to search for pretty, out-of-the-way things. I also know that with Uri in a wheelchair, we will never have to leave Jerusalem, and I am always afraid we will. (Both of us would like to stay, but because of Uri's work, we will probably have to leave Jerusalem one of these days.)

As much as these details are painful, the most awful thing is the fear that Uri might be totally in despair and might wish to die. During the war, there were several times Uri did not call me (he used to call me every night), and then I felt a devastating fear. All this time I kept thinking: If only he comes back to me somehow, I won't mind if he is wounded or crippled, even a total invalid, let him only be. A very bad feeling. Helplessness. Some of the same feeling comes back now as I imagine Uri in a wheelchair. As much as I fuss about him and love him, it's as if a barrier exists between us—the barrier of his silent despair. I cannot do anything about it. I cannot give him the pleasure of making love together as before.

I also think we would adopt a child, and I can see Uri playing with him. But I am so sad, because if Uri were not handicapped, he would have played with our child in a different manner. He would have lifted him and thrown him in the air and taken him for a walk on his shoulders. Uri the invalid is playing with our adopted child differently, quietly, in his chair. The thought about the child was, however, brief.

I also see Uri sitting in his chair and getting fatter and fatter, like the chief of some African tribe. But he is completely white —the sick, fat whiteness of a person who cannot move.

When I imagined myself in a wheelchair, several months ago, it seemed very probable that I would want Uri to leave me. As much as my life would be completely screwed up, it would be a pity that his life should be the same. Yet now, as I see Uri in the wheelchair, I am afraid he might want me to leave him for my sake, might want us to separate. There is one thing that I feel now very strongly; namely, I don't want Uri to have any doubts about me. I want him to know, to take for granted, that I want to and I will stay with him, whatever happens.

Now I'll try to review what has happened to me in the last couple of hours. I read the paper and felt anxious. In my attempts to work it through, the image of the wheelchair returned, with Uri in it. I tried to gloss over this fantasy with an idyllic picture of springtime; but later, in spite of my resistance and unwillingness, I let myself stay with the images, penetrating the real, technical details and the emotions accompanying it all. This fantasy is very similar to the one about myself in the wheelchair, which I had experienced in the group. I also realized the significance of our home for me. The most meaningful point in this fantasy was my fear of the barrier created by Uri's despair. If he despairs, somehow he will be partly dead for me.

I ask myself: Did the image of the wheelchair attract me so much at the time because it hid my implicit fear about Uri? And did reading your paper, which stressed the war, a war in which Uri—not I—participated, lead to the awareness that the fear of the wheelchair is a fear for Uri and not for myself? Before Edna told us about her wheelchair dream in the group, I had never felt myself drawn to this subject in any way.

I don't think any answers are necessary. I cried for Uri and I cried for myself; and I learned that the wish to die is, in itself, a half-death, and this is the meaning of the barrier of despair.

Now I ask myself: So what? This business remains unfinished because of the different wars we, in this country, have to live through, and not only because of things within us. I now feel how easily I can accept Yuval in his refusal to talk about his war. I don't think it helps. This business should be buried in the deepest of all places. Maybe now that I exposed this to daylight and developed it with all its details and felt it deeply, I will be able to bury it more easily. Perhaps this is the true meaning of "finishing the business" in this case.

Now I don't want to return to the fantasy or to think about it. I feel empty.

New Group, Old War _____

Introduction

These last two sections of "The Unfinished Business of War in Israel" cover cases which deal with effects and manifestations of the war from one to three years after the actual fighting had ceased. Throughout this period, it was evident that war, for us, was very much on our minds.

A new psychology students' group started in November 1974 and was scheduled to continue until July 1975. It was thus formed one full year after the October War. The country, in general, continued to feel the impact of war; and the political attempts to achieve some peaceful arrangement in the area underlined this awareness.

Yet, when I selected my students for the new group, I had the impression that the majority of the members were bothered with problems of identity and growing up, and not with war, death, or bereavement. In other words, I expected a group like the ones before the war.

The noticeable exception was Tamar, who was a war widow. Actually, her husband had died only eight months before. He had been an officer on a patrol in the mountains of the Sinai Desert, and during the night he had fallen off a cliff and died. I hesitated to accept Tamar into the group and talked openly about it with her. I explained that I was convinced that she needed more personal attention than a group could offer to any one of its members. I knew she would stand out in the group due to her situation, and I wondered how this would affect both her and the group. On the other hand, I have never believed that therapy exists in a social vacuum; and inasmuch as war widows, invalids, and other unfortunate individuals are part of our social reality, they should naturally be included in therapy groups. Since Tamar told me that she was in individual therapy at that time as well and that she saw the group partly as helping her to re-establish ways of relating to others, I decided to accept her.

Inside the group, Tamar became a living memorial to the war; and the group, although further from war in time that the Wheelchair Group, provided its members with the place, atmosphere, and methods through which people worked quite openly on their war experiences—more so than in the other group, which related to the war almost exclusively through symbolism. Whereas unexpressed fear was the main issue of the Wheelchair Group, the second-year group dealt with the experiences of grief and mourning, and the sense of guilt of those who remained alive. Retrospectively, it is hard to say whether all this happened because of Tamar or because of the interaction of other individuals who happened to be in the group. I tend to think that Tamar was a catalyst for a process that would have begun anyway; and, with a certain distance from their actual experiences, people were finding it easier to relate directly to war and its meaning for them. This greater openness of the 1975 group may, furthermore, lend support to the idea that for functional reasons, emotional expression is blocked during and after a crisis; but if appropriate channels and atmosphere are provided, a gradual healing process through the release of tension and feelings will eventually occur. Whatever the reason may be, the group members that year worked constantly on their unfinished business of war.

From my point of view, Tamar and Avi, the main characters in the drama of the new group, represent much more than their individual histories. Tamar is struggling with her own image of the hero/heroine. She asks for permission to be weak and receives a medal for heroism. She again asks for permission to be weak; but when granted her wish, she declines, fearful that she might totally collapse. Then, finally, she allows herself to collapse into a torrent of self-blame, and from this pit, she slowly begins her ascent.

Avi is a hero in his own way. A competent soldier, he is shocked to discover that he has repressed his human feelings. To be emotionally blocked is "functional" during the war, he is told. But back home? There he is proud and aggressive until he allows the iceberg within him to melt a little and comes to terms with his own insecurity. Do heroes have to be rigid? Are all rigid heroes insecure underneath? Can this be said for an entire country or generation?

Avi's work leads us into the core of the issue, for Israeli men, of strength versus weakness. We've had earlier glimpses of this issue, and it is also the focus of David's dream ("Unknown Driver in the Desert"). Later, this issue will be exposed in its full colors in Ben's and Avinoam's interviews ("Peacetime Conversations About War"). In all these instances, men struggle with the personality stereotype, which is a product of the frequent wars in Israel and requires physical strength and courage, seemingly precluding the possibility of free emotional expression and awareness of inner conflicts. Israeli men are frequently obliged to function in roles and situations which are alien to their natural tendencies; to make war and to withstand tough discipline, which might be the unlikeliest things they would do out of their own free choice. Some men, like Avi, may become "heroes" to the point of being unable to feel, whereas others, frequently educated abroad, like David, have difficulties in adopting the tough-guy front. Thus, in many ways, Avi is the opposite of David: David identified with the schlemiel, the antithesis of the hero, and tried to recapture his strength by finding within himself the brave driver of the command car in the desert; Avi, whose strong self is up front, is now bent on letting go, allowing his weaker parts to emerge. Both men, as well as Ben, Avinoam, Mory, and others in this book, search for a balanced expression of power and vulnerability, doing and feeling.

As this second year after the war draws to an end, it is clear to everyone in the group that the war, which is now more distant in time, is still very close to many of us. This realization is something we share, an inner secret, while reality outside maintains its normal appearance.

Tamar, A War Widow
(November through December 1974)

The subjects of death and bereavement were up front for Tamar. They were, at this stage, important parts of her identity. She does not hesitate to present her problems right from the start. In fact, sometimes I think she does not have control over her behavior; she is simply wide open. This fact has a major impact on the group. Groups usually enter into more intimate and painful areas very gradually, but not this one.

At the third meeting of the group we are playing with clay, doing some group projects to help us learn more about each other. One group is making animals. Tamar is making a rat; and as she places it on the table, she says: "I made a rat. Look, it's a dead rat. I'll make more dead rats for you." And someone cooperates with the suggestion "Let's make a killing machine for the rats." I am sure everybody notices the extraordinary statements, yet all of us prefer to ignore the incident at that time.

Two weeks later, we enter another stage, where people are required to work on the hot seat. There is a long silence, as nobody wants to be the first one, and I wait. Tamar is the one to break the silence.

TAMAR   I told Sara I'd be among the first ones to work in the group, but I didn't want to be the first one. I don't know, I feel I'll be able to relate to you better, to all the others, after I throw off some of the burden, relieve some of the pressure.

Tamar's first presentation, together with the group's reactions, takes two whole sessions—altogether about three hours. It is, of course, too long to report verbatim, but the following extracts represent much of the content and spirit of the whole picture. Generally, Tamar feels great pressure to tell us about her life as a widow, as if to let off steam; and the group, as well as myself, fight to accept yet to remain outside, not to be flooded by Tamar's grief. Some of us are anxious to face her fully and directly; and as I read the record of these sessions, I feel that I hesitated to direct, to offer so-called professional help, and simply supported Tamar whenever I could. I see these sessions mostly as mutual adaptation: Tamar presenting her tragedy, and we facing her as human beings. The resulting sessions, as far as psychotherapy is concerned, may appear disorganized, although Tamar feels greatly relieved after these meetings; and a few weeks later, she is able to proceed to an even more painful and intimate area.

TAMAR   I think I can start. With all the things that have happened to me this last year, I think I need a *teudat misken.* *
Until two years ago I had such a happy life; and then, recently, I got knocked down by three misfortunes, one after the other, and I feel I cannot stand on my feet any more. I wish I had a *teudat misken.*

Tamar briefly describes the two earlier tragedies that befell her family in the past two years. I prefer to omit this part, since it may disclose Tamar's identity.

TAMAR   And then, less than a year later, my husband was killed. I see these events as one inseparable chain, and I feel completely vulnerable. There is no longer anyone to rely upon, to trust. What happens to me now? I do everything. I tend to my housework, take care of my daughter, come to the university for my classes. I do everything half-heartedly, yet I keep feeling everybody owes me a special award, reinforcement, for any minor thing that I manage to accomplish. On the other hand, I am very proud and sometimes feel pretty unique to have been hit with so many personal tragedies. I look at the people around me and forget that they, too, may have problems, that

---

*This is a term I cannot translate from Hebrew. It is a sarcastic idiom that means "certificate of poverty or misery," indicating that the carrier of such a document is entitled to special rights and favors from society.

they may be tense and worried. I feel that the burden anyone else may be carrying is nullified in comparison with my lot. This approach distorts my feelings and activities among people. I want to receive much—attention, support, evaluation—and yet I myself am not pleased with my work, my behavior. When I fail to accomplish something, I am angry with myself, then announce: "Well, I am so unfortunate." Obviously, this makes me even angrier.

I   Suppose you got the *teudat misken*: What would you like to have written on it?

TAMAR   I am a world champion of misery and trouble.

I   Could you imagine yourself walking around with this document?

TAMAR   Yes. Whoever sees me with this will immediately admire anything I do or achieve.

I   Do you feel that people don't give you enough respect or admiration?

TAMAR   Yes. For instance, as I sit in a staff conference, I am fully there, am able to follow the discussion, to say something to the point, and I feel: Tamar, *ḳol hakavod.* * Yet other people accomplish the same with no visible effort. Or I do my chores —I clean the house, such trifles—and I feel people should applaud all of the things I do.

I   Here in the group, too?

TAMAR   Here, too, I caught myself exhibiting my *teudat misken*. The minute I got here—unintentionally, by the way— I made a dead rat so that all of you would pay attention to me. Even if I try to disregard the past for a while, I immediately find a way to announce how miserable and unique I am.

I   You have tried to disregard the past?

TAMAR   Some people I know give me the feeling I should. They say to me: "Why do you keep dragging this flag of misery all the time? You have to live in the present and ignore the past. Don't cling to your past."

I   And your answer . . .

*Another untranslatable idiom, meaning "all the respect," and used in admiration

TAMAR   This, now, is another part of me, or, if you wish, some other people who, I imagine, must have this reaction. When I start to live in the present and dare feel a little better, I feel guilty. And I can almost hear these people saying: "So soon? We can't see how you participate in your present life so completely when you know that the ones closest to you are dead." When I feel a little happier, this part of me takes over and reminds me that it is forbidden for me to enjoy myself.

I   What do you feel now?

TAMAR   I think I can't stand the pressure, I talk too much. I bet you're glad that I talk so openly, since it's good for the development of the group.

I   You sound very angry now.

TAMAR   The anger is the outcome of my feeling of invulnerability, the feeling I had before it all started, before all these things started to happen. I was so sure I'd never have any problems. I was proud, secure that no misfortune could happen to me. I got pregnant when I wanted to, was sure I'd have as many children as I had planned. My marriage was perfect. People who knew us used to notice our beautiful relationship and were jealous of it. We knew we could cope with problems, we had the power to and lots of energy.

She is quiet now and looks downward, absorbed.

I   What are you thinking about?

TAMAR   I have the feeling God is punishing me for my former attitude that I could control my life completely. From the start, from the beginning of this chain of disasters, I told myself: You ruined your chances for a good life, you got punished for your over-confidence, and the good life is over.

I   Are you religious?

TAMAR   These recent holidays, on the day of the New Year, I went to synagogue and heard all the people praying to God, imploring Him that He give them a good year, a year in which they won't die, and I thought: Nonsense! Who can tell God what to do? If He so wishes, He'll kill us all. I wanted to talk to Him, too.

I   And say what?

TAMAR   Very simply, that one more disaster, and I won't be able to stand it. That's all. I'll certainly collapse.

This continues some more. The following occurs later in the same session.

I   I keep hearing different parts of you. One is the heroine, the strong one. One is the angry Tamar, angry at God and also at herself for being sure of her invulnerability. I don't know what else, probably the non-heroine, looking for support. Try to stay with one . . .

TAMAR   The heroine.

I   . . . and exaggerate it, maybe by talking with someone here and bragging about how strong you are.

TAMAR   Avi . . . Avi, I feel bad today, I have a cold. But I didn't let myself stay in bed. I got up early and drove all the way up to the university. I did all that was necessary at home, took my daughter in the car with me to her grandmother, talked with her on the way—she had fun and was pleased to skip a day of school. The other night I went with her to a Chanukah party. I wanted to cry but controlled myself. I lighted the Chanukah candles, bought presents for the little one. I cook a hot dinner for the two of us every evening. On Monday I had a group of people meet in my house. When they left I cleaned the place, washed all the floors. I highly appreciate my ability to get so well organized for this first Chanukah alone. And finally I found somebody to fix the roof where the rain leaked in.

I   How do you feel?

TAMAR   Pleased with myself. What a list of achievements, *kol hakavod.*

I, however, hear some sarcasm in this comment and ask:

I   And you're fully together, behind this feeling of achievements?

TAMAR   I guess you are saying it's all nonsense, a list of trivialities.

I   No, I am not saying that, not at all. I appreciate very much what you have just told us, I truly do. I think there is a part in *you,* however, saying: "It's all nonsense, a list of trivialities."

TAMAR   I think that's right, but I don't know.

I   What is not a trivial thing, from your point of view?

TAMAR   To be cheerful and happy with my daughter. Why can't I?

I   And can you be sad with her?

TAMAR   Not when other people are present.

I   And for yourself, can you stand, and live with, your sadness?

TAMAR   Sometimes I can. Once I even said to Avi: "Help me, I am sad, do something about it."

I   To me this sounds like running away from the sadness. But I would like to hear what the others feel, what their reactions are.

URI   I feel admiration. I was sharing your suffering while you talked, almost to the point of crying, especially when you talked about you and your daughter.

RUTH   I think you are truly a heroine, yet I feel that you yourself are not convinced of it.

I   I feel the same. When you played the role of the heroine, there was this sarcastic undertone all the time, adding: All these things are not really important. At the same time, we here are convinced that the things you have accomplished are indeed important.

AVI   That's exactly what I was thinking, and I know Tamar better than many of you.

TAMAR   Do you mind if I tell what happened between us when we met in the cafeteria the other day?

AVI   No, go ahead.

TAMAR   We talked about my feelings, and Avi was listening very attentively. Then suddenly I felt that Avi was trying to penetrate into all this, into my world, because he was thinking about his wife, trying to estimate her reactions in case he himself got killed in the war. And Avi admits it.

Some of us are too shocked to react, while the others add supportive remarks, commenting on Tamar's courage.

TAMAR   You know, as we talk here, I feel that instead of a *teudat misken,* you are finally going to award me a decoration of valor, a citation.

I   Decoration for the heroine. Could you now show us the non-heroine, the one who needs this *teudat misken?*

TAMAR   This is more difficult. I washed the floors after midnight because I am crazy; I thought I would collapse. I run away from my daughter once a week, for the whole day, and dump her on different people. I drove to Jerusalem and gave a soldier a ride and immediately told him I am a war widow. Why did I have to do these things?

I   Are you the non-heroine when you do things you feel like doing on the spur of the moment?

TAMAR   Like staying in bed for a day? Yes.

I   Is there something between the heroine with her decoration and the unfortunate with her *teudat misken?*

TAMAR   Yes, forgetting the past.

I   Do you believe this?

TAMAR   Yes. It would make me normal again. I'd do things just so and not to be admired for the doing because of what happened in the past. All my behavior these days, all my feelings, are dictated by past events. I am stuck there. I have to change that.

I   Do you feel that's possible?

TAMAR   It must be, otherwise, how will I get out of this situation?

I   And your feelings right now?

TAMAR   I wish it were true, all I said just now.

I   Your face is skeptical again.

TAMAR   I thought about another war widow, a new friend of mine, who gave a birthday party for her little boy. I told her: "You are great to be able to do this." She said: "It's nothing." And I admired her for giving the party and for what she said.

I   She must be another heroine, or let me put it this way: she preferred that day to show you the heroine part.

TAMAR   Yes.

I   I think you are a heroine, yet the non-heroine part is also important.

TAMAR   The easiest thing for me would be to give up, to sit at home all day, to cry and feel sorry for myself.

I   I am telling you again, Tamar, there must be a middle way, but perhaps we are still far away from the crossroads. I feel your pain and your courage, and I don't think you are ready to forget the past, not for a while.

People in the group comment:

RUTH   If I were you, I'd be afraid to stay at home alone and cry. I'd be afraid I'd never emerge from that situation again.

MICKI   That's true. But you need friends, like us here in the group, in front of whom you could expose the non-heroine as well. They'll accept you, we'll accept you, and you won't be so alone.

RUTH   Are you afraid that you may break down completely?

TAMAR   This is something that never even crossed my mind. I can't allow myself to break down: I am a mother. Sometimes I feel that being a mother is the only thing that keeps me together, you know.

RACHEL   What happens when your daughter feels you're sad?

TAMAR   First she asks why I am sad and if I am angry at her for saying or doing something to upset me. Then she hugs me, kisses me.

RACHEL   Did you ever tell her that you miss her father?

TAMAR   Yes, I did in the beginning, and now she knows.

URI   I didn't know you before, so I didn't know till now that you are a war widow. I saw you in the library, and you looked and behaved like any other student. What you told us today is so strange and new. I never saw you as an unfortunate.

RACHEL   These things are not transparent, you know.

TAMAR   Why, I am pleased to hear what you said, Uri, that I am like any other student, just a human being.

I We'll have to finish now. I hope you feel that you got a lot of respect from me, from us, for what you are and how you are. I am glad you talked to us about it. I did not expect you'd be able to do it so soon. I thank you for trusting us, for feeling that your problem is not too big for the group.

TAMAR I am glad it's all out in the open now.

The next week Tamar is late. Several people say they have more to say to her and cannot see how we can work with someone else or talk about her in her absence. While this discussion is going on, Tamar steps in. She looks more composed, less tense, than she has in past weeks.

I Have a seat. People here were waiting for you. They feel they want to talk to you. Ben, you were the first, and then Daniel.

BEN I know I should have said these things last week. I could not, however; it is such a sensitive issue, and I felt blocked. I didn't know about your tragedy before. My feelings in the session were shock and empathy . . . admiration for your coping . . . but then, I got angrier and angrier; and only later that night, at home, was I able to get in touch with my anger. I am angry at you, Amia, mainly, and at the people here in the group, for supporting you in your suggestion that Tamar show her weak, non-heroic side. I don't know why you suggested this step. What psychological rationale is there for it? I know Tamar won't fall apart if she admits her weakness, but what's the use?

I I prefer that you find out first, by asking Tamar, if that's the main message she received last week.

TAMAR No, not exactly, but I did a lot of thinking in the meantime. I am pleased with what you feel for me, Ben, but I don't see exactly what there is to be angry about.

I That's because a whole week has passed since these feelings were aroused. Ben, I am not trying to avoid your point. It is true that I personally believe that many of us are heroes excessively. Sometimes we are required to be, but I believe we all could let go a little more. If you have a different opinion on the matter, then we are in disagreement, and that's OK with me.

DANIEL   I, too, did not express my feelings last week. Like Ben, I was too moved to speak. I felt for you, Tamar, that's all. I used to think that war was easier on the women. I never saw or felt myself in the position you described here last week. You have changed my perspective, somehow. Now I want to ask you how you felt after the session, if you wish to tell us.

TAMAR   I received two documents from you last week, a decoration of valor and a *teudat misken*. And I know that to integrate the unfortunate with the heroic in real life takes more than two hours of work, so I'll work on that. One thing that really warmed my heart after the session was what Uri said, that I look, to him, like any other girl, that he didn't know I was a widow, wasn't too impressed by me, that I was just another student in the library. It's good to know that for some, I am still me, Tamar, not a symbol of whatever I represent to them. And what you, Avi, said, that I am OK, and since you know me better than all the others, this made me feel good about myself. I figure I have to find the source of my need for approval and appreciation from others and the way I ask for it, so that I can stop myself . . . then I'll do things simply for me and be whole.

I   That's a nice statement for your goals in your growth. You sound as if you're on your way, too.

TAMAR   This is a growing-up process I still need to go through. For me, society is still Mother and Father, handing out rewards. I want to be independent.

I   In the group, too?

TAMAR   Yes, I don't want to depend on the group for reinforcement. It's a process I see I have to go through, for myself, in order to appear in society as a human being, not as a widow.

URI   This dependence you speak about, did it disturb you before . . . before your husband got killed?

TAMAR   I guess it did, but only recently did I start to feel displeased with the way I behave with others. I think I first formulated it here, last week.

URI   I find it interesting that now, after the disaster, you have this need to grow up.

TAMAR   The situation changed for me, drastically. Before the war, my husband fulfilled the role which I now require that you, or the whole society, play. You see, if I got a high grade on a paper, I didn't have to let the whole world know. It was enough that I came home to my husband and told him. Or if I washed the floors, he would come home from work and notice the difference. As if together with my husband, I was whole and accepted myself. Now I am not so any more.

Nothing more was said; and at that stage, I felt that Tamar would not go any further, and I was ready to work with someone else.

The impact of Tamar's opening was, however, so great that the next week nobody was able or willing to take the hot seat and to work. The best summary of the prevailing feelings was given by Rachel and Ruth, who were highly involved with Tamar while she worked.

Rachel said: "Last week, when Tamar worked, I had the feeling that to proceed from that to any new topic would be extremely difficult. When one hears problems like these, I mean real-life ones, I feel like saying: "Forget your own problems. They are a bunch of childish nonsense." I know it's a stupid comparison to make between us, since it's the inner situations that count most; still, the transition from Tamar's to my own presentation is, for me, too difficult."

And Ruth said, some time later in the same meeting: "I feel an unwillingness to cooperate today. I feel disappointed at what we were unable to do for Tamar. We did not finish the business for her, did we?"

I   Obviously we didn't.

RUTH   But I wanted to ask you, Tamar, did you feel that all that exposure was worthwhile for you? Did you get anything out of it?

I   You feel doubtful, maybe guilty, for not being helpful enough. I admit we all feel this helplessness, since we cannot really change the reality for Tamar.

TAMAR   I want to answer Ruth. You said that so little was done for me here. Well, you can't change my life, yet it was one step forward for me. I left with the feeling that I got a whole reservoir of support. It was a good feeling, something I didn't have for a long time. What we did here was very significant for me. Also, I feel that now I'll be able to listen to others. I am relaxed and waiting. I am thinking especially of you, Avi. I feel you need to work, and I want to hear you. I know you others have things to work on, too; and as you go on sitting here, quiet, resisting, I ask myself: What have I done to the group? I have cast a spell on you; nobody can work any more.

Surprisingly, this somehow unlocked the group, and Avi was the next one to work.

The next time Tamar worked was about eight weeks later. It would be a distortion of the developmental process, a forced continuity, however, if I present this later, dramatic session, right away. So the next section is an account of Avi's work, which actually occurred right after Tamar's first presentation.

The Melting of an Iceberg (January 1975)

Avi is a young man of twenty-five. He is married and the father of two children. Like most of the others in this group, he is an advanced student in clinical psychology.

In one of the first sessions of the group, I asked people around the room to stay for a few minutes with their present awareness and to report what was happening. For most of them it was the first time they took the hot seat, in the sense of being the focus of the group's attention. They found it, therefore, quite awkward, even threatening. Most statements in this new group were like the following: "I feel uncomfortable . . . I don't know what to say . . . My hands are shaky . . . My skin is hot . . . I am anxious and don't know what there is to be anxious about . . . Now I am blocked, have nothing to say . . ." From more experienced people, I usually get totally different reactions, something like: "My body is very relaxed; I feel the weight of my body in the chair . . . I see you all looking at me. I see eyes, brown, blue, brown again . . . I hear footsteps in the corridor, approaching. I imagine somebody standing at the door . . ."

As Avi's turn came, he said: "I am hot. There is pressure in my chest. I am aware of my arms, heavy. I am heavy. I feel excited. I feel! I know suddenly that I am capable of feeling, and I am glad, happy . . . I am not dead inside. You don't know what this means for me. Since the war I felt as if all my feelings were dead, I thought forever. Maybe I could work on all this in the group, sometime."

This was Avi's introduction to the group. I expected him to work pretty soon, but he started only after Tamar worked and seemed to be finished. As he takes the hot seat, he announces that he wants to work on his poor self-image.

AVI   Today, for example, I was working on my thesis, and I conducted this experiment. The results support my hypothesis, but I keep telling myself: There must be something wrong in the design. I am never sure I am OK. The same thing happens at the clinic. I leave the session after an hour of therapy and say to myself: What have you done? You're not fit to work with human beings. Then I meet my supervisor and tell him about it, and he says—

I   Be the supervisor.

AVI   I wish he'd say I was OK.

I   Be him, and talk to Avi when he thinks he has failed.

AVI   OK. You are doing fine. There was no other way, for one thing. And you have so little experience, what do you expect? With more time and experience, you'll get a better perspective on what's happening.

I   Does it make you feel better about yourself?

AVI   No. In my heart I say: Bullshit, I don't believe you. And I still don't know if I can become a good psychotherapist.

I   Like Freud?

AVI   No, like my standards demand. I see this young girl; she is my patient. As she sits there, weeping, confused, week after week, I feel impatient. I don't accept her feelings; I don't know, actually, what she feels. All I wish to tell her is: For heaven's sake, pull yourself together! I have to quit this profession.

I   Could you tell several people here: I am no good. I am worthless.

Avi hesitates. Members of the group encourage him, saying that even if he doesn't feel that way, maybe it's worth trying.

AVI   I don't want to say this to anyone here, not now.

He is silent for a few moments.

I   Where are you?
AVI   I have this pressure in my chest. I don't feel anything as I am talking. I pick things out of my head—stuff that I have been thinking about for a long time now. Perhaps something is happening to me here and now, yet I am out of touch. I am hot, my legs are heavy, but I don't feel anything.
I   Are you aware of the way you are sitting?

Avi's posture on his chair forms a diagonal with the floor, his weight seems to be supported mostly by his right arm, which is leaning on a low table next to his chair. I sense this is a very odd way to support his large body.

AVI   The fact is my back hurts badly today, that's why I sit this way. I am aware of tension in my body, but I don't feel anything. This is more important to me than what I started with before. I doubted if I could bring it up.
I   Or wanted to.
AVI   The problem of feeling: this is really more of a problem than what I told you before. Now I start to feel the impact of the strongest experience I have lived through in my whole life. It was during the war. I don't know if you care to hear about it, it's pretty strong. Now I am angry at myself for saying this. I know I'll tell you anyway. In the war I went through a very tough situation, lots of people killed and wounded. I had to evacuate a pretty big unit. On my tank were people in different shapes—wounded, burned, dead. I evacuated them, went back to the front, and kept fighting. Then I got wounded myself and arrived at the hospital. As I lay there, at the hospital, my sole preoccupation was evaluating my performance. I wanted to know if I was good, competent or not. I didn't feel any of the pain or grief about what I lived through. I tried to . . .

I   To feel pain?

AVI   Yes, anything. I wanted to feel sorrow or to dream, to have nightmares like the others—I never had one dream about the war. And I ask myself: Can a person like me treat others? Feeling is the main thing in psychotherapy, I think. I'd have quit a long time ago if not for the positive feedback I kept getting. If I were really a block of ice, as I feel now, would I get this feedback from others?

I   Be a block of ice.

AVI   What do you mean? What do you want from me? I can't add anything to what I told you about the war. This is the actualization of the image of the ice block. There is nothing to add. I talked about my inner freezing to the army psychiatrist at the hospital, and he said it was functional . . . a functional reaction. It is, perhaps, functional for a computer, but I don't want to be a computer. I want to be a psychotherapist. I feel I am avoiding now, running away from what I have told you about the war.

I   What do you feel now?

AVI   I feel empty.

I   Stay with it.

AVI   Immediately Avi-the-functional pops up and asks: What will you gain if you follow these directions? What for?

I   And you answer—

AVI   I won't gain anything. So what?

I   Put this wise guy in the corner for a while.

AVI   I'll try.

I   Did you pay attention to the timing, to the moment he appeared?

AVI   Yes, when I was trying to be with myself.

I   When you were trying to feel empty.

AVI   I am forbidden to . . .

I   Continue. I am forbidden to . . .

AVI   I am forbidden to feel empty, to feel bad, to fail.

I   Where are you?

AVI   I arrived at my wall, the inner wall inside me.

I   Be the wall and talk to Avi.

AVI   I can't.

I   Visualize first. There is a wall, and you. On what side of the wall are you?

AVI   I don't know what you are talking about.

I   You said you've arrived at your inner wall.

Avi is silent. He looks as if he is suffering immensely.

I   Where are you?

AVI   One minute . . . I can't do it . . . I am unclear about how to be a wall. Something is preventing me from being on the other side.

I   What is on the other side? Can you guess?

AVI   I am stuck in front of the wall. I can't move.

I   You don't want to move. You also don't want to be a wall or a block of ice.

AVI   I am trying. [*very angry and tense*] I can't be a wall, damn it!

I   How does the wall look? Your breathing has changed, you're excited.

AVI   I don't understand you.

I   Don't try to understand. Just tell me how your wall looks and where you are. Is it like the Wailing Wall?

AVI   No.

I   So describe it to me.

AVI   I can't!! I don't see the wall, I don't feel the wall. I just know it's there.

After a long silence, while Avi is so obviously fighting with himself, breathing heavily, I say:

I   I am very sad for you.

AVI   I don't feel your sadness.

I   You don't believe me?

AVI   I believe you and I don't feel . . . [*Silence. His breathing becomes more relaxed.*] I am coming out of it, slowly.

I don't ask what the "it" is; I feel tired of pushing. I ask the other members of the group for their reactions.

Most of the people say they feel frustrated or sad; some try to provide interpretations. A few are angry with me for pushing Avi up against his wall so hard, demanding that he do something he obviously could not do.

I   When I asked Avi, asked you, to feel empty, or be ice, or be a wall, it wasn't for the exercise. My strongest impression from you today has been the feeling of your strong boundaries, your limits. Up to here I'll go and not a step further. You said some strong things, and I believed you. At the same time I felt you were saying to yourself: These are my limits; I'll stay on this side of the wall. That's the strongest feeling I get working with you.

AVI   I never went beyond these limits, never in my life. I am worried that I don't feel—that feeling, too, is beyond my boundaries now. Again I am thinking about the war. I was holding my dead friend in my arms. He had been killed. I did not think about it, only about how to save the others; and later, when I went to inform his parents, to tell them about what had happened to their son, I did not feel much either. From then on I've been trying to get at this barrier, or better still, to cross it, to find out how and why I prevent myself from feeling. At the hospital I had a lot of time to think about it. When I was evacuated from the battlefield—I was, perhaps, the last one alive to be evacuated—the other guys at the post hugged me and kissed me, and I did not believe them, didn't believe all the good things they were saying about me.

RUTH   As you find it hard to believe us here, or to take the word of your supervisors when they praise you. You shut yourself up and say you don't feel, so we can't reach you.

Avi has withdrawn into himself and does not seem to be listening to Ruth.

I   What is happening now?
AVI   I am not here with you. I am there, in the war, again . . . living through those last minutes before the evacuation.
I   You were afraid you'd be killed.
AVI   Yes, and that my wife would remain alone. I was also

afraid I'd get burned. I did not think then, consciously, about death—one cannot fight that way—just the fear of being burned alive and that my wife would be a widow.

TAMAR   It's a pity my husband didn't think this way in his last minutes.

The group is dead silent for a long time. I am in conflict whether to attend to Avi's needs or to Tamar's.

AVI   What Tamar said, it hit me . . . it hit me very strongly just now . . .

I   You want to talk to Tamar. She is here.

AVI   No . . . no words . . .

TAMAR   I have shut you up.

AVI   No, it's not that. When you talked, I felt as if I had one body with you, knowing . . . but after words like these there is nothing more to say.

I   Then be with the silence.

TAMAR   I may, however, talk to you, Avi. What I wanted to tell you, and my remark a minute ago slipped out unwittingly, is that I feel it is beautiful that you thought about your wife at those moments.

The time limit for this session passed a long time ago. Avi still sits withdrawn, and the group is quiet, waiting.

I   Do you feel you can stop for today?

Avi nods, smiles sarcastically, and says:

AVI   You think I feel something? You'll be surprised how easily I can discontinue now or any time.

I   You know, either you're a great actor or your feelings are all right and you're simply mislabeling what's been happening here. Anyway, it's time to go. Sometimes we end our work at an impasse. It's frustrating, yet it's true. We did not solve your problems, but at least we felt them.

During the week I met Avi once. I could not look straight up at him and hardly said hello. This was an impasse, and we both felt it; it was a genuine feeling, though very hard to take. I hoped Avi would find his way out.

Next week, nobody starts to work. I express my feelings that apparently we are all waiting for Avi to continue. People are smiling at each other as if in tacit agreement not to take Avi's time. Avi notices the situation, and it infuriates him.

AVI   What a bunch of weaklings! In the corridors, as well as just now before the session, you people were telling me things, pushing me to go on, and here you all sit, quiet as mutes!

I   I also had an encounter with you in the corridor and was surprised to discover that, somehow, I could not face you. I wanted to find out how you felt, but I decided to wait and hear about it here, in the group.

AVI   Yes, I noticed. You didn't even smile. Last time, as I left the group, I suddenly found myself facing this immense wall, this iceberg, and you didn't provide me with a rope to climb to the top, to pass to the other side. You found an empty chair to talk to for everybody in this group, but not for me.

I   I wanted you to talk to your wall.

AVI   I know. Those were two very difficult hours for me, last week.

I   And what do you plan for today?

AVI   Not to work, not today. Maybe in a month, I don't know.

DANIEL   May I say something? My strongest impression from last week is how you refuse to accept anything from us. When we say pleasant things, stroke you, you refuse to accept; and when we criticize you, you call us all a bunch of weaklings. Is this a joke? I didn't enjoy it, and I don't know what you meant. I think that if you were to go to a priest or a rabbi, he would tell you that you lack humility, you are so proud and unforgiving, as if you were playing the role of God.

Avi looks at Daniel very attentively.

AVI   I don't think I am proud. I am hard and aggressive, and I wish to change.

Some people continue to make various comments, while my attention is once again drawn to Avi's posture in his chair.

He is, as last week, sitting at a diagonal, one leg crossed over the other, leaning very heavily on his right arm. Last week he said he had a backache; still, I decide to try to work on his posture.

I   There is something in the way you sit. Last week you said you had a backache, so I let it go. I noticed when you criticize yourself, assume the role of God and put yourself down, as Daniel said, you take this diagonal posture. You don't support your body; you almost fall off your chair. Try to sit straight, to support yourself.
AVI   [*moves about in his chair*] Like now?
I   Put your two legs down, feel the earth.

Avi follows my example and sits, reflecting.

I   What is happening when you sit straight?
AVI   It's not the way I sit, it's the words you said: "support yourself." You gave me an awful shock.
I   Leave the words alone. Try to feel yourself as you sit balanced, supporting your weight by your contact with the ground. Remain with your body.
AVI   I feel good. I feel strong and remember some good feelings.
I   Can you tell us?
AVI   Well, it may sound idiotic. Still . . . when you said support yourself, I felt the tank climbing on the hills, me and my unit behind me. There in the tank, in its turret, I felt in full contact with my body, every single part of me, and I was straight.
I   Can you remain with this feeling and look at us here?
AVI   I feel funny. I said I didn't want to work today, and here I am working again.
I   This is once again the part of you that is putting you down or interfering. You are again reclining to the side of your chair.
AVI   Yes, I'd like to get rid of this part of me.
I   I'll tell you how you look when you face this part. You move away, recline, lose your balance and support. Here, look, you

are a diagonal again. [*I imitate his sitting posture, while he looks unusually attentive.*]

AVI   This is the part of me I am trying to avoid. [*talks very slowly as if discovering something*] I'll tell you about him. He is small and husky, rolling like a fat ball.

I   Talk to him. You wanted to talk to an empty chair. You sit up straight and face him on the chair.

AVI   I am facing you Avi, Avi-boy. [*Avi follows my directions and can do it. I am glad, and feel his immense difficulty and his forceful overcoming of it.*] You are a spoiled little boy. Everything is done for you by others, even in the boarding school. You are spoiled and lazy. All you read is Tarzan stories and the sports news. And you're fat. You're not willing to accept that the situation has changed now—I am changed. You are locked there in your feelings of inferiority, your lack of confidence. I am not like you any more! You don't see how I have changed; I have all the evidence. Don't infect me with your insecurity.

I   Now switch chairs and be him.

AVI   (as "Avi-boy") Forget it, you are just like me, as before. Every single student knows more than you do; your IQ is zero! You're not sensitive to others. You're spoiled like me.

—[*changes chairs and roles*] Shut up! You make me mad. I am sick and tired of your hanging around me. How can I get rid of you? You spoil everything, prevent me from feeling! You reduce every experience I have, asking what it is good for. Don't you see I became what I wanted to be and I don't want you here? You annoy and disturb me.

I   How old are you when you are him?

AVI   He is me from fourteen to eighteen. I see him as fifteen now.

I   Ask him if there is anything you can get from him now.

AVI   What I get from him is criticism all the time, a destructive approach. I want to send him to hell.

I   No, you don't understand me. What do you want to get from him now?

AVI   Now? Nothing. I can't stand this part. I simply wish, Avi-boy, you'd leave me alone.

I   Is there nothing?

AVI   Yes . . . no . . . There is something. [*looks at the empty chair*] Give me back the ability to cry.

I   Talk to him.

AVI   Give me back the ability to cry. You used to cry for any stupid reason. You made me think that to feel was to be weak and a cry-baby. I fought against this weakness, and now I don't cry any more. And there is something else you took away from me when I sent you away—my love of music, the ability to let go and play for relaxation and the practice of listening to music a lot.

I   He is not so horrible then.

AVI   [*very gently*] I found some things I want from him but in moderation . . . that I won't close up immediately when I see somebody crying, or when there is a good reason to cry. Oh, I hate him!

I   What is it now?

AVI   He is laughing at me while I am talking. He is saying: "Why are you play acting here? You feel none of it anyway. You know both of us are worthless." That's why I hate him.

I   I think that you can't get rid of him. Maybe you'd be able to make an agreement with him.

AVI   An agreement? What kind?

I   I don't know. He is your part, not mine.

AVI   The only thing I can think of is: "Leave me alone for three years, and then we'll see."

SARA   May I ask a question? Is he yours, or are you his?

I   Yes, who is bigger?

AVI   He is smaller but smart.

I   And you're afraid that if you don't expel him, he'll take control.

GABY   When you let him control you, you sit diagonally.

AVI   He makes me sit that way.

RACHEL   Why don't you offer him a partnership? Let him feel he helps you in some ways, so he won't feel like fighting you all the time.

AVI   I don't see how.

RACHEL   Don't you have children? You know how to deal with children. By giving him the feeling he is nothing, you make him rebel. Let him feel helpful to you. This will make him feel good, and he'll relax his hold on you.

SARA   Ask him for his conditions.

RACHEL   No, you tell him your conditions, since you're bigger.

I   That's enough. I think we gave Avi a lot of suggestions, and he'll have to find his own way. What is going on within you, Avi?

Avi is silent for a while, but he looks more relaxed and pleased.

AVI   I see the direction you are pointing to. Yet now, on the spot, I still don't see what kind of a contract I can make with him.

I   With me.

AVI   With me.

I   I wish you'd say to your Avi-boy something like: "I know we have to live together, and we'll work on the conditions later."

AVI   It's done, that's what I feel I have said to the smart little fat fellow.

I   Very well. I want to tell you that today I did not feel your wall so much; it wasn't as visible. I feel relieved. Now, you probably want to hear from the others.

The others have, indeed, a lot to say, with very much feeling. I'll quote just a few.

GABY   When you talked about this small smart fellow, I didn't feel you hate him that much. I feel that, somewhere, you may even love him.

RUTH   I would like to see more of this Avi-boy around. The two things that strike me about him (or, you, isn't it?)—the ability to cry and some sense of inferiority—would add a lot to you. I am glad to find out about this part; it makes you much more likable. Don't throw him away.

GABY   Hey, did you notice how you sit there smiling at people? You look so much warmer and open now.

I think that our feelings just then were expressed beautifully in a poem, written by Daniel about the group. I'll quote several lines.

> Sometimes there is silence; is this work, too?
> Sometimes there is humor, which helps for a while.
> Relief: somebody starts to work.
> I feel with him. He works for me, too.
> He looks so alone, focused on himself.
> Am I a witness? A partner?
> Avi works. He stumbles at a wall. Avi is feeling his way
>   along the wall, looking for an opening.
> It so happened that a wall tumbled down in front of us,
>   a wall simply disappeared.
> There were moments of celebration.
> A flower opened up.

Tamar: Immersion (March 1975)

It is during a marathon session late at night that Tamar wishes to work for the second time.

TAMAR   Remember the time I cut into your conversation, Avi, with my remark? When I said I wish my husband would have thought about me in his last minutes.

Avi and I respond; we remember.

TAMAR   For a while, I was angry with myself. I did it again, I disregarded the right that you, as well as all the others, have for attention. My problem always has to come first. Well, we worked on that, and I hope I can control myself much better now. But basically, the slip I had then is very significant for me; it is something that has been bothering me a lot.

I   Would you like to talk to your husband about this now?

TAMAR   Yes, I would.

I   You never use his name. What is his name?

TAMAR   His name was Benjamin, and you're right. I still find it very difficult to mention it.

I   Speak to him now.

TAMAR   Benjamin, for the last couple of months I have been very bothered by this. What were your last minutes like? Did you suffer a lot? Did you know you were dying? I wish I knew. I would also like to know some other things. Did you think about me then, and about our daughter? Did you imagine how we would be left alone without you? Did you?

She is quiet for a few moments, looking very tense, sitting with her hands over her face. Then she continues:

TAMAR   Sometimes, I imagine you didn't think about us; you couldn't have. If you had, I know you wouldn't have gotten yourself killed like that. I know for sure.

I   Tamar, do you believe that?

TAMAR   Yes, I do.

I   What are you actually telling him? You sound as if you're blaming him for something.

TAMAR   Yes, and I'll talk to him directly. Benjamin, I feel that if you had had our image, mine and your daughter's, before your eyes that night, you would have been more careful out there in the desert, you would have saved yourself somehow— if not for your sake, then for ours.

I   How do you feel, saying this?

TAMAR   Very upset . . . angry, and I know I shouldn't be. You're probably all shocked by my attitude. But you don't know the things I know.

I   What are you referring to? Talk to Benjamin about these things.

TAMAR   I'll talk to him. Remember, Benj, the times we used to talk about hiking and the ways to take care in the desert? You used to say that an intelligent human being can always survive if he has enough water and maintains his clarity of mind. We used to hike a lot together, sometimes in the Judean Desert, and we talked about that. You knew how to be careful. If you had only tried to, you could have tried harder. And I have this feeling that you didn't try, as if you gave in to the night and the desert. There was nothing worthwhile to fight for, to survive for, any more.

I   How is that?

TAMAR   Just a few more meters and you'd have found the light and the camp, and you could have been saved. Why didn't you make it?

I   Can you answer for him?

TAMAR   I can, but I don't want to role play.

I   Do it your way. I am listening.

TAMAR   I blame myself horribly. I feel so guilty. If I had been nicer to you . . . if I had given you more reassurance . . . if only I had shown how desperately I needed you, I know you would have been alive today. But I didn't. I acted as if everything was taken for granted—life, happiness, our relationship. I didn't even worry about you any more, since the actual combat was already over and you were just mopping up. I didn't show my love for you. Now I feel it so strongly. I didn't let you see how important you were for my existence. I didn't know myself. I just discovered that now, too late for both of us. And I have this nagging feeling, this certainty, that it was up to me to give you more energy to cope with these circumstances, to keep you alive.

I   Tamar, look at me for a minute. Do you really believe what you're saying?

TAMAR   Yes, otherwise I wouldn't say these horrible things in front of all of you.

I   I was not quite sure. As far as I know, his death was an accident.

TAMAR   Yes, but accidents don't just happen like that. He wasn't the type of a person to get lost in the worst conditions or to fall off a cliff. You didn't know him.

I   You're talking as if he committed suicide.

TAMAR   More accurately, as if I killed him.

I   You feel you're responsible for his death, yet you know that's not true. You have some other parts, I am sure, that deny this responsibility and can see the death of Benjamin as a terrible accident.

TAMAR   I guess you're right. There are external, more normal parts, which I show everyone. Here, I let myself show you the other parts, too. Are you too shocked?

I   Yes, I am shocked, it's true. This is my emotional reaction, understand. I am not judging you. I am reminded of books I read about children's reactions to sudden death in their family. They frequently say: "I was a naughty boy; therefore my father died. I am guilty, I am to blame."

TAMAR   I am not a case in a book. I really feel this way. I am sure he didn't think about me during those last couple of minutes, when he still could have pulled himself through. He didn't, and it's my fault.

I   I have mixed feelings about that. Part of me wants to say: That's how you feel, I am pleased you can express yourself, share it with us. And another part of me, my adult, reality-experienced part, wants very much to change your perspective. I also want to say: Tamar, that's impossible. You've convinced yourself of all this. You built this theory with which to punish yourself, and you're simply incorrect. There is no factual basis for your theory.

TAMAR   I know what you mean. I didn't dare say all this to anyone . . . and it's been inside me so long now. You know, when it happened, when he got killed, I wasn't even home. I had gone away for the weekend to visit some friends, and they had to look all over the place for me to inform me.

I   That's not your fault either. You couldn't have helped Benjamin out there if you had sat home all day. It wouldn't have made any difference.

TAMAR   I know. But can you understand how I feel—and how I felt then? When I was having a good time with this family, he was dying there with no one to help him. I didn't give him a minute's thought that night.

I   So you're sure he didn't think about you either.

TAMAR   Well, maybe.

I   It is a horrible feeling, I think I know. Yet I want to take the role of your ego tonight, of your healthy, adult part, and I say: All this has nothing to do with reality, with the fact that he was killed. You just keep punishing yourself, in addition to the objective disaster, which is bad enough as it is.

TAMAR   Don't you believe that people who aren't strongly motivated to live, who do not see any purpose for their lives, would be more likely to be careless about their survival, and then die?

I   In certain extreme cases, that's true. But does this describe Benjamin—having nothing to live for, to look forward to; a young man, healthy, successful, with a family of his own?

TAMAR: No, I guess not. I am so upset, I don't know what I am talking about. And it's so late. Nights are awful for me.

She starts to cry at this point, for the first time.

I   That's all right. You're entitled to be upset, you're in great pain. I feel it, too. And I think it's good you expressed your guilt and anger, all the hidden emotions. I hope you can be in touch with the other parts, which are so-called healthier and more reality-based, you know.

Tamar is silent; she isn't crying any more.

I   Would you like to continue talking with Benjamin?
TAMAR: No, not now. I wish to hear the others here, especially the men. You must be feeling I am awfully dangerous, some sort of a witch, perhaps. Tell me, what do you think?

Tamar's manner, when she speaks, is highly provocative, as if she is begging to be punished more. The group is silent; nobody takes the challenge. I feel in a bind, too. If we want to accept Tamar, should we say: "Yes, you're horrible?" And if we say: "No, you're imagining all that," aren't we denying her internal reality, the great confession she's just made? After a long silence, Dori starts, as if talking from a great distance.

DORI   You know, my father died of cancer some years ago; I was in high school then. The doctors told us there was no cure for him; it was just a matter of time. I was a child, the oldest of my brothers and sisters. My parents never had much education, particularly in European medicine. We just had to take the word of these wise doctors and leave my father with them at the hospital to die slowly. It was horrible, that sense of helplessness, that whatever we'd try, there was nothing we could actually do. Then, one day, Mother went to a rabbi of some sort, someone who was known to advise people and who practiced some sort of primitive Oriental medicine. The old man gave her some herbs and instructed her to make a drink from these herbs which could help Father. I don't think he promised anything, it's just that we wanted to believe him so much. So Mother used to cook these herbs, make some tea from them, and every single day after school I would take my bike and the small jar to the hospital, and give this drink to Father. Obviously the doctors weren't aware of the whole thing. Father died a few weeks later, and I witnessed the whole process; from day to day as I visited him, I saw how it was coming. But Mother used to make this medicine with the utmost devotion and I used to carry this jar to him till the last day of his life. I didn't think about that for a long time now; and tonight, as you talked, Tamar, I suddenly remembered. I felt the urge to tell you about that. I felt it was relevant to you, somehow.

TAMAR Thank you, I feel you as being very close to me.

I Dori, I am very moved. If you can, I wish that you'd tell Tamar how you see your story as relevant to her now.

DORI It's difficult to formulate; perhaps it's like this: it's hard to accept one's helplessness when someone very dear to you is dying, so we convince ourselves that we can do something to help, to prevent. In my case, it was before Father died. We sneaked this medicine to him to save his life. In your case, it all happens after your husband's death. You convince yourself that you might have helped if you had behaved differently, if you had loved Benjamin more, maybe if you'd been a better wife to him, whatever. So, what I am trying to say is that actually, for you as for me, the death of our dear ones was inevitable, something we couldn't prevent or stop by any means. We just have to learn to be sort of humble, to accept our helplessness, to admit that we can't stop death. It's very painful and difficult, I know.

Tamar thanks Dori again for his personal approach. She does not fight any more, does not try to prove her guilt. We all sit silently for a long while, immersed. I am thinking about religion and how it may provide some support in facing death and helplessness. Tamar has to go her own individual way about it, and she does. At the end of a long pause we all get up for a break. No one feels like adding anything.

Tamar did not remember the path she traversed that night in the group. She asked for my notes some time later and took them home to read. She said she had found it difficult to believe that she actually had been there, had said all those things.

There was a gradual change in Tamar following this immersion. By the next week she had changed her hairstyle and bought some new clothes. She wasn't as tense as before; and most important, she started to listen to others in the group, was able to see their lives and difficulties from their point of view, without making constant comparisons with her own lot. As if following this deep immersion into the pain, only one way remained open: upward.

The Shadow of War _____

Introduction

As I leave Israel for a year, in the summer of 1975, I carry
with me the awareness that war, although somewhat removed
in time, is still very much present for many Israelis. I return a
year later to a similar atmosphere. It is now the fall of 1976, and
a new group forms. Without any warning, this group is "in"
again when David announces: "I had a dream about how I
missed the war." (This dream, "Unknown Driver in the Desert," was presented earlier in Part II.) Following David, the
group of 1977 is again treading this by now familiar path, with
Esther voicing her mourning and the whole group participating
in expressing their fear of death. The presence of Dana, another
war widow, endows these new/old encounters with additional
intensity. Clearly, this year's work has pointed to the amount
of personal strength and vigor necessary to confront the fear
and pain, which are an inseparable part of our life in Israel, in
the shadow of war.

●　　●　　●　　●

People around my office at the university who knew I was
working on a book about war expressed interest and used to
inquire about my progress. One Sunday morning, Taly, a
woman who was not a member of my group, came to me. "I
had a strange dream on Friday night," she said, "and I remember it with unusual clarity—colors, textures, and all. It was very
frightening and has something to do with the ten-year memorial
ceremony for my brother-in-law, which I attended the other

week." Since Taly was a friend and had never been my client, I was somewhat hesitant as I asked her whether she would like to tell me the dream.

Taly lit up a cigarette with a trembling hand and told me the dream, quietly depicting the details of the horrible picture which was of an unusual surrealistic quality. I listened carefully, expressing my dismay, and then asked Taly if she would be willing to write the dream down for me so that it could be included in the book.

Taly asked just one question, whether I would provide an interpretation of her dream. "No," I replied, "only you can provide your own interpretation."

An hour later she brought me the transcript of the dream, which I later translated. In a way, I find that the lack of interpretation adds to Taly's vision, which I entitled "Where Have All the Young Men Gone?" and chose for closing this part of the book.

Four People at the Doorstep (March 1977)

At the beginning of our student group in the fall of 1976, I asked people what issues they would like to work on in the group. Ester said: "On death," and then added: "If I am able to." For four months she did not say much about herself, just stared at us with her intensely expressive eyes.

The following are several excerpts from her session in the group.

ESTER   I feel divided. I am two parts. One works and studies. It's—

I   Say, "I am."

ESTER   I am sometimes happy or sad, like everybody else. I grow plants. I enjoy my life with my husband. In short, I am alive.

I   And the other part—

ESTER   The other part of me . . . death is my company. I am always with death. It started during the war, I guess. I am with the dead. I refuse to believe they won't come back again.

I   This is very moving. Can you pick one of these dead?
ESTER   Yes. It is Alon, my cousin. Actually, he was a brother to me.

Her eyes become clouded with tears, yet she does not cry as she adds with devotion:

ESTER   I love him so much. And I have problems. Sometimes it is like my two parts make contact and the dead me tries to take over. Like the following instance. In the school where I teach, a young man was recently hired as a gym teacher for the boys. His name is Alon. This simple fact blocks me completely. I cannot work with him. I ignore him, as if he weren't there; in fact, lately, I just don't call him by his name. And I am angry.
I   At what? At whom?
ESTER   At myself, naturally.
I   Be your angry part. Sit here and express your anger at Ester.

Ester smiles for a moment, then starts looking at the chair.

ESTER   I am mad at you, Ester, for forgetting those who died. I am also mad at you, Ester, for still remembering them so much. When will you take your mind off the dead and resume your activities, your life, in a normal fashion?

She looks at me and says:

ESTER   You see, I am in a bind. I am angry when I forget, and I am angry when I remember.

I ask Ester to be the forgetful part. For a few minutes she remains terribly confused, the distinction between the parts becoming obscured. Finally she reaches the following point:

ESTER   To forget and to remember: this reminds me of the different memorial ceremonies in the family. I do not attend these ceremonies. For the last three years I have not been able to make myself go even once. I don't visit Alon's parents either. When I am by myself, the memory of those killed is very vivid in my mind, and it is this way all the time. So what do I need the rituals for? The rituals are for those who forget all year

round and need to be reminded one single evening a year.
I   Is there someone you want to talk to about these matters?
ESTER   To Alon, of course.
I   So talk to him now.

There is a very long pause. I suggest that Ester visualize Alon
sitting on the chair in front of her.

ESTER   This is very difficult.
I   So tell him.
ESTER   Alon, it is very difficult for me to talk to you like this.

Her eyes are glistening with a most sorrowful expression. To
our dismay, she does not fix her piercing look at the empty chair
but at one of the men, Dor, who happens to sit across the room.
She continues as if in a trance.

ESTER   Alon, it is so difficult for me to accept your death, to
believe that you really got killed. I am so sorry we cannot meet
again, talk to each other. I want you to understand my not
visiting your grave or your parents' house. It is because of the
emptiness I feel now in these places, the void which takes your
place. While in my house, among my living things, you still
exist as if you are alive and may come in any minute.

She is quiet now for some time.

I   What do you feel?
ESTER   [*pale and trembling*] I am afraid. I feel a great fear
. . . I fear the next war. This feeling is like panic; it paralyzes
me. I have a feeling of doom. For me, disasters come in a row,
and I feel that in the coming war my husband or my brother
might be killed. I will never be able to cope with another war.
When my husband was wounded, in the last war, I was sort of
happy. I said to myself: We have paid the price now, so nothing
worse will happen to him. But since then, I again have those
nightmares, and I never let myself stay with my fears, my
imagined catastrophies, to the end. I rush away, I distract
myself . . . the same way I avoid meeting people who remind
me of the dead, refuse to visit places that are associated with

them, and so on. I keep avoiding all these external things, places, or events; yet, actually, the fears are within me all the time anyway.

I   This fear, how do you feel it?

ESTER   It is choking me, right here in my throat.

I   And how does it look?

ESTER   It's huge.

She makes a motion with her arms to enfold all the space in front of her.

I   What color is it?

ESTER   It's blue. This surprises me. Blue is not so gloomy.

I   Talk to your fear.

ESTER   Now you look as if you fill all the corners. Behind my clothes, in the closets, in all the dark spaces, you thrive there, you hide peering at me.

I   Keep talking to your fear.

ESTER   I would like to come to an arrangement with you. I will give you a certain area for your existence, and you will let me exist also, sometimes without you. [*She looks at me.*] This is just a game of words. With whom am I negotiating? This fear is part of me.

I   That's right. And what do you do about it?

ESTER   We co-exist? No. That's not so. I exist in its shadow. This fear is bigger than I am. It is as big as . . . four uniformed people standing at the doorstep.

There is an outburst of sobbing from the other side of the room, where Dana, a war widow, is sitting. Somebody goes and hugs Dana, while Ester sits there dry-eyed, as if visualizing the scene in her mind.

ESTER   I was at my uncle's house when they came to tell him about Alon. It was the last day of the war, and we had talked on the phone just the other night. But as I saw these people at the door, I knew immediately what their message was. I guessed right. Fear is this sight.

She is quiet for some time, then looks around and adds:

ESTER   Now I feel relieved. The pressure in my throat is gone. Maybe some of the fear is gone.

We are silent for a long while, very moved, feeling bad for Dana at the same time.

I   We could go on working in several directions. There is just one thing, however, I would like you to do today. Say *shalom** to Alon.

ESTER   That's not fair.

I   Fair? To whom?

ESTER   To Alon. No, from his point of view it is fair. He would have liked us to go on living as usual, to be as happy as we could be. It isn't fair to me, maybe.

I   Talk to Alon about that.

ESTER   I can't. I want him to stay with me; I don't want us to separate.

I   The things you have within you, nobody is entitled to take away. I am not trying to. They will always remain yours. Perhaps this is a good starting point. Tell Alon what parts of him are now alive within you.

ESTER   Alon, you gave me so much. I obtained from you the trust you had in me, which built my confidence. When I had no parents, you were somebody to rely on. Now I have myself to rely on. You gave me your optimism; now it's mine, too. You always told me I have the right to live my own life the way I choose to, and I own this belief now—it is mine.

Silence, with a peaceful note.

I   Now, are you willing to let him go?

ESTER   Yes, I think so.

I   So take your time and say good-bye to Alon.

Ester is quiet, absorbed; and a little later I add:

I   Now look at the people around you here in this room.

*Good-bye

Ester is making the rounds with her eyes, stopping at each one of us, absorbing our unsaid messages. Slowly she starts to smile. As she reaches Dana, she says:

ESTER   I feel you have been crying for me, too. I could not cry here today.

DANA   This was such a horrible session for me. I wanted to run away, yet I also wanted to stay and witness how you cope with all this. When you mentioned the four people at the door, I felt like fainting. I received such a visit, you know. I wanted to faint. That would give me a way out. Yet nobody forced me to hear you out; I chose to stay.

In the encounter between the two women, Ester replies that she did not know about Dana's loss. She apologizes for causing her all this grief. Most of the people in the group are too shocked to react verbally. There are two comments from the group, though, which I want to cite.

Noam is the first one to talk; then Dor, on whom Ester focused when she started to talk to Alon, shares his reaction with the group.

NOAM   I am also afraid, like you, Ester. But I am afraid for myself. I am sure that the next war will get me. I was comparing our reactions. You felt sorrow, grief for the killed. As for me, I do not feel that—I just sense a void . . . or maybe it is not a void but simply the awareness that I had some friends who aren't any more and I forgot them, as if they never existed. Sometimes I ask myself if that's human. I guess this is my way of coping. The fear, however, which you also experience, I did not repress. This part of me, my concern for my safety in the future, identified with you all the way.

DOR   I was afraid of your eyes, Ester, when you looked at me so piercingly as you talked to Alon. I had the feeling you were confusing the two of us. Maybe I am the dead one. Then I felt guilty, the same feeling I had for months after the war. This guilt is formed as a question: Why am I alive when he, Alon, as well as a great number of other guys, is dead? And then I felt this immense hatred for the Arabs for doing this to us, to you, to me. Perhaps I should not say that. I know I am childish and naïve; we are also to blame for what has happened. But in my fantasy, my naïve part imagines how perfect it would be if all the Arabs were gone—transplanted, so to speak, to Australia or further. There would be no bloodshed, you know. And at the far horizon of my fantasy all will be quiet and peaceful.

The week after Ester's work and Dana's outburst, we start our session with very heavy feelings. Death is still lingering in the room. I begin by mentioning the heavy atmosphere.

AMOS   I wish to ask Ester: How do you feel? What is the result, so to speak, of opening up this way for you?

ESTER   I had a good week. I am pleased that I talked here with you. I feel as if an awful load has been lifted from my shoulders. I do not feel like continuing today; I am finished for the time being. Yet I know that my presentation last week opened up unmentioned topics for many of you and that I caused you pain. And I imagine that today some of you might want to use the time to finish your unfinished business from last week.

DANA   For me, this was horrible, and I can't work on this either.

I   I feel how difficult this is for you. The problem is that it was not your choice to bring up the topic which Ester chose. This is the risk of being in a group. And yet, wherever you go in Israel, among friends, and especially with the clients you will be treating soon, you may encounter other bereaved people, and you'll have to cope with this somehow.

DANA   No, I don't know. It didn't do me any good to talk about it, to hear about it, maybe because it was not my timing. If I start to work here, I am afraid I won't be able to go back home later.

Here she starts to cry violently and adds between her sobs:

DANA   I feel like a double traitor . . . I have been betraying both of them . . . my dead husband with the new one, and the present one with the fact I still long for the first one. I cannot go to my husband and cry with him for my former one, the one I lost.

I   Are you sure this cannot be done?

DANA   At least, that's the way I feel now.

I   I feel bad that you had this experience in the group. I think, however, that it is all the better for you, just the same.

AMOS   Some things you just never want to face again or think about. I had a very close friend whose name was also Amos. Some ten years ago, right after high school, he was killed in a car accident. And he was such a wonderful person—I wonder why he got himself killed and not me. Just the same, I never went to visit his parents—never, since the accident. In the *shivah,** I could not face them, and I have never been able to since. So I understand you very well, Dana.

DANA   Yes, I know what you mean. When my husband was killed in the war of 1973, I did not cry, I did not fall apart. People came to tell me about his old parents—how horrible their situation was. I was expected to be there as someone to lean on, someone strong enough to support them during the crisis. And I did, too. When someone does not show the pain, people don't see the wound. I myself didn't know the wound is still so painful. That's why I am surprised I cried here so much for the last couple of sessions. And now it is enough.

Where Have All the Young Men Gone? (June 1977)

TALY   On a very hot summer's day, at noon, I am in the kibbutz in which both my father, who died in 1972, and my brother-in-law, who was killed in the 1967 war, are buried. I am on my way to the kibbutz cemetery for a memorial ceremony in honor of my brother-in-law. The way from the kibbutz to the graveyard usually takes about fifteen minutes; but in my dream, the road seems incredibly long. On my way I cross an army camp (which does not exist in reality), where I stop to ask for

*Traditional Jewish week of mourning

directions. An officer inquires why am I going there, and I tell him about the memorial service. He then offers to give me a ride on his military motorcycle, since he, too, is on his way to the graveyard. We reach the place together.

In the kibbutz burial ground there are about ten people gathered for the occasion. Of these, I have a clear picture of only four, all women: myself, my mother, my sister, and a childhood friend and neighbor whose husband has been serving for years in the same combat unit with my own husband. The women are the only living people there. The graveyard, which in reality is situated in the midst of a splendid park overlooking the Jordan River, has been moved into a huge hall that encloses it, its floor paved with large red-brick tiles. Most of the graves do not stand out higher than the floor, except those of my brother-in-law and a few others.

Toward the end of the ceremony, a very young soldier in full battle dress suddenly emerges from his grave in the corner of the hall, just beyond the burial place of my brother-in-law. His face is very innocent and handsome, his uniform is slightly disarrayed, and he is barefoot. One of his legs is bandaged, the bandage having been bound quite loosely. My sister turns to him and says that because his memorial service is not today, he has to return to his grave. She speaks to him very gently and calmly, and he lies down on top of his burial place and slowly becomes transparent until he vanishes completely.

And then, many of the buried get out of their graves. All are men, all uniformed, only their hats are missing. They are of all ages, and some of them are wounded. My mother, too, talks to them in a very pleasant, quiet manner, persuading them to return to their graves. They obey. Each one lies on top of his burial place and slowly fades away. One of them, who seems to have been seriously wounded in battle, puts himself into some sort of a long burlap sack and disappears with it into thin air in the same fashion.

My friend turns to one of the dead, points to a corner grave bounded by small white stones, and says: "Tomorrow, or next week, I'll be here again to bury someone there, and then I'll visit you."

Later, we are walking on our way back to the kibbutz. The beautiful road is dotted by fish ponds, palms, and orchards, which run along a canal. Here I see my father standing in the canal with pajama pants, army shirt, and hat in camouflage colors. In his hand he is carrying a big bag, and he tries to get out of the canal. He seems to be angry and makes some signs with his hands, but I woke up before he had a chance to talk to me.

_____ Part **3**

Peacetime Conversations About War

Introduction

This last part of the book is a record of interviews in which I asked people about their war experiences and their perceptions as they feel or remember them. The spring of 1977, when I conducted these interviews, was a relatively peaceful period, yet peace has always been a relative term in our area.

The interviews were not used as a test to support or reject ideas which came up in the clinical material. By its nature, the method of the interview often uncovers different levels than those of the group-therapy sessions. I had mixed expectations when I started interviewing—that people would be more superficial than in the clinical setup, alluding less to intimate experiences; that they would tend to form one-sided statements of opinion as answers to my questions rather than the complex, frequently ambivalent picture that emerged in the groups; that in the neutral atmosphere of the interview, people would focus on subjects which are usually secondary in therapy, such as ideology, general beliefs, or political analysis. However, the resulting correspondence with, as well as the contradiction of, attitudes and themes expressed in the groups was of great interest. Moreover, since there is a process of natural selection in joining groups voluntarily, the people who are the "characters" of the previous part of the book may have been overly sensitive or in urgent need of sharing their emotions. It was, therefore, intriguing to glimpse into the world of those who didn't join a group or go for therapy, and find out if they were, indeed, so different from the others.

I looked for people who were similar to the members of my

groups in terms of age, education, and occupation, and limited myself to my acquaintances—colleagues, students, and friends. I did not feel comfortable opening the topics which interested me with strangers. All the men and women whom I contacted were willing to cooperate and to have their interviews recorded. They sat with me for long sessions (of which only portions will be presented) and frequently became quite involved and excited in the process.

We talked about many subjects: war memories and personal bereavement, attitudes and feelings concerning the possibility of a future war, the image of the hero, attachment to the country, attitudes toward the Arabs, and the influence of war on roles and relations between men and women. We also mentioned the book and discussed their reactions to some parts they had read.

Twice, with two women, I felt the need to apologize for intruding into very unpleasant spheres; but even then the conversations continued. By and large I believe that people were willing to talk about the issues under investigation, since they were personally affected by them, as all Israelis are. Four of them had previously attended groups of mine, so they were already used to an open discussion. Almost all of them started, however, with the statement that they rarely thought about war and its effects on their lives. This introduction seemed rather shallow, given the depth of the ideas, memories, and emotions which were revealed directly afterward.

The interviews are divided into conversations with men and with women; these, in turn, are followed by records of conversations with people who read the clinical part of this book.

All the men interviewed had participated in the wars of this country, some in 1967 and all in 1973. By and large, they were combat soldiers, talking about their own experiences. As Shay put it, describing his feelings during the last war: "Those who didn't fight can never know this kind of feeling, cannot understand what I'm speaking about. You can't learn about it from books."

First among the men interviewed was Ben, a young psychotherapist and painter. In our long conversation, he unfolded the private history of a soldier, spanning ten years of service. His factual account, which is omitted from most of the other interviews, serves as a picture of the reality to which all the others are reacting in their fears, hopes, values, and opinions. The themes and feelings that are uncovered may serve as an introduction to the military experience of young people in Israel. They also touch upon many of the issues that emerged in the clinical setting.

For Ben, the military service was a period of masculine adventure. A son whose parents fought for Israeli independence, he was raised to follow in their path, with his father's expectations for heroic performance manifested above the surface, and his mother's anxieties hidden well beneath. His story begins with great enthusiasm for his "romantic" occupation, which cooled off somewhat once he faced heavy fire on the Suez Canal. Later, in his new position in the Jordan Rift, he regained his sense of excitement and devotion under the outstanding influence of one of his commanders. Ben enjoyed his role as a conscript soldier, the freedom and the manly adventure, although it was far from popular to admit this attitude among his friends.

Some years later, Ben was mobilized for the Yom Kippur War. In spite of his admitted fears, this war, like his previous military activities, was mostly a positive experience for him, one of growing strength. He discovered his willingness to abandon demands for outstanding military achievements and realized a powerful potential of a sort he called "feminine strength."

Ben provided some very candid responses to questions regarding the future and his outlook on life in Israel. He acknowledged his concern over the future of his baby son. Life in Israel, as he conceives it, more than anywhere else, brings death into awareness. Therefore, he feels obligated to make his life as meaningful and worthwhile as possible and to review again and again his decision to live here. Both in the relatively positive account of his war experience and in his expressed doubts about his future in Israel, Ben boldly put forth his somewhat unpopular views.

A second, clearly different perspective is offered by Avinoam, the only enlisted man whose interview is included here. A unique Israeli product, Avinoam presents a combination of roles and traits that is probably rare elsewhere. His current occupation is that of a military psychiatrist, but for years he had been a paratroop commander of high rank; and he continues to serve as a parachutist in his original battalion during reserve duty.

The opportunity of conversing in depth with Avinoam provides our set of profiles with a rare glimpse into the private world behind the public image, the inner space of a hero. An unforeseen story is revealed: a weak child builds his strength and achieves an outstanding reputation in the army, all the while still carrying his internal image of the incompetent boy; a wounded soldier fights his way back to his military career; a man is stubbornly driving to conquer those realms of life which strike him with terror; a hero is subconsciously praying to be hit so that the whole miserable adventure will be over.

As in Ben's story, Avinoam's interview is replete with expressions of a love of the military and its adventures. But the dichotomy between weakness and strength, the discrepancy between the public image and the inner world, which we've already seen in Avi's ("The Melting of an Iceberg") and David's ("An Unknown Driver in the Desert") work, receive their most profound expression in Avinoam's "confession."

Another aspect of Avinoam's personality is unfolded later in the book, when his psychiatrist self comes forth as he shares with me his reactions to the book ["Avinoam (II)"]. There we discover a completely different layer—the adult mental-health professional who uses his rich experiences as a soldier and a commander in consultations regarding various difficult interpersonal situations in the army. It is hard to believe that these two interviews, conducted a couple of months apart, were given by the same person.

Avinoam referred very little to the experience of war in our first conversation. The internal war was much more apparent, while the external events appeared as a long, continuous chain of battles, training, and maneuvers. Most of the other men referred specifically to war as a distinct phenomenon, treating it as a necessary evil which they had to accept but never enjoyed.

Shay is, in a way, the antithesis of Ben. He talks about war as a dreadful experience of paralyzing terror which he believes he will be unable to face again. He expresses a very complicated web of conflicting attitudes and predictions: another war will never come, yet another war is unavoidable; he will not be able to function in the next war, yet he knows he will; war is terrible, yet he will hate himself if he misses it; he abhors the tension of recurring war, yet he knows he could not live anywhere else. From this divided state of mind, he is rescued by a sense of boundless loyalty to the group of soldiers for whom and with whom he is capable of doing anything. More than the admitted inconsistency in Shay's attitudes and expectations, the striking quality of his interview inheres in his frank disclosure of fear of the coming war, fear of combat, and fear of death.

Illan is more guarded than the first three, picking his words with great caution. He talks about emotions with much reluctance, as if he were not used to that kind of conversation; and when he does address himself to his feelings, the emotions described appear removed from his immediate experience. People, he claims, tend to repress their fears, their pain, the whole topic of war. Keeping himself well out of the picture, he is worried about our future national existence and does not mention his own future or that of his family. The outcome of his analysis is in terms of the need for political action and a gradual building of trust with the Arabs that will ultimately put an end to war.

Illan agrees that our upbringing stresses a norm of heroism. Long before military service begins, school and youth-movement ideology centers around volunteering, to the point of self-sacrifice if necessary. But, Illan claims, in his case this standard had been completely internalized without doubts or conflicts regarding its value or fairness. All the same, he remembers years when he seriously considered emigrating from Israel, being disappointed in the way the country was evolving.

Paradoxically, the increased danger he perceives in our life here since the Yom Kippur War has changed his thoughts about emigration; and since then, he has felt a growing attachment to the country. There seems to be an irrational core in every Israeli when pressed to confront his decision to live in Israel.

Moshe goes one step further than Illan in his analytical approach to the circumstances of our life. As a scientist, he presents a highly rational perspective. Neither war nor the threat of it affects him personally any more than do daily car accidents. War's main impact on our lives, as far as he is concerned, is in the economic sphere, in our reduced income and standard of living. Moshe is confident of his personal strength, his ability to cope with rough battle situations, although he never has had to do so. As to those people, like the ones in this book, who react differently, he believes they are alienated individuals who focus on their private world of feelings and pains. There are vast individual differences in such "self-involvement," and he, Moshe, stands at one far end of this spectrum. In his interview, one detects his sense of superiority in not feeling, and some criticism and disdain of those who concentrate on emotional expression, which may hinder the required perfection of military-technical skills. He does not allow for the importance of other, psychological factors and deals with the image of the hero in the same way.

Within the framework of this rational analysis, Moshe introduces an original concept to describe the Israeli existence, that of the "desperate ghetto fighter." We must become a fortified stronghold so that no enemy can overrun us. It is rather outstanding that this term, which for me was emotionally provocative, was introduced by Moshe as another rational outcome of his analysis: "That's only due to the very high odds against us, in this land, surrounded by enemies." I found it admirable, if somewhat hard to believe, that someone could hold on to such a set of opinions; and I wondered whether there was an additional hidden layer in Moshe that the interview did not reveal.

Last among the men interviewed was Matan, an archaeologist by profession and an Armored Corps commander, who has recently started building a new village in the desert. Matan accepts war, like death, as an integral part of Israeli existence and sees the preparation for war as an ongoing process in the building of strength. While the act of destruction is an aspect of human nature, the act of construction is the remedy for despair and spiritual collapse. War demands personal achievements and the overcoming of fear; therefore, to be a good soldier, spiritual integrity is required more than technological training or any other material component. It is the Jewish faith and an understanding of our religious and historical roots which provide the basis for such integrity.

For Matan, the Jewish faith is a way of life, a system of values he uses in normal, as well as in extreme, circumstances. It is this basic faith that lends Matan's words a sense of depth as well as a high level of consistency over wide-ranging topics. Matan's life is structured around three interlocking foci: the process of building, the preparation for war, and the Jewish faith. The various parts of his tale, such as his face-to-face struggle with an Arab soldier in the alleys of embattled Jerusalem or the planting of trees in his young desert settlement, can be viewed as expressions of his all-embracing ideology and historical awareness. This approach is, naturally, in accordance with specific background, personality, and educational factors, the combination of which makes Matan quite special.

Matan's interview concludes the men's presentations. Evidently, each of the six men is unique, with his own set of background factors, personality traits, educational training, military experiences, and political beliefs. Each has his own feelings about heroism and fear, although they all share these feelings in some way.

Their diverse approaches are most visible in their image of the good soldier: he has inner strength due to successful coping with his fears, according to Ben; he is fighting for the sake of his fellow soldiers, according to Shay; he is a highly trained and effective technician, in Moshe's view; and he is a true believer in the Jewish faith, according to Matan. As to Illan, he was educated to be that way; to be a good soldier is the most natural thing for an Israeli. From Avinoam's point of view, a crucial distinction must be made between inner and outer realities. The good soldier is, perhaps, an illusion.

For me, these men are six Israelis answering my questions with a great deal of sincerity. A common characteristic is, perhaps, their tone and style. Even while talking about their deepest fears, the men seem to be personally out of the picture, putting an emotional distance between me and them. In this respect, the women I interviewed came through more strongly, more emotionally; they were more "there" with me. This is such a familiar distinction, in the groups as well as in reality, that it is tempting to generalize that women are simply more open and sensitive than men. However, at this stage, such a statement seems unwarranted. It might be possible that the women identified more with me, that our rapport was easier, or that some factor in the selection of the interviewees produced this apparent difference.

The women offer a different perspective on the issues of war and peace. Clearly, they might end up losing their loved ones in war—brothers, boyfriends, husbands, or sons—rather than their own lives. They never experienced combat and fire from close range. By themselves, these facts create a certain barrier between men and women in Israeli society.

• • • •

Two unconnected episodes from the past came to mind while I was conducting these interviews. The first one was during my conversation with Moshe as we spoke about the education for heroism in youth movements. I suddenly realized that during my adolescence, boys faced demands completely different from those made on girls. In the youth movement, the boys were encouraged to volunteer for combat units, while the girls were taught that their role was to go to a kibbutz or, better still, to start a new one along the border. Both of these demands were implemented as parts of the same ideology, guided by the needs of the country rather than those of the individual, by patriotism rather than egoistic choice. But the message was clearly different for boys than for girls, although at that time nobody doubted the inevitability of this distinction.

In the twenty years that have passed since my youth-movement education, I have not been especially bothered by the military role division between men and women. I saw it, and still see it, as part of our reality, which, though not always fair, cannot be changed. Maybe I have implicitly enjoyed my protected feminine role and have preferred it to that of the soldier; yet nobody challenged this situation or attempted to alter it, and I was never made to choose between fighting and waiting at home.

Interviewing Dina, I remembered, however, a social gathering that was held right after the Yom Kippur War. Quite innocently, I was speaking about my difficult experience during the last weeks—the tension, the constant worry and anxiety, the heavier load of household chores due to my husband's mobilization. Perhaps I used very strong terms; I don't quite remember. Suddenly, one of the men present attacked me aggressively, saying: "I can't stand this bullshit. What are you talking about—did you ever sit in a tank? Did you ever sleep in a ditch under fire? What do you know about war?" I was startled and ashamed. I don't think he was attacking me personally as much as women in general. He was saying mockingly: "How frightful was your suffering, indeed! You sat at home and knitted sweaters. You could not open the windows because of blackout regulations. And you had to take care of the family car all by yourself. Big deal!"

I did not argue with him; I forgave his outburst, seeing it as a postponed shock reaction of some kind. Weeks later, in my 1974 group, Yuval expressed a very similar reaction against the women of that group. So truly, roles are allocated in a rigid way in our society. Bluntly, men defend women; women, like children and elderly people, are passive and helpless. Can one measure and compare, though, the amount of fear and courage, the sacrifice of women on the home front? The women interviewed in this section provide their own answers.

• • • •

Yael was born and raised on a kibbutz. She was educated using the same formula that turns kibbutz boys into first-rate combat soldiers. The kibbutz population is 3 percent of the total Israeli population, but they suffer about 25 percent of the losses during war. They raise their sons to be up front as soldiers and officers in the most dangerous assignments, and they pay very heavily for it. Yael herself lost her brother and her boyfriend in the Yom Kippur War. She also speaks about the loss of a whole group of classmates and acquaintances, people who were part of her past in the kibbutz and who were killed in the different wars.

During Yael's interview, she spoke very slowly and succinctly. She was very excited yet assured me she wanted to continue. There is no trace of victor's pride in her words, not even when talking about the Six-Day War. We hear about bereavement and mourning, termed in the simplest phrases, as when she tells about her father, who said at his first-born's funeral: "We raised our sons for that, to go first, to be the leaders." Neither the ideology of the kibbutz mission to defend the country nor the personal grief is presented in pompous wording, and therefore her story is all the more heroic and touching.

Michal, too, formulates her story and opinions in a very personal manner. She seems to answer all my questions in terms of her immediate experiences rather than in terms of political or ideological significance. When I ask her about her attitudes toward the Arabs, she answers that she would never think of going out with one socially; or when I question her about attachment to the country, she answers simply that she could not live anywhere else, and that tourists whom she meets in Israel seem to have a foreign, distant mentality.

Generally, she thinks very little about war and its impact, and she blames herself for a superficial handling of these topics. Her answers to my questions are very brief and rather fragmented. Somewhat contrary to Yael, Michal presents the picture of a person with a very high potential for recovering from traumatic experiences. A social worker in a hospital in Jerusalem, she talks about her very difficult job during the war, caring for families of the seriously wounded, participating in the most tragic events in the hospital—and going back to business in the university, where she was working toward a master's in social work, with surprising ease.

Michal is not clear about the effects of the military roles on the relations between the sexes in Israel. She feels drawn to combat soldiers, whom she sees as more masculine and physically attractive, but she does not feel the need to compensate them for their tough experiences in combat or training. War in Israel serves as a reinforcement of the conservative male-female stereotypes, which exist, according to Michal, all over the world. The general impression is that Michal is willing to accept the situation in this area.

Dina, like Michal, relates to my questions in a very personal manner. A somewhat older woman, she is the mother of two teenage sons and a daughter. She, too, refers to the relationship between men and women in our society. One step further than Michal's awareness of the issue, Dina represents the loyal wife-mother who unquestioningly accepts the obligation to care for her fighting men. She condemns women who complain of their hard lot during the war, who forget that their men lived through more severe hardships.

She talks extensively about differences in our perspective of life in Israel before and after the Yom Kippur War. Before, we were always victorious, so we became accustomed to that situation. This sense of security, the feeling of omnipotence, has broken down due to the last war, although Dina claims that she never doubts the existence of Israel as a national entity.

There were two interesting occurrences during Dina's interview. Toward the end of our hour together, Dina developed a slight trembling, which became rather awkward later and disturbed her speech. It started after she admitted worrying about her sons' future service in the army, a few minutes before she told me about the death of her father. The later occurrence was a very remarkable chain of associations, or rather, lack of associations where I expected them to be. Dina was saying: "Well, thank God, I don't have anything to complain about, so far. From all the wars I've lived through, I, and the ones dearest to me, have emerged untouched." As I was listening, I thought of a fact known to me from other sources that very clearly contradicted this positive summary. Delicately, I hope, I inquired about Dina's childhood, and within a moment of the statement above she was telling me the missing part of her story. "My father was killed in the riots of 1938. . . . He was walking to work and was murdered by Arab terrorists." I did not confront Dina with the contradiction. She herself added that since she had never known her father, she did not feel his death as a personal loss. I find this a very profound example of the traumas Israelis have to live with and the extreme mechanisms sometimes needed to cope with our reality.

My final interview is with Ronny, a young woman educated in Europe, who came to Israel at the age of eighteen. Still somewhat of an outsider eight years later, she has a very keen and detached point of view on problems which other Israelis tend to ignore. Politically she is Left-oriented and active in the women's movement, and it is obvious that she has given much thought to the topics we discussed, using her private experience to test her ideas. She feels that many areas of our life are in need of urgent change. Unlike all the other women interviewed, she is less personal and more intellectually analytical in her approach to my questions.

Ronny sees war as having far-reaching repercussions on the Israeli character structure. As a result of being educated to fight the enemy, Israelis develop a certain cognitive narrowness that can be detected in elementary schoolchildren, who tend to see only one dominant point of view. This early induction of taking sides, of distinguishing "right" from "wrong," blocks creativity and the willingness to change, as well as tolerance toward others who do not conform with the norms of the mainstream.

Furthermore, war and military training have serious effects on sexual roles and relationships in Israel. Ronny thinks that the high tension in our life finds a release in sex, as well as in hazardous driving and reckless competition. The sexual behavior of the Israeli male is modeled on his military role, so that he sees women as objects to conquer, lacks tenderness, and is afraid of deep emotional involvement. Women hesitate to demand rights and changes in their men's behavior toward them because they suffer from guilt feelings vis-à-vis the fighting men who protect them in war.

Ronny is a great advocate of change, starting with greater openness in talking about emotions and doubts. She characterizes the Israeli mentality as superficially optimistic on the one hand—"Everything will work out in the end, you'll see"—and falling for the "no-choice" justification on the other. By working against repression and by facing the difficulties, she feels change could be achieved both on the political and the personal levels.

Do the women interviewed have something in common? I do not see more similarity here than among the men, although as a group I found them talking more about personal experiences and feelings than about philosophy of life or ideology. Generally, women I know, in the interviews as well as in groups, are more open in their expression of emotions and find it easier to admit fear, weakness, and grief. Men have a long way to go in this respect. They are capable of expressing occasional fear but find helplessness quite unbearable and grief almost impossible to show. As Michal put it: "Behavior seen as gentleness in women is looked upon as weakness in men." Or, as Illan said: "Men don't cry."

But this is not always true in the clinical material, and a sweeping generalization is always unfair to most individuals. So we will let the people who made this book possible speak for themselves.

The Men _____

Ben

I Could you start by telling me about your military experience?

BEN I was a senior in high school when the Six-Day War broke out. Listening to tales of that war, I was impressed with the importance of the Armored Corps reconnaissance unit, which seemed to have the most dangerous and important assignments. So, when I was drafted for regular service in July 1967, a month after the Six-Day War, I volunteered for it, and I was accepted.

In the beginning, I loved every moment of my service. I enjoyed driving jeeps in the desert—it was very romantic. Even after the War of Attrition started, I still felt a love for my job. At that time, however, I was thinking in terms of loyalty to my unit, a strong desire to be of help, or the wish to get ahead in the army. Actually, I loved doing what I was doing then, and I was a good soldier.

As a result of this, I was sent to squad leaders' training course; and when I rejoined my unit, a couple of months later, the War of Attrition had reached a more severe stage. We were under very heavy fire; and for the first time, I began to be afraid [*laughs*]. It is very interesting now to think about all this, ten years later. In the middle of 1968, before the rough period began, when we had some relatively minor skirmishes, I used to exaggerate them in my imagination, thinking about a total war and feeling sorry that I had missed it. But when the skirmishes became more severe, I really didn't know what I wanted. When these attacks took place, I felt like running away; yet, when things were very quiet, I wished for more action. I had many fantasies. I used to talk about them with a friend, who once told me that he had a fantasy, or an absurd wish, that we would all hit a mine and everybody would be killed except himself. Naturally, I was very angry at him for expressing the wish that I be killed. But later, his fantasy bothered me a lot, because I sometimes had the feeling that I wished for the same thing.

I   Would this mean being a hero?

BEN   Yes, being a hero.

•   •   •   •

BEN   Later I was sent to officers training course. It was the beginning of 1970, after a period of very heavy shelling. During the course, it gradually dawned on me that I didn't want to go back to the front and rejoin my unit. I had many dreams at that time, and I still remember one that was quite clear even then and awakened me to my true feelings. In my dream, I was looking at my head from above, from the outside, and it looked like the desert landscape; and underneath, it was full of underground fortifications. My head was completely hollow and full of mice. I took this to mean that I did not wish to return to the war, as if my service there were eating [the inside of] my head away. I wasn't brave enough to formulate it openly. Mind you, I was in officers training course then, where the pressure to be a good soldier and a good Zionist—to conform—was stronger than all the pressures of former stages of my military experience. So, although I didn't want to return, I couldn't admit it, even hardly to myself. But I started to neglect my duties and got into all sorts of trouble until I was kicked out. This wasn't done intentionally, although sometimes I preferred to put it that way. I just wasn't fit to continue and was thrown out.

To my surprise, I was then given the choice of either returning to the reconnaissance unit or going on another assignment in the Jordan Rift. I became a sergeant at the headquarters of another combat unit, not as exposed as my former one. I served there for a year and regained both my positive attitudes toward my army life and my love for it.

I   In other words, when the situation wasn't as hazardous, you enjoyed being a soldier.

BEN   Yes. We were chasing Arab terrorists, and there was an intense sense of adventure, of fantasy. There was also more room for individual initiative, which had been completely lacking in the passive condition of being shelled at the canal. At that time, however, I was not as "sold" on the army as I had been before. I was frequently bothered by moral speculations—feeling guilty that the upshot of my activity was man hunting, which was despicable and cruel. I considered the chases to be unfair and imagined that if I were a Palestinian, I would probably become a so-called terrorist, too [*laughs*]. I became very confused because of these moral dilemmas, but they didn't keep me from performing my job well and even enjoying it.

At that time I met M., who was my commanding officer and whom I respected greatly as a "good" person. He was a very wise man, and he had found the balance between being a professional soldier and enjoying it on the one hand, and being a sensitive human being on the other. He was not bloodthirsty—by no means, although this was somewhat the atmosphere in the valley at that time. It was our duty to stop the terrorists from infiltrating through the Jordan and reaching the population centers. Some soldiers behaved as if they were involved in a game of cowboys and Indians, as if they were realizing some childhood fantasies. I, too, tended to be carried away with this excitement; and only M. introduced a human, sensitive approach, which balanced the scales. Yet, we lived through a period of a long masculine adventure, which had its strong attractions for me as well.

•   •   •   •

BEN   After three years, I was discharged, and I went to the university. When the October War started, I was called right away. At the gathering place, we found out that this was a massive war on all fronts. I was sent south to join my original battalion. I felt as I did in high school in 1967 or at the beginning of my regular service—very excited. Not only was I going to take part in a war, but I would be doing it with the Armored Corps reconnaissance unit! There was, of course, also some fear. Even before we started out, while we were still loading the jeeps, I felt the excitement and the mounting fear, which increased as we drove down to Sinai.

The process of joining combat was very slow, waiting for the tanks and hearing the sounds of battle from far away. Only on the evening of the fourth day were we sent to the front. We were directed to the top of a hill to zero our artillery in on the enemy, and we were to stay there until located by them. Once discovered, we were supposed to escape immediately. Sometimes we had to evacuate the wounded, which was harder, since we had to stick to the mission and couldn't run away from the shells. You see, running away, escaping, was foremost in our thoughts. There was an atmosphere of horrible fright. I was in charge of communications in the commander's jeep, and all the time I kept hearing two questions over the radio: Have we been located? Has the order been given to run away?

I   It sounds like such an anti-normative term!

BEN   Well, the actual word used was "break contact" [*laughs*]; and naturally, it was all in code. But what we had in mind, honestly, was to run away from the hill. Yet all the kibbutz members, those "heroes" who were the majority of my unit, never admitted they were afraid. Naturally.

As to myself, I was in the clearest state of mind, sharply aware of everything that was happening to me and to the others. I remember every single event or thought of those long days. I especially remember observing very carefully our commander, who was in my jeep, searching for signs of confusion or mistaken judgment; paying attention to see if he weren't just displaying bravado and thus risking our lives. I felt I had to supervise his actions, observe them very carefully. If I noticed that he was tense or nervous, I would talk to him, almost as if providing therapy. This went well with my role as communications man, since I had, naturally, all the information needed for the decisions, and I felt very responsible. Simultaneously, I thought of escaping myself, even before the order was given. I could get off the jeep and run down the hill, out of the range of the shells. This was a great temptation, but I never did it, and I knew I wouldn't.

I enjoyed this sense of control, that I could experience terror without denying it and, at the same time, not be overwhelmed by it. I felt the fear to the end, without all the doubts and the defense mechanisms I used in my former service. Yet, I also had an awareness of some rational control over myself and even the ability to be responsible for others and to help them. Altogether, I felt more powerful and competent than ever before, and I think this feeling, and the responsibility I undertook, had a basis in reality, since I really was more "together" than most of the other soldiers around me. This feeling of strength stayed with me until the end of the war.

So now you understand why I sometimes say that I loved the war. I finished my regular service in 1970 with the realization that I'm not a great soldier nor a risk taker, physically; and gradually I accepted this. But I had been insecure in many ways; and this war built my self-confidence more than any other experience. I emerged from it a different person.

•   •   •   •

I   What are your feelings concerning another war in the future?
BEN   Well, lately I've had severe back problems; and when I finished my M.A., I was transferred to the military psychology unit. I'll probably sit out the next war in a clinic somewhere.
I   It might be a front-line clinic.
BEN   It's still so different from being exposed in a jeep on the top of a hill. It may sound immoral to say so, but the amount of fear for my own safety has decreased a lot and, with it, my sensitivity to the whole issue of war [*laughs*]. You won't believe it, but even my political outlook has changed since I don't belong to a combat unit any more. I know it isn't fair to those who will risk their lives in the next war; it may sound very egoistic. But I feel quite remote from it all. You see, if I think

of myself as a seismograph for tension on the borders—a seismograph that is constantly checking for the probability of war in our area—I have become a much less sensitive instrument since I was transferred from my combat unit.

I   Are you implying that people who have to risk their lives are better seismographs in this respect?

BEN   I didn't mean it as a generalization, but for me this is certainly the case. I imagine that mothers of soldiers are even more sensitive than the soldiers themselves. At least, that's how I feel about my son, although he is just a baby now. I think I'll be more afraid for him than I ever was for myself.

•   •   •   •

I   Did you ever think about society's demand for heroism?

BEN   Yes, I certainly did. For me, the act of volunteering to the most hazardous task was certainly an attempt to show that I could be as heroic as my father, with all his military achievements in the past. As a child, I used to hear about his heroic deeds during the War of Independence and before, in the Hagana,* the illegal *aliya,*** the fact that the British put him in jail for eighteen months. I was made to see his tremendous sacrifice for this country, something I felt I would never be able to compete with. Only once did I try to talk to him about his own fears. This was toward the end of my service. I asked him two questions and put a lot of pressure on him to answer. One was whether he was afraid, and the other was whether he felt guilty about killing people. To the second question, he said that he never felt any guilt, and this despite the fact that he had many more face-to-face encounters with the enemy than I did. I felt very helpless when I heard this answer. I realized I was more of a sissy than he ever was, since I was bothered by these matters, while he wasn't. As to fear, he had a very simple answer to that, too: he felt fear was something one had to overcome, and that's it.

*The pre-state underground Israeli army
**Immigration to Israel, which was very limited under the British government until 1948

I   What type of soldier did he want you to be?

BEN   Well, he never said it openly, but I know he was very ambitious for me. When I was kicked out of the officers training course, he was very hurt. He was ashamed and searched for ways to "explain" it to his friends.

I   So he didn't have enough of his own wars. He wanted you to fight some more?

BEN   That was how I felt. I felt like a complete failure when I was kicked out.

I   Are you really sure that it isn't a fantasy you have invented about him?

BEN   [*laughs*] Yes, I'm sure it isn't a fantasy. He made up justifications for me, as if to console himself and overcome his disappointment—such as that I failed because I was too intelligent—all sorts of excuses, which he needed more than I did. Clearly, there was pressure from my home to do well in the army.

•   •   •   •

After my discharge, my mother told me something which she had kept from me for two years while I was in the army. She said that during the War of Attrition, while I was at the canal, she saw one morning, when she was returning from her shopping, a big car parked near our house and two people in uniform asking to see my father. She fainted on the spot, with her grocery baskets in her arms. She was sure they had come to inform them that I had been killed. The men, who actually were looking for my father concerning his business, were startled and took my mother to a neighbor's to recover. The astonishing part is the fact that when I came home the following weekend, she didn't say a word about it, and she kept this episode a secret. She told me only when I was discharged, and then she explained that she hadn't wanted to burden me with worry for her, that she didn't want me to know about her anxiety so that it wouldn't affect me. You see, she didn't want me to worry about her worrying about me.

I   Maybe there are also some superstitions involved here. If you talk about death, you may "open your mouth to the Devil." Recently, when a client told me that he was sure he would be killed in the next war, I felt hesitant about writing it down, as if I might, thus, be somehow affecting his actual fate.

BEN   I had the opposite feeling; namely, that nothing could happen to me during the war [*laughs*]. But I never counted on it.

•   •   •   •

I   Is there anything else you would like to add?

BEN   I feel I didn't respond to your question of a few moments ago about the next war. I said I'm less involved today, since I don't serve in a combat unit. But I know that this is avoiding the issue.

I   Well, you mentioned your worries about your son.

BEN   Yes, my son's future already creates a certain burden for me. The most difficult question is: Given all these fears, what am I doing in Israel? What are my beliefs about Israel's future? What am I willing to sacrifice—not in the sense of sacrificing my son or myself but sacrificing in order not to sacrifice? Because the truth is, I don't do much to push my political opinions except by voting for a certain party once every four years [*quietly*]. And now again I catch on to easy solutions, such as that I myself wouldn't be risking my life or the fact that my wife is an American and so our son will have the choice of not serving in the army if he so decides. I know this is avoiding the issue. I don't dare cope with this question. I continue to be frightened by the war.

A few weeks ago, I went on a trip to the North, and I was amazed to see so many tanks and fortifications all over the place. It wasn't like this before 1973. Well, there I was. It was springtime, and I had planned to see parks, waterfalls, flowers, and birds—and what I found instead was tanks! This was, for me, a reminder of the fact that while I live my normal life, others plan for the next war. Ninety-nine percent of my time, however, I manage to avoid thinking about it. And when I don't avoid, I just feel afraid. I say "just" because the real problem is what then do I do about these facts and fears? Sometimes, quite rarely, I do think them through. During those moments —and it may sound pompous to you—I tell myself that life in Israel requires that I be able, constantly, to give an account for the meaning of my life. My wife, who is an American and loves Israel, feels it even more than I do. I am not sure it's a result of the war, but I keep asking myself: Are the things I'm doing with my life truly worthwhile? Are these the proper ways to achieve what I want to become? Are these choices of mine of any help to others here, too? I keep asking myself: Am I not wasting my life? I think this is related to the fear of death but not exclusively.

From time to time, I think of going elsewhere to live. America, perhaps. The temptation is great. When we talk about it among friends, we really don't get to the root of our attraction to Israel and to our lives here. I know that for my parents it would be a catastrophe, "a knife in their hearts" as they say, if I were to leave the country. But I feel that the external pressure, the brainwashing, the shame involved in the act of treason, these don't cover all the elements involved. There is something positive beyond all this, some positive attraction in this country for me, but it's something that I can't pinpoint and say, "For sure, that's it." Anyway, it's a matter of choice. It's not automatic. So far, I have chosen to live here, but I may reconsider my choice sometime in the future. Who knows?

Avinoam (I)

I   I have been working on the image of the hero, and I heard you're also interested in this matter. I'd like to hear your point of view.

AVINOAM   I'll tell you my personal history, some points which are, perhaps, relevant to your search. Clearly, in my case, I have done all sorts of "wild," "bold," maybe "heroic," deeds, out of the need to become the opposite of what I was meant to be according to my natural tendencies. The way I see it now, the things I accomplished in the army, as well as many of my activities in civilian life, could be essentially characterized as an attempt to brave exactly those areas that frightened me most. Actually, this is still going on. Recently, I took a scuba-diving course in the Red Sea just because I find the sea so frightening. This is very typical of me.

Until I was drafted into the army, I was a very fragile, miserable child. I had all kinds of accidents; my physical fitness was simply zero. I was really screwed up. I was a good student, that's true; but outside of school, I wasn't worth much. Naturally, at that time, I didn't believe I had a career waiting for me in the army, of all places. I expected to become one of those pale, weak soldiers, an office clerk of some kind, you know. Then I went to basic training and I saw, to my amazement, that I could take it. I gradually started to develop some ambitions. I volunteered for the paratroops, and later I got accepted to officers training course. This process seems quite normal for the majority of young men in Israel; but for me, with my background, it was pretty unusual. I went through the various stages with uncanny ambition, always fighting my fears and weaknesses, struggling to stand out. I see it now as a wish to erase my previous history and personality, to build new ones instead. The cost was tremendous, and the effort I put into all this was unbelievable. My body had been so weak. But these extreme efforts led to my finishing the various courses with distinction [*laughs*].

• • • •

I   Did your success change your image of yourself?

AVINOAM   That's very complicated. It didn't change completely, only partially, perhaps. Gradually, I realized that my success worked like a tranquilizer, putting my old personality to sleep for a while. But that was all, because even through periods in which I really stood out in the army and became famous for various things, my basic self-image didn't change. Underneath all that reputation, in my private secret way, I saw myself as weak and incompetent, just as I had been as a child.

I also expected the whole world to discover the truth about me —it was just a matter of time. This feeling stayed with me for a long time. Even only four years ago, in my reserve duty, when I commanded a very successful maneuver with my battalion and received much positive recognition all around, I realized how it made me feel "high" for a day or two, and then I recommenced torturing myself: if "they" only knew about this confusion and that mistake, their opinion about me would immediately reverse or, at least, they wouldn't be so admiring. Worse, perhaps, I sometimes expected to be caught as cheating, when my real weakness would show through. So, I finally realized that all my efforts were invested in producing some change in my negative self-image; and, at best, I could achieve only a temporary respite from it. My lack of confidence always loomed large within me. I could never perceive myself as really strong and competent without all these doubts. My achievements in reality didn't, basically, change my self-image. So, recently, I think I have started to give up, in a way. I know I was pursuing an impossible goal, and I'm trying to accept myself as I am.

[*thinking*] But here I skipped a central fact. My strong drive to excel in the army doubled in force, actually, since I was wounded.

I   When was that?

AVINOAM   It was in 1964, when I was in officers training course, two months before its end. One of the trainees was demonstrating something with his machine gun and forgot it was loaded. He shot me from very close range, the distance between you and me here, in the room. I was hit by two bullets in my abdomen. Rather, it wasn't in my abdomen but closer to my genitals [*laughs*]. I spent a month in the hospital and was then released from military service.

I   But you recovered fully, didn't you?

AVINOAM   Yes, I did. Yet the army has regulations in these matters; and in my case, after this kind of injury, I had to be released for good. That's when I started to fight and struggle in order to get back into the army and into the officers course. As to the injury itself, I had a massive block in this respect. I don't remember any emotions or apprehensions I had at the time or right after—just the bureaucratic headache of army rules and regulations. I started my struggle to get back into the army even before it was clear that I would completely recover from the injury, and these stubborn attempts gave me a great reputation. I fought my way back for seven months until I got back in.

I   What did you do during those seven months?

AVINOAM   I was at home. Besides running after various military medical committees, I took some classes at the university and just waited. I read a lot—that's when I built the foundation for my future education. I also undertook vigorous physical fitness training; this is something I almost forgot. Just recently my mother reminded me of that, of the long hours of exercising at home.

I   Did you have any guidance in this physical fitness program?

AVINOAM   None, I was completely on my own. My mother used to worry that I might harm myself, but I had to recover fast. Finally, I got back into officers school and finished it. Since, by that time, everybody knew me, I was assigned as an officer to one of the top paratroop battalions.

That's when I started to go into wilder and crazier things all the time. I got myself into a special course for sports trainers, allegedly to help build my body, and later into a course for hand-to-hand combat, where I learned to hit—and get hit—face to face. You see, as a child, I abhorred physical struggle. I never touched a child; and when I was hit, I didn't know how to hit back. And here I chose to go into this program and, again, finished with distinction. I took it very seriously, although I was afraid. I was very violent, all of a sudden. I also got hit very severely: I was the only one to be really knocked out once, as in boxing. All this, I see now, as if I were trying to destroy Avinoam-the-child and construct a new personality.

When I returned to the battalion, with my new skills, I became the expert on all these. For me, however, this behavior served a central need: to prove that I was a man. At that time, as I think of it now, I had the least amount of doubts about my real strength.

Later, as I was promoted and assigned more responsibility, my doubts also increased. At that time, around 1966, I got a few months' vacation and went to Europe on a trip. There I took a course in free-fall parachuting in my spare time, of my own choice. Again, an attempt to prove something—I was extremely afraid. Taking this course was like taking a big aspirin against my deep fears. People didn't realize that, of course. For all they knew, I was a great fighter, and it added to my reputation. Soldiers imitated me. But in my new, more responsible position, I was very aware of the gap between my external image and the real me. I felt that if I'd commit the least error, I'd be thrown out.

I   Did anyone notice how you felt inside?

AVINOAM   No, I'm pretty sure nobody ever guessed. I remember one particular incident. I was on a chase in a cavernous area; it was some sort of an old mine. I went alone into a cave in search of terrorists. They were shooting, and my rifle suddenly didn't work. The cave was full of smoke, and I almost suffocated. For a moment, in this cave, I felt paralyzed with panic. I was alone, and I immediately recovered and functioned efficiently. But the feeling of panic remained with me later on, and I tortured myself with the notion that I was a ham. As long as I have an audience—my troops—I'm a great hero; but once I'm on my own, my true, fear-filled self emerges. I was ashamed of my fears and of the knowledge that I couldn't cope with the stress.

I   Do you still feel that, that you couldn't cope?

AVINOAM   Well, yes and no. It's complicated.

I   Because to me it sounds as if your self-torture is not at all justified.

AVINOAM   I know. I'm more balanced now.

This incident in the cave stands out in my mind for other reasons as well. [*The following is spoken very slowly, with a great amount of effort.*]

This is something still very vague, something I discovered

only lately. As I said before, I had repressed my injury and its meaning for me, all the fears and feelings I must have had. Yet, since then, in all the many events in which I participated, something always happened to me in the last moments before battle, before we started shooting. At the last minute before firing, I had this fleeting thought—almost a sensation, a wish: this is going to be my last battle; let me be hit quickly and get it over with so that I won't have to stand it anymore. Usually, I forgot this thought as soon as it appeared; but there, in the cave, I became aware of it more than ever before. I wished to be hit directly in my head. Later, when I went into this fantasy in more detail, however, I was actually able to feel the blow in my lower abdomen, the place where I had been wounded before. I could sense the blow again, the pain, the heat, the very loud noise—and then the pleasant awareness: it's all over and done with; I'm dead.

In fact, during many of my battles, although I was always as careful as one can be under the circumstances, I had the feeling that my caution was never real, since I was always going to be hit this time. For truly I felt like lifting my head, uncovering my body, so that I'd be hit and the whole story would be over. The only time I clearly remember being careless in real life was in that cave. I got into the cave chasing the terrorists under heavy smoke; I nearly suffocated. And there was no need for it, really. We could have blown up the entrances to the cave from the outside. Yet I didn't issue that order, and I went in alone. Perhaps that's why I panicked. Later, my commander also expressed his astonishment when he found out what I had done; it was really careless and unnecessary.

I   I knew someone who was killed this way, in a cave, in 1969.
AVINOAM   Yes. In fact, one of the officers I admired most was also shot to death in a cave [*ponders*].
I   Take care.

• •

Shay

I   Do you think much about the war?

SHAY   I think I have developed some formula for dealing with that. I'm a "graduate" of the War of Attrition. I was an officer on the canal in the fire zone for a long time. I used to get up every morning to patrol the front line. At that time, I somehow managed to overcome my anxiety. We were all very cynical. We used to go out to our daily morning patrol smiling at each other, saying, "Well, today is our day. The cannon shell, which is after us, is on its way." Inside, my firm belief was the opposite, that this couldn't happen to me—or rather, it could happen but so far hadn't, so there was no reason why it should happen today. This belief, that I was somehow invulnerable, was what kept me going in those difficult days. If I should have seriously thought that I might be hit, I don't believe I would have been able to go on with it, day after day. We used to do our patrol daily for three or four months, then go up north for a while, and back to the canal again. Once I got wounded in an accident, so I was away longer; but I demanded to be sent back to the front with my cast still on. I felt I had to.

I was released shortly before the cease-fire agreement of the summer of 1970. I remember that as I took off my uniform, I had the feeling that I would not be able to return to this type of existence again. I went on a trip to the States, but the recent events were very much with me. From time to time, I would ask myself what would happen if another war broke out. I had the strong feeling that it would be impossible for me to go back and fight, that I would not be able to function. First of all, I was very pessimistic about the next war. I didn't want to be up front when the two immense forces clashed, because I was positive that whoever would be up front would be killed. Since I knew the masses of troops and arms involved, I wasn't surprised at the outcome of the first days of the Yom Kippur War either. So, I was trying to prepare myself psychologically for the next war. I knew I would go when issued the order, but I thought I would be useless, paralyzed and unable to function. Of course, I didn't think about it all day long; but periodically this thought would occur to me, even during my trip to the States.

In the States, I lived for a while near a huge airport and constantly heard the sound of jets taking off, landing, or flying in at low altitudes. For the first few weeks, I was afraid of these sounds. It took me some time to adjust to the fact that I was in America, and the airplanes were not after me or my tank.

Since my return to Israel, after a year abroad, this threat has been brought to my awareness, especially when I'm called up for reserve duty. This made my fears rather concrete, for, obviously, one does not train just for fun—it is for some purpose. I usually don't think about the war; and when I do, I hope very intensely that it won't break out again. On the other hand— without getting into politics—I see two enemy armies building their strength up constantly, getting bigger and better all the time, and I feel that this by itself has to lead to an explosion. On a different level of consciousness, I refuse to believe that another war will break out; I refuse to accept this for a fact. I cannot live with it.

I   So you don't think about it?

SHAY   No, I pretend that war won't break out, and most of the time I don't give it any thought. This armor has, however, some cracks, and feelings do come through from time to time. Then, it is very frightening. I know that the next war will be even bloodier than the last one; and for me, personally, I feel that my luck may run out. How many times can I be saved by sheer luck? I was in the War of Attrition and in the Yom Kippur War; another one might be one too many. The probability of getting hit increases all the time.

•   •   •   •

I   You said you didn't believe you would be able to function in another war, and then came the Yom Kippur War. What happened?

SHAY   I found myself part of a group and behaved accordingly, sitting on the tanks, driving down south. Luckily, our share of the fighting wasn't too bad; it was a clean, sterile sort of war. My battalion engaged in what I might rate as a medium-to-difficult level of fighting. Some had much tougher battles.

I was OK. In the beginning, right away, I sank into a state of apathy; I didn't care about what would happen to me. Actually, I felt that I might as well get hit and finish the war fast rather than go through the whole experience of the tensions and anxiety, which are part of surviving. This was a very miserable state of mind. Those who didn't fight can never know this kind of feeling, cannot understand what I'm speaking about. You can't learn about it from books. It's this nasty, despicable feeling of being stuck there in the middle of endless sands, constantly shelled by artillery. With all due respect to Zionism and such, when you're there, you don't have Zionism in mind. You are simply miserable.

But I recovered pretty fast. I didn't run away or chicken out. I managed not to show how afraid I was. And again I feel that I won't be able to face war once more.

•   •   •   •

I   So what are your conclusions about living in this country for the rest of your life? I understand that you now plan to serve in the army for the next year. How do all these parts fit together?

SHAY   They don't. I know I sound irrational. I might be continuing here just out of habit. It would be such a drastic step to try to change something, and I'm unwilling to do it. I guess my education is too good; it has attached me to this country for life. I have adopted the norms of going to the army and being a combat soldier. My brothers are like this, and my parents are like this, too. It's too much for me to be able to get up easily and leave it all behind. Notwithstanding the fact that I am aware of injustice in some aspects of our life here, and I have despaired of solving these through wars, I cannot leave. I solve this contradiction by clinging to the belief that there won't be any more wars. Yet I know that there will be another war, just the same.

I   And yet you volunteer to go for a year—

SHAY   As an army psychologist. And I hope this year will end safely for me.

I   Does this provide you with a transfer from your tank unit?

SHAY   It could, but I requested not to be transferred. I have many reasons. After serving for seven or eight years with these people, I feel very attached to them, and I don't want to have to adjust to a new set, even if it's less dangerous. You see, I don't give up the norm so quickly. I know I keep contradicting myself. On the one hand, I sit here for an hour telling you how I hate wars, and yet I know how I'll curse myself if I'm not actually in combat in the next one.

In the summer of 1973, before the Yom Kippur War, I was working on a boat; and, by chance, I returned from a long stay on board two weeks before the war started. I could have been in a remote place and avoided all the fighting, but I was, in fact, satisfied it didn't happen that way. I would never have forgiven myself if I had missed the war.

I   You wouldn't have considered yourself lucky?

SHAY   No, certainly not.

I   So what is the essence of this devotion, this need to be among those who fight the battle?

SHAY   I think that this is the meaning of adopting the norms. If you live in this country, you have to fight for it. On another level, it has to do with masculinity, being a man. To participate in wars and be good at it is one of the signs of masculinity in our society, of being one of the good guys.

I   This norm of the military life, the masculine stereotype, does this demand a denial of feelings?

SHAY   I think it does. The norm is that a soldier doesn't experience or express feelings. But I don't agree. I think I have been a good fighter and sensitive human being at the same time. I've held this belief even before I started studying psychology, maybe due to my personal problems. Who knows? I could always talk about fears quite freely.

I   And your friends?

SHAY   They never discussed them in depth.

I   And sorrow, mourning for friends who died?

SHAY　I've lost many good friends in my lifetime. Too many. I reacted very deeply to the first losses, although basically I see myself as a person who finds the expression of grief very difficult. I don't know how to mourn for people who are gone, in war or otherwise. Before I became a soldier, I did, however. I even remember crying when I heard about one of the young men of our village who left a widow and a little girl. The little girl's fate, especially, moved me very deeply, and I cried. But it hasn't happened since, even when I lost very good friends. I would feel gloomy, but I think that I wasn't expressing myself, that I was blocking my pain.

I　Do you think it has to do with the number of losses?

SHAY　Yes, there is an accumulation of losses, and then you become sort of immune to them. It's as if your emotions are dulled. This is functional, since tomorrow the list of losses will keep growing, and I don't know who's next.

•　　•　　•　　•

I　Earlier you mentioned your education in terms of accepting life in Israel. Do you feel we are educated to be heroes?

SHAY　It's not an education to be heroes but to accept the norms of the military life, to be willing to take on combat duty, to fight. This is, at least, true for my generation, but I believe it's the same way for the younger soldiers as well. We always have a tendency to see ourselves as the last generation of real soldiers. The norms are the same. In the village in which I grew up, the proportion of boys volunteering for combat units was indeed enormous.

I　Does this act involve a feeling of mission or other values?

SHAY　In high school we sometimes had a sense of mission. But once you grow up and experience life in war and peace, this mission loses its meaning. During the Six-Day War, I was in high school, and I remember feeling that I missed the war. I wanted to participate, especially in that war, which was so clean and glorious. One night I woke up alarmed from a dream that from now on we would have no more wars, and that I had missed my chance once and for all. I wouldn't have a way to prove my masculinity as demanded of an Israeli. But this is something that belongs to my adolescence. I don't feel it any more. I hope that my children, when they are born, will never have to experience military life.

As an adult, there is a deep sense of obligation. I am needed and I must go; nobody could do my share for me. And the group of fighters, as I said before, is today more significant for me than any ideology. When you sit with people on a tank, a half-track, or an armored personnel carrier, they gradually turn into a very cohesive group. When you fight, you measure your behavior against the norms of this group, not against any sort of general value system. The "what for" of war doesn't mean a thing during combat or under fire.

I   So, in order to perform well in war, a soldier must be well trained in the technical skills, without a deep sense of mission or devotion to a cause of some sort?

SHAY   The deep devotion is toward your group, the battalion you fight with, and through it, toward the whole military system. I have the feeling that if my unit were hit or disassembled for any reason, and I were placed with strangers—as a soldier and not as their officer—I would be tempted to desert my post; or perhaps I'd enter a condition of shock, which is, from my point of view, very similar. The army fights the way it does not because of its sense of mission but because of its cohesive groups. The more closely knit the group, the higher the quality of the fighting. The ideological mission is perhaps somewhere underneath the system, but it's not on the soldiers' mind.

•   •   •   •

I   Do you feel that war influences your relationships with the Arabs?

SHAY   During the long months I spent with my soldiers, I don't remember that we discussed the nature of the enemy, but I'm sure that nobody hates the Arabs. Maybe others are different.

I   You come back from the war, where they are the enemy,

and then you walk the streets of Jerusalem among them. Isn't it a strange feeling?

SHAY   Well, I sometimes feel, as I walk through the Arab bazaar, that if they had the chance, they would stab me.

I   But don't you feel you want to kill them?

SHAY   I could never imagine myself just facing someone and shooting him; but if I have to defend myself in war, that's different.

I   You said you don't hate Arabs, yet you feel that they hate you.

SHAY   Because of our respective roles of conqueror and conquered. I know of people who don't trust Arabs, and my father is one of them. I think he represents the older generation, which is very distrustful. They sense the hatred of the Arabs, and they believe they are revengeful and unforgiving. I'm more flexible, but maybe I'm just fooling myself here, too, because if I say that the Arabs will hate us forever, then I have to hate them and prepare myself for a fight.

Illan

I   Do you think that the fact that war is a real possibility in our area affects your life, or life in the country in general?

ILLAN   That's a very difficult question to answer, since many factors are involved here. Let me say first of all, it's very clear to me, especially after the Yom Kippur War, that war affects our lives. I believe that these effects are not completely apparent. There are tremendous forces working to repress them, as they are not easy to live with. The effects of the Yom Kippur War were mainly in the very severe shock it gave to our sense of security. During the years before 1973, we lived through different phases of the Israeli-Arab conflict with the fear of war, which is a very rational fear. But, basically, we felt secure. It was clear to me, as to other people with whom I spoke, that even if another war were to break out, which would certainly be disastrous, with many people being killed and wounded, there was no doubt that we would come out on top. In other words, we couldn't imagine that the State of Israel would be destroyed.

I feel that this basic confidence has been shattered by the Yom Kippur War. It suddenly dawned on us that if all the Arab states open fire one day, catching us unprepared, they could destroy us as a national-political entity and, perhaps, on a personal level as well. Who can imagine the outcome for women and children, let alone the soldiers, if the Arabs were victorious and entered our cities and towns? Actually, this didn't happen —the war was still far away from the population centers—but there was a feeling that it had almost happened, that by sheer luck, or thanks to a miracle, a small tank unit was able to stop the Syrian forces at the edge of our settlements. Maybe the Syrians themselves didn't advance as far as they could have, since they didn't know how unprepared we were for their attack and therefore how open we were for it. So, the last war has undermined our sense of security as a nation for a long time to come.

I   Are you saying that you, personally, take into account the possibility that the State of Israel may cease to exist?

ILLAN   Well, obviously, since the war of 1973, several years have already passed, and some lessening of all these feelings has taken place. They don't openly disturb us now as much as they did right after the war. I remember thinking and talking a lot about all this right after the war; and many people, both soldiers and civilians, had similar feelings at that time. People don't enjoy exposing these fears openly, of course, and often I just sensed them behind their words and deeds. I think that today people have simply stopped speaking openly about these things, although deep down their confidence has been shaken.

I   So what conclusions should one draw for one's own life under these circumstances?

ILLAN   Well, for one, many people have decided to leave the country. We all know that the number of the *yordim* has increased significantly since the last war. There are also economic factors that affect emigration, but I believe these are secondary.

I   Do you personally know anyone who emigrated because of the war situation?

ILLAN   No, not personally. I know people who went to the States to study and didn't come back. I met some of them last year during my post-doctoral studies. They don't mention the military problem as the reason for their prolonged stay; but, you know, this is the kind of thing people don't talk about. And actually, they don't have any convincing reasons for their decision to live in America.

I   And for those of us who are aware of the problem yet do not leave the country, what is happening?

ILLAN   As I said before, there is, first of all, a massive repression; we don't think about it. Those who remain aware of the threat translate it into political language. They draw political conclusions, believing that a different administration may lead to some kind of peaceful agreement with the Arabs, which would minimize the probability of war and therefore the disastrous outcome that we spoke about before. I think that the only way for us to feel secure in this area, in the sense that we are a state like any other and not one which might be erased from the face of the earth one day, is through a peaceful agreement with the Arabs and not by any of the military and other methods which the previous— as well as the present—governments of Israel have tried. I know it will be a very slow and difficult process. Perhaps it has started already, at least from the point of view of the Arabs, whose style of speech about us has changed noticeably in the last couple of years. We are all aware that this is a complicated process that involves not only trust and agreement between the Arabs and ourselves but also all kinds of international guarantees and, of course, changes of the borders. All this can be achieved only very gradually. Anyway, I believe that this is possible and, moreover, that this is our only chance to survive in this area.

I   What you're saying, then, is that getting more involved in politics is one of the outcomes of the decline of our psychological security. Wouldn't you agree that this increased political involvement affects both ends of the political spectrum, the Right as well as the Left?

ILLAN Yes, that's right. Some people may feel that our chance is in growing bigger, stronger, and arming ourselves to the teeth in preparation for the next war. I just failed to mention it because my own opinion is the opposite, as I explained before. Actually, this is a very interesting observation; namely, that most of the people I know had the same political convictions before the Yom Kippur War. They didn't change directions from Right to Left or vice versa; rather, there was some polarization of the political attitudes and more involvement on both sides. This may be one outcome of the traumas of the last war.

I And people whose political-ideological awareness is not well developed—what do they do with the immense anxiety they must be feeling?

ILLAN I really don't know. I mentioned denial and repression as possible mechanisms. And besides, some of the day-to-day tension of people here, the sense of pressure and stress, the lack of tolerance toward each other, these might be related to the situation we have analyzed, although many other factors are probably involved as well. This is something I noticed during my stay in the U. S. last year.

I Well, what you are saying is that from a rational point of view, to live in Israel is not the best choice.

ILLAN That's certainly right [*laughs*]. I must admit that something paradoxical happened to me. I don't have an explanation for it, and it stands in contradiction to most of the things I have been saying. The Six-Day War awakened in me the conviction that we couldn't go on as we had been till then, that the war situation must be stopped. It was the stunning victories of that war that convinced me that we cannot rely on such victories and that future wars would be more dangerous as the weaponry became more sophisticated. A situation in which the Arabs could threaten us with war every few years is intolerable. All this brought me to the conclusion, at the beginning of the seventies, that it is irrational to remain in Israel. Politically I'm a leftist, and so more of a cosmopolitan and less of a nationalist.

Neither does religion tie me to the country. All these factors together started me thinking about leaving Israel. I also discussed the idea with my wife, who had reached similar conclusions.

Paradoxically, however, the Yom Kippur War changed my mind about that. I don't know why, though I talked about it with several people. They asked me, and I asked myself, but I'm unable to explain it. The fact is that since the last war, I have stopped considering the possibility of leaving the country. It is completely out of the question for me, and I don't know why.

I   Maybe it's like escaping from a sinking boat.

ILLAN   Yes, but why shouldn't one escape from a sinking boat? It's the most rational thing to do! What would you be looking for in a sinking boat?

I   But there is a sense of treason associated with leaving.

ILLAN   Yes, probably. Treason versus the sense of loyalty, that's how we've been educated. But it is not a rational explanation.

•   •   •   •

I   Tell me, do you ever think of your own son vis-à-vis your own dilemmas and your decision to live here?

ILLAN   [*laughs*]

I   It's a difficult question, and you may prefer not to answer it.

ILLAN   It is difficult, yes. Sometimes, perhaps. Again, this is one of the things one keeps repressing. We tell ourselves there is a long time before us, maybe we'll achieve peace before our children are drafted. My son is just six years old now. Twelve years is a long time. But actually, I'm not too optimistic regarding a peaceful termination of our conflicts within twelve years. But it's easy to pretend there's a long time ahead. Actually, I feel we are not completely fair toward our children, but I have to admit I usually don't think about it.

•   •   •   •

I   Let's move into another area. People in my groups worked on the image of the hero. They claim that they have been educated to be heroes, and for some of them this ideal is too big to fit. Consequently, when they sometimes feel weak, afraid, or just fed up with the situation, they automatically feel they are deviating from the norm. Did you perceive this message, in yourself or in the soldiers you fought with? And if so, how is this message transmitted?

ILLAN Well, yes. I think this is a correct observation. In those of us who are sabras, who went through primary and secondary schools, with a strong involvement in the youth movements especially, the image of the hero was clearly implanted.

I And not during your army service?

ILLAN Yes, surely, but the roots are from much earlier. Moreover, if you accept this ideal, you volunteer for a certain kind of army service, as I did for the paratrooopers at that time. Yes, I think this is very true. Almost all my friends from school and the youth movement tried to get into combat units. This was what we felt was socially demanded of us. We wanted to conform with the image, to serve up front, and not to let others risk their lives for us. I felt it personally. The question is, of course, whether there is any contradiction. During the wars I was in a paratrooper unit, and I never felt this private wish, which contradicts the norm of heroism. Maybe because we weren't exposed to direct fire so very much. I remember one particular day that was very difficult. The battle was from very close range, and we were under fire all day. Naturally, I was afraid, hearing the whistling of the bullets and mortar shells. But I didn't feel any internal conflict; the fear was appropriate. I expected to be afraid under fire, and this feeling was not in contradiction to the image of the hero. You see, heroism, at least from my point of view, is not the unreal type of feeling that sends you rushing into the fire. My concept of heroism is to contribute to the safety of this country with all my might and ability, to volunteer for necessary and even unpleasant duties whenever possible, and to be willing to risk my life for the country. This was how I was educated; this is how I understand heroism.

I And you have accepted, internalized, these values?

ILLAN   Yes, I have, and I've tried to behave in accordance with these values as much as possible. But that doesn't mean that under fire I may not feel any fear! This is exaggerated and untrue, for we are taught to jump into the foxhole when bullets whistle near us. Otherwise, it would be stupidity, not heroism. I saw, however, people in the war who were struck by fear much more severely than I was, who were almost paralyzed. We know that there are individual differences in fear and other reactions to stress, and it could be that some people did experience the conflict we mentioned before. I don't remember hearing about it from people who fought with me during the war.

I   Does the image of the hero imply suppression of emotions other than fear?

ILLAN   Like what?

I   Like grief, sorrow, mourning and crying for those who fell. People in my groups spoke of the image of the male hero which excludes this form of feeling as well as fear.

ILLAN   Again, I must disagree with that from my own experience. When a very close friend of ours was killed by direct fire right in our midst, everybody expressed their sorrow. There was a sense of shock in the unit. Nobody cried at the moment—that would really be incongruous with the image—but there were many other manifestations of grief. Men do not cry on other occasions, either. But the whole unit reacted very strongly to his death. However, it could be that in units where people were being killed every day, like among the pilots, some toughening takes place, and people try to deny their losses and stop mentioning them. But for us, he was the only one who was killed from our small unit. We had shared plates and beds for many weeks before he was killed so suddenly, and the reaction was intense. Don't think that men are cold inside just because they don't cry!

•   •

Moshe

I   My basic question is what effect does the fact that we Israelis constantly live under the threat of war have on your life and on the lives of the people here in general?

MOSHE   Well, first, on the general level, it's very clear. Because of the threat of war, 40 percent of the national budget is used for security expenses, thus directly causing very high taxation and, as a result, a standard of living which, very clearly, is lower than in countries of comparable quality of population. This is the most outstanding manifestation of our situation.

I   You mean, then, that the main effect is economical?

MOSHE   Yes. This is a very severe outcome of the situation. You notice it all the time.

As to the rest, I personally do not remember myself in a situation without war, except for the two years I spent in the U. S. during my sabbatical. It started with the Second World War, which I remember although I was a young child then. I remember the adults talking about it, anyway. Later, I remember the British soldiers with their firearms in Tel Aviv, the curfew and shooting in the streets, the resistance movement, the posters on the walls. Still later, the Egyptian air raids on Tel Aviv during the 1948 War of Independence, staying in shelters, Arab marauders, Zahal,* and on and on. I don't recall one day without these facts; it's all one long continuum.

I   And how does it affect you?

MOSHE   Personally, I'm not aware of any specific effect. I lived in the States for two years; and except for feeling that I had to engage in some sort of propaganda for Israel, I didn't feel in any way different from the people I met there. I didn't feel I was more sophisticated than they were, more immune, tougher, or anything else. Maybe I am somewhat less naïve about certain processes, military or political, the significance of

*Israeli defense forces

which Americans don't perceive as readily. But I didn't feel different in any other respect.

I   In other words, it is your opinion that we, in Israel, live normally.

MOSHE   Well, that's a bit of a generalization. I see vast individual differences here, ranging from people who are completely insensitive to the threat of war—and I think I am one of them—to others who are very sensitive, are anxious every single moment and over-react.

I   Why are you unaffected?

MOSHE   I don't know. I don't know what makes individuals more or less sensitive to the conditions of their environment.

I   I wonder, though. Objectively, our lives here are in greater danger than the lives of people in most of the world. The lives of our children are in greater danger. How can you disregard the facts and claim you are unaffected?

MOSHE   I don't think I'm irrational. I know, for instance, that the probability of getting killed on the roads is higher than that of being killed in war. Although our casualties in war are concentrated in a short period of time, the absolute number is not very large, and there are people being killed in accidents every single day. And I, as well, take to the road, and I don't think about all this. I relate to the risk of war in exactly the same manner I relate to taking a car ride to Haifa or Tel Aviv. My car is a thing that can kill; I can get killed in it very easily —and I still drive. This is, perhaps, our microcosm. It is as if the State of Israel were riding on a certain road. Just as we drive cars without being afraid every moment of the time, so I live in this country, riding on the axis of time, without the continuing feeling that any minute we may have an accident in which I, or somebody else, might be killed.

I   I have heard some people claim that the extremely high rate of car accidents we have here in Israel is, perhaps, related to the strain created by war.

MOSHE   I don't think this is so. I think there are other factors —road conditions and maybe the Jewish disrespect for external discipline.

I   So here again you claim we are, more or less, normal.

• • • •

I You were saying that for you, war is not such a threat, that you are not too sensitive. Could your attitudes be related to the fact that in your war experiences, you have not been that exposed to physical danger?

MOSHE That may be so. There is a difference between being in a tank and being in an office. Personally, I was never assigned to fight in a tank and shoot Arabs. But there were certain situations in the previous wars in which I was under fire. I firmly believe, since I know myself, that I wouldn't panic under fire. It wouldn't affect me that much, I'm sure. Yet, whether the experience would be a severely traumatic one, I cannot say. But most of the soldiers are not exposed in this way. Such a belief is based on ignorance, because the army is built so that the proportion of soldiers thus endangered is very low; and the vast majority are involved in services, transportation, office work, etc. Very few are in the spearhead of the army, and I don't think they are the most sensitive to our situation.

• • • •

I In my groups, there were many people who were affected by the war in some way or other; and they had many things to work out in terms of their experience of war and their reaction to it. How does that fit in with what you just said?

MOSHE I don't know if it's all the people in your groups, whether it's for a certain period of time, or how many there were.

I That's right, and I don't claim to have a representative sample. But just as cases, single instances, what is your reaction?

MOSHE I think these are people who never thought seriously about our general situation or of the significance of the total Israeli system within which we live.

I Can you enlarge on this point?

MOSHE In my opinion, they are very alienated and, in fact, very much withdrawn. What matters to them above all is how *they* feel, what's going on within in their closest surroundings. The image I have of these people is of those who trail behind the entire camp because they are in some little pain—their leg hurts, they stubbed a toe—all the while in perpetual awareness of their own selves. These people would have behaved in a similar way in totally different environments. For instance, in the States, they would feel hurt and dissatisfied because of their boss, the slowness of their promotion, the competition, money problems, whatever. They are crybabies, very self-involved people.

I   Do you see any connection between this kind of introspection and the fact that many of the people in my groups were psychology students?

MOSHE   Probably. And clinical psychology students even more so. This is their focus of interest in life, their driving force —to understand themselves, to understand others.

I   Is this a healthy tendency?

MOSHE   I cannot say.

I   What's your judgment about it, though?

MOSHE   Let me put it this way: these people will not get much out of this introspection, these ruminations. It only causes people to be less effective when they have something serious to carry out, physically or mentally.

I   You have heard about people, normal people, who might sit for three or four hours working on their inability to feel, to feel sorrow, to admit fear. What do you think about them? Maybe it's more adaptive for them not to feel? This would go well with your criterion of effectiveness.

MOSHE   Well, I don't know. Perhaps it's good for these people to develop their sensitivity to feelings, but on the whole, I think that this kind of introspection stands in the way of efficient functioning. I don't see any poems or good stories growing out of these ruminations, and I'm not even certain that they feel any better for having expressed themselves.

•   •   •   •

I   One of the main themes that emerged in these sessions was the feeling that here in Israel our education demands that we be heroes, both from the point of view of our achievements and performance—to be the best and strongest—and from the point of view of emotional balance—never to express weakness. They claim that this image of the hero is a very heavy load to carry throughout our lives. Do you agree?

MOSHE   First of all, the statement that our education demands that we be heroes needs proof. I don't accept it point-blank. I don't think we educate toward heroic destination. Instead, we are trying to prevent something from happening. It's not heroics.

I   You mean the holocaust?

MOSHE   Yes, of course. I think that basically, people in this land want to avoid following in the steps of the Jews of the Diaspora. In order to achieve this goal, just to become normal like others, we don't have to be heroes. I don't see here any special attempt to educate a generation of heroes. The opposite is true: I think we have too little heroism.

I   But when war breaks out?

MOSHE   In wartime the standard is that you have to perform as well as possible.

I   And when someone gets killed?

MOSHE   We then say he did his duty. If we say he was a hero, I see it as a minimal tribute to the families who paid such a high price. For, you see, the soldiers who do come back safely are not given a hero's reception. I remember movies showing the return of the French soldiers to Paris. People were out of their minds with joy: they threw flowers at the soldiers, had the streets flowing with champagne—the heroes were back. We don't even have a victory march. I don't see any emphasis on heroism in all this—no medals, no marches, no special uniforms or insignia. We all look alike, and pretty worn out, too.

Even in officers training course, which I went through some years ago, never were the terms "hero" or "heroism" brought up. The same is true in other courses.

I   It may have been implicit all the time.

MOSHE   No, I don't agree. Other ideas were underlying our training, such as perfectionism, competence to the maximum of our capabilities, but with a sense of implementing technical skills above all, implicitly as well as explicitly. I recall only one instance that was out of line with these attitudes, and this occurrence was so out of place that I was startled at the time. It happened during officers training course, where I was a machine gunner. We were on a very long and difficult march, miles and miles. I had to carry the machine gun the entire way. We were given a short break and sat down to rest awhile. Just then, the commanding officer drove up in his jeep for an inspection. I was sitting on the machine gun, simply relaxing there instead of looking for a rock to sit on. The commander came out of his jeep and started screaming: "Get off of the machine gun! It's not a chair! Don't you know what a gun is? Respect it! It's a very important object, and for all the effort we put in to obtain it, you should not sit on it!" He didn't say you'll break the gun, for that's nonsense, I couldn't break it by sitting on it. It was as if our firearms were holy—some old-fashioned values from the Hagana,* perhaps. I got up and found a rock to sit on, but I felt his outburst was ridiculous. And, mind you, he was a real hero, so to speak, a very important officer. I think that this is the only time I have encountered something I can associate with the concept of heroism. So, I ask myself: Where did your clients, the members of your groups, get the idea from? If they say it comes from the army units they served in, I wonder why didn't I get the message?

The central idea is that we must survive. If we don't act, we'll be attacked and murdered. It's somewhat similar to a ghetto but a fighting one. A fighting ghetto. Is heroism the idea that we must survive, must defend ourselves?

I   To me it's more than that. It's the idea that we must be superior, an example to the whole world.

MOSHE   That's only due to the very high odds against us in this land, surrounded by enemies. That's why I see the image of the desperate ghetto fighter. We are a kind of stronghold, a fortified ghetto, so that if the enemy overruns us, this whole, closed-in world will cave in. Yes, that's the ideology with which I grew up.

*The pre-state underground Israeli army

I   I see a lot in common between the hero and the ghetto fighter you described: a sense of immense loyalty to the cause; the conviction that there is no way back or out, that one cannot give in; that if you break down, you would never be able to forgive yourself; that you would never want to betray your homeland.

MOSHE   Maybe. But I don't usually think in terms of homeland or forgiveness, and I don't remember these ideas from my education. As I said before, I think in terms of effectiveness. People who are more psychologically oriented are, perhaps, more aware of the other things. I guess I am different.

Matan

I   War is part of our life in this country, and it affects people in different ways. Do you think about war?

MATAN   Yes, war is constantly a part of my awareness. It's been this way since I was a child. I still remember the sound of shooting, the struggle against the British, and then the War of Independence.

I   How old are you now?

MATAN   I am thirty-five. War, as I see it, and this has been my outlook for years now, is an integral part of life. I'm not talking about it's being good or bad. We have to live with war and cope with it; excel in it and win; and, through all this, maintain our sanity. War is inevitable as a human phenomenon. It might be temporarily avoided if one is strong, if the political situation is stable, or if one lives in another country, in another period. But generally, war is a human imperative. Construction and destruction, peace and war, are all aspects of human existence.

Obviously, I personally don't want to have to go to war. But war here is part of life. It may erupt at any moment. Just now I went for coffee and heard on the news that the Jordanians are in a state of military alert. I just happened to catch it in passing —it's as if my ears were built to listen for such things. I am always on the alert. The next war may start tomorrow. It's already second nature to me. Therefore, my life is dedicated to being prepared as a citizen. I have never wanted to become a professional soldier.

Right now I'm a company commander in the Armored Corps. I got into that after the Yom Kippur War, when many of my friends were killed, and it was said that the tanks are most important of all. In my position, I'm completely exposed in the field. It's a very tough job. But those are the preparations for war in this country. I see myself continuing for the next twenty years in the field, like today.

I   And then?

MATAN   Then my sons will take over. Personally, I could easily get a softer job in the base or the office for the next war. Civil Defense Corps or something. I have a bad ankle; I could have been disqualified ten years ago. But I'm not cheating anyone; all these facts are meaningless. One cannot avoid facing the war. One cannot escape. That's the point. And if someone does escape and remains alive, and if he's truthful—and let's assume that all people are truthful for some moments of their lives—then he knows he's a coward.

We encounter fear in a hundred different ways in life. If I run away, then I run away, and I haven't coped with fear. Fear exists, it's a natural feeling, but one has to overcome it. That is one of the manifestations of man's superiority to the animals.

I fought in difficult wars, and I have tested my ability to overcome fear. In the Six-Day War I fought in Jerusalem. I was walking down an alley, and an Arab soldier called from the corner: *"Man hada?"** He was as close to me as you are now, and I walked right toward him. He wasn't standing there with a candy bar, that much was clear. I was the platoon commander, and the procedure was that two scouts are sent ahead of the commander, who is at the head of the platoon. One of the two, who were between me and the Arab at the end of the alley, whispered back to me: "I just have a rifle." He was afraid. A

*Who is it? (in Arabic)

rifle wasn't enough; he needed some magic, too. So I moved up front. I had only a second to make the correct decision, otherwise the whole platoon would go to pieces. I told my soldiers to move out of my way; then I jumped forward and killed the Arab. At that time and place I was better than him, faster than him.

War demands utmost concentration and ability. Under immense pressure and tension, you have to perform at your best. It is exhausting. I'm not talking about those who underwent shell shock, nor about rumors and news broadcasts and stories that spread back at home. That's where fear rules supreme, especially among people who have never experienced the fighting itself. Everything is uncertain and unknown, and that's what causes fear. I experienced such fear before my first battle, a paralyzing fear. But in war itself I overcame it, thanks to long training, my years of regular service in the paratroopers, etc. Yet basically I struggle with myself before each battle. Strength is something one builds gradually and through hard work. And then one has certain expectations of oneself.

I   Abroad people refer to this as heroism.

MATAN   I take my concepts from Judaism, the Torah, the rabbis. According to them, a courageous person is he who conquers himself. My teacher in this area is Maimonides. He speaks about three types of people: one who is a coward, one who is brave, and one who is foolhardy. This is very important because, you see, the brave one, perhaps what you termed a hero, is in the middle, between cowardliness and foolhardiness. Here in the army, too, sometimes people name the foolhardy one a hero, while in fact what he does is unnecessary. I don't admire that type.

When the war was over, I realized that I had changed. All experiences change a person, and this war certainly changed me. Before the last war I did only what was minimally necessary in terms of the nation. I rested a lot, so to speak, or went butterfly hunting, bird watching under the trees. After the war, I drew some personal conclusions from the whole thing. Up to then I had relied on our leaders, the politicians; I paid my taxes and let them do their jobs, assuming that they were doing them well. I always thought that theirs is a dirty job, while all I have to do is my reserve duty. I am an archaeologist, I dig quietly, and the world goes on its merry way. Whether they did an outstanding job or only a mediocre one, I didn't interfere. But when I realized that our leaders were leading us toward catastrophe, I had to change my ways. I couldn't continue in my relaxed way of life, not if I wanted to survive. Moreover, the relationship between the individual and his community is anchored in Jewish law. One cannot keep to himself. The American dream of each one for himself, as long as you don't kill your neighbor, doesn't work in an emergency situation. For Jews it's different. Jews are responsible for one another.* I know this from my studies in Judaism, and here it came to the test.

I   So you emerged from the war with the awareness that you had to dedicate more of yourself to the public welfare, even between wars and reserve service periods.

MATAN   Yes. As soon as I was released from the army after the war, I returned and volunteered as a tankist. I said to them: Teach me to be a tankist; that's where I'll be needed next time. Following this, during my yearly stints on reserve duty, I carried out a three-year program, which I finished just recently: to become a tankist myself and to build a combat unit out of people with no combat experience, people used to the easy life in the army.** I was used to a different type of soldier. The paratroopers with whom I had served till then had all volunteered for their elite fighting units. They were noble, so to speak, compared to these others. My real task was one of re-education; and this is my contribution to politics, building all the time, doing what I can do to build our strength or create it where it does not exist. In the same way, I have been building a new border settlement in the desert. I plant new trees around my house. Strength has to be built. This is good, fair, and just—the

*A maxim from Jewish law
**After the war, when there was a great dearth of combat soldiers, many non-combat soldiers were transferred to combat units and had to be trained accordingly.

right thing to do. We Jews lived so long in the Diaspora that we developed habits which fit that kind of existence. But in our literary sources, which were written when we were a free people in our homeland, our kings and sages talked about building strength and preparing for war. "A time of war, and a time of peace."*

The way to remain mentally sound after the war, instead of going to psychiatrists, is by building, actually building, and begetting children. My youngest son was conceived during my only day of leave in the last war. I didn't plan it that way, but I used to dream it might happen, and I'm pleased it did. A few weeks later, I was very far away across the canal in Africa;** and when my wife called to tell me she was pregnant, it was a life-giving serum for me.

This was a very difficult period, and I had to reach down to the depth of my faith in order to remain sane and on my feet. There was a feeling of total collapse. My unit, made up of civilians in uniform, people used to the easy life, was totally demoralized. They were under such pressures that they were living on tranquilizers, under the supervision of mental-health officers. We were the last ones to be released, after 179 days, in the spring. But I must say, during the following three years, they have mostly recovered, not through slogans or lies but by facing an old bald head like me, who could survive the conditions and do his job faithfully. Living with me, they had to change, too. That's the only way. Their prior education, at home and at school, was completely worthless, I tell you. I am not referring to the whole army, of course, just to my battalion, which was assorted the way it was.

I   For you, personally, is it the Jewish faith that keeps you mentally intact? By the way, do you consider yourself an observant Jew?

MATAN   I don't like the term. I am a believing Jew, and I keep part of the commandments.

*Ecclesiastes 3:8.
**The Israeli army succeeded in crossing the Suez Canal during the Yom Kippur War and established itself on the western bank, which is geographically part of Africa.

I   So your faith, as well as the historical perspective you maintain, helps you preserve your sanity?

MATAN   Definitely. The Torah* is the path of life.

I   And you claim that the role of the warrior is not alien to the
Jewish faith?

MATAN   Definitely.

• • • •

I   Soldiers may be trained for superior technological performance without stressing the national-historical aspect of their
role. Is this against your approach?

MATAN   It simply won't work. Our best soldiers are the yeshiva students. They don't have the best training for the me-
chanical-technological aspect of war; the kibbutzniks are best
prepared for that. And yet every tank commander will tell you
that the yeshiva** students, pale, thin, and spectacled, are better than many other soldiers. As a group, they are superior.
Yes, the kibbutz is a good preparation, too, but who would
believe that those yeshiva guys would be able to acquire such
technical skills? Those who have brains and who know the
historical importance of our mission are the best ones to lead
the way. Confronting death requires more than technical competence, which is just one element of it all. Here we are talking
about the complicated man-machine in combat; it demands the
utmost of human talent and abilities.

So, to summarize, my position is that it's impossible to survive in this country, physically as well as psychologically, without the Jewish faith.

I   Is that what's missing in people who join groups to talk
about the war?

MATAN   Maybe. We tend to adopt foreign norms and values
instead of following our own traditional ways. Let me give you
an example. While visiting my in-laws, who live in a very nice
neighborhood near Tel Aviv, I noticed their gardens, not because I'm a botanist but because I live in the desert and gardens

*Written Jewish law
**Religious study center

excite me. So what do I see? I see all kinds of exotic plants, imported from far away, Africa and South America. The amount of care they need—water and shade and protection from winds and people—gives you the impression that the owners would go to no end of trouble to provide all these needs so that the plants may succeed in this foreign soil and climate. Now, on the other hand, look at an Arab garden. You'll find a fig tree, an olive tree, pomegranate trees, a vine, some wheat and barley—that's all. A beautiful garden that belongs right here. This is what I call the traditional culture. In Gethsemane we have olive trees that are two or three thousand years old.

I   So what conclusions do you draw from this comparison?

MATAN   That the Jewish culture is part of the country of Israel; they are inseparable. Moses knew why he brought us here, and I know, too. As I study the Torah, I imagine Moses talking to me—we get together once a week at least [*smiles*]. This is my culture and my tradition. I don't have enough time to study as much as I would like to, but I do what I can and my roots are here. The conditions here in this country, especially after the Yom Kippur War, are so difficult that without permanently studying our books, our sources, with or without faith in what's in them, life is completely intolerable. This isn't mysticism; I don't accept mysticism. It's dealing with olive trees.

I   And are there many people who share your beliefs?

MATAN   No, I don't think so. But our number keeps growing, it's a process of growth. Right now I'm working on building a Yeshiva in our settlement, to have a "tent of Torah."

•   •   •   •

I   There is just one more question I'd like to ask. How do you feel about the Arabs?

MATAN   We have to live with them and cope with them. Better in peace, but if that's impossible, then in war. I don't hate them; I don't eat them for breakfast or for dinner. Presently they are the enemy, within as well as without; a stubborn enemy, a cruel one. That's true for today. But I keep checking it everyday, watching for possible change. So far, I haven't detected any changes. In my work I have a lot of contact with Arabs, and we are friendly and kind to each other—when we like each other personally, of course. I live nearby, I do my shopping in Arab stores, and they know what I think as much as I know what's on their minds. I'm more accepted by the Arabs than most of those liberals who speak in favor of a Palestinian State within our borders. I understand the Arabs; this is their region, no doubt. But my grandfather came to this country, and my father lived here. Each one of them suffered here and paid the price for returning to this country. And when I was eighteen, I thought about the whole question and I made up my mind to remain here, with all that follows from this decision. It was, as it is now, a matter of choice, of my own free will. I have a sister who lives in Australia; maybe she'll never come back. She also made her choice, you see. Free choice is a very Jewish concept. It's such a rich concept, I just barely begin to understand it. When I grow older, I'll study more.

The Women _____

Yael

I   I would like to talk with you about the war. If you feel uncomfortable with any of the things I ask you, please feel free to stop me at any time.

YAEL   Ask me some specific questions.

I   Does war, or did war, affect your own life?

YAEL   Yes, yes. In my case, I started feeling it in 1967, when I was doing my army service. This was the first time that people I knew very well got killed in war.

I   You knew them from the kibbutz or from your army service?

YAEL   From the kibbutz and from other kibbutzim. They had been part of my social group as I grew up. Well, it started in the Six-Day War, when first one friend was killed, then another and another. [*She mentions their names.*]

I   Really, so many young men whom you knew were killed in that war?

YAEL   In the Six-Day War, there were two young men from my class; their deaths were the hardest. One of those two classmates was really close to me at the time he got killed. We had been together a lot. And the second—it was such a shock when I found out about his death, he was so full of life, the type of person whom everybody admires. I was very friendly with his girlfriend as well. I remember thinking: Now the men of my class are beginning to go, and we'll see how many will be left. Then there were several other men whom I knew fairly well. One was an older man from my kibbutz.

I　The fact that you grew up in a kibbutz is probably the reason you know so many men who were killed.

YAEL　Yes, men of our kibbutz have been killed in every war; they just have that kind of role. It's also because we know more people, I think. Many activities are shared by parallel age groups in several kibbutzim; and by visiting each other, we get to know a great number of members from different kibbutzim. So, if you ask me about the effects of war, at present many people who belonged to my group, the social group I felt a part of, are not alive any more. Sometimes, this is even harder to take than the dear ones who are gone. It's like two different kinds of sorrow.

I　Do you refer to the sheer number of those who were killed?

YAEL　Not just the number, because the names are very important. But somehow, this list of names keeps growing, and then I stop and say: Who else? We were a tightly knit group of friends. [*She mentions about six names.*] And I frequently feel that there, with those who have died, I had my roots, my basic feeling of belonging. Today I don't have this kind of relationship; nothing is left.

I　These six names you have just mentioned are of men who fell in the wars?

YAEL　Yes, and all were kibbutz children.

She then tells me the circumstances of the deaths of several of these, not including those of her brother and boyfriend.

YAEL　Two of those who were killed were close friends and neighbors. Whenever I visited one, I would see the other as well. Dror was also my younger brother's commander. They all served in the same select reconnaissance unit, so we were very close. Three of them were killed during the same week in 1973.

I　So there's a sense of a group of people growing smaller.

YAEL　Yes, that's it.

It's very difficult to explain. I would have left the kibbutz anyway and put some distance between myself and my place of origin. I didn't like my life in the kibbutz; yet maybe because of the wars, I can't separate from it psychologically. I keep thinking of it. I don't feel completely at home in the city, and sometimes still have a sense of surprise that I'm here, as if it were new for me; and I enjoy city life, since it's very different from the kind of life I had before. It's as if I were still celebrating the change. But my basic sense of belonging is to those kibbutz friends, to that group which suffered so many losses, whose central figures are gone. With it, so many other possibilities are gone, terminated. The number is, of course, also important. It's as if a whole group has been wiped out. All of them.

I   Weren't there any women in this group?

YAEL   Yes, but I was never as friendly with the women at that time as I was with the men. I was quite close with two of the wives of these men. But now I feel very reluctant to visit them, because I used to come to see the men, not them. With the women I had only superficial ties.

•   •   •   •

I   The kibbutz has this standard that men volunteer for the most difficult military assignments, and they are a large proportion of the officers in the army. How is this standard communicated?

YAEL   It's somehow self-evident that they should volunteer. I don't know how it all started, but today it's part of the lifestyle that this is an important image for the kibbutz. It's also crucial for a kibbutznik to reach a really important position in the army —some combat function, not just any job. "What will the others say?" is quite strong and significant.

I   How do you educate for that?

YAEL   First, there's the example set by the older generation— the stories we hear, tales of the War of Independence. But I really don't know. The War of Independence was a very important part of our upbringing, with memorial services and memorial books for those bygone heroes. This is central. And then, in high school, officers of elite army units visit the kibbutz, talk about their duties and importance, and try to persuade people to volunteer for those units. The paratroopers were popular at the time. There was some sort of competition among the boys, who would volunteer for a more hazardous position. A lot of it was imitation of older age groups, too.

I   Do you believe that the men went wholeheartedly to these units? Did they ever talk about doubting the need to go, express resentment that they, in particular, had to go first? Or was it a forbidden subject?

YAEL   I don't remember that sort of conversation. I know that my brother, who volunteered for the naval commando unit, actually didn't want to serve there; but it was a position of the highest prestige in the army, so he volunteered for it, with a great amount of conflict. It was flattering to his self-image, and also, one of his great childhood heroes served in that unit. It was very difficult for him to admit that he actually didn't want to go there.

I   And did he, finally?

YAEL   No. Somehow he was placed in a reconnaissance unit, which wasn't a bad choice as far as prestige goes. In that unit he followed in the steps of our two older brothers, and he had another dilemma: Would he be as good as they were and not shame the family? My oldest brother got a medal there, and the young one didn't want to be recognized only for his family name, to be in his big brothers' shadow. But he did very well himself. I'm sure that some boys would rather get a softer job, but they wouldn't admit it. There were, for instance, a number of kibbutz members who were assigned to the Fighting Pioneering Youth [Nachal].* This was considered a relatively non-combat role. They were forced to do this, and they were terribly ashamed and frustrated. It bothered them a lot. I remember one of them who disliked his role as a Nachal commander, but he admitted that it was a safer job, saying: "Who needs to be killed?" He was pretty cynical about the men who run ahead to take the riskiest positions, who have to stand out. He hated the army and waited for the day of his discharge, maybe because he wasn't assigned to his preferred combat unit, who knows. But he was a pretty unusual type. And what do you

*An army corp which serves, after basic training, in agricultural settlements

think? He got killed as well! I was the last one to speak to him before he was killed in a stupid accident.

I   But the others you know, would you say that they loved the military life and enjoyed it? Those who had the most prestigious roles?

YAEL   No, certainly not. Basically, it is a sense of duty. A few of them love certain aspects of the military life, but by and large, they don't.

     •   •   •   •

I   We were talking about the attitudes of the men who go to the army. But the others who stay behind—the girlfriends, wives, parents, the kibbutz community—how do they react to the whole thing, to the great loss of life they have always been suffering? To the fact that their sons and husbands stand right in front, performing the hardest jobs for us all?

YAEL   It's very difficult to generalize. My sister-in-law is recovering from her loss perhaps, but very slowly. The other day I visited the kibbutz, and there was a Friday night party with folk dancing. For the first time since the war, she joined the dancing. She used to be such a fine dancer, but she always danced only with my brother. That Friday night, when she accepted an invitation to dance, I had the impression the whole kibbutz was watching her breathlessly. Or, perhaps, they all felt somewhat relieved. People differ in their reactions.

My father, who lost his oldest son in 1973, says that he had always taken this possibility into consideration. He always knew this might happen. He says: "We raised our sons for that, to go first, to be the leaders." I think this is fairly characteristic of the kibbutz in general. I don't know how sincere it is—well, I suppose it is sincere, only I'm upset by this sort of argument. I feel that when people talk about the national mission or destiny, our values and aims, our education, that we knew it might happen, they are proud. I feel all this is a cover for the sense of terrible loss. It's easier to talk this way than to admit that the pain is too bad to bear.

I   But you believe these people, like your father, when they speak this way?

YAEL   Yes, it is, perhaps, true for them. Yet it's a question of how *much* one speaks that way. Sometimes it sounds exaggerated and untrue.

I   People like these don't talk about their pain but only about their ideology?

YAEL   Yes, it used to be this way, but recently I've noticed some slight change. I don't know. People seem more willing to acknowledge their sorrow.

•   •   •   •

I   Would you say this is a culture of heroism?

YAEL   Yes, in a way. It's a culture of heroism with a stress on self-sacrifice. As if we had some historical mission which is more important than individual lives. I personally find it hard to live with the knowledge that we send somebody else to be killed, to defend us. With all the possible rationalizations, I find it somehow unacceptable. I don't know how parents, like my parents, take it.

I   Is there any choice?

YAEL   No, there isn't. But the feeling is still there. Sometimes it's expressed by bereaved parents when they say: "I would rather have died in his place." And, in the same way, I ask myself: What is the justification for my life going on while these men are being killed, since this is my war as much as it is theirs? Why should men be more exposed? This creates a very basic inequality, an unbridgeable difference, between men and women in our society.

•   •   •   •

I   So for you, personally, if you had been born and raised in another country, your life would have been completely different?

YAEL   Yes, of course.

I   Yet there are people who claim that their lives here are normal.

YAEL As I said at the beginning, my life started to take its special course during the war of 1967, and this process has grown much more pronounced since the 1973 war. I live with a permanent sense of loss and a constant fear that another war may break out and more people will be killed. Even when friends or relatives of mine just go to the reserves, I'm more nervous and anxious than I used to be. I am afraid all the time. This is the central tone of my life.

I Don't you think that such conditions may drive some people to leave the country?

YAEL Yes, possibly. I wouldn't know how to formulate the answer if you asked me why I stay. I feel I have to, but I can't explain it verbally or reason why. I remember a period when B. [*her boyfriend, who was killed in the war of 1973*] was very critical of what was going on in Israel. He used to talk, then, about going away, leaving the country, and it was a real possibility for him. I used to tease him: Why don't you go, then? His answer was that he didn't know why, but as long as people were called to the reserves, as long as he was needed by the army, by the country, he couldn't leave. He would have the feeling that at any future moment, if some tension arose in the area, he might have an urge to return. This wasn't said as a Zionist declaration; it was a simple, down-to-earth statement of fact. He hated to go to the reserves. He was afraid, and he used to ask himself how many more times he would be lucky, as he had been several times before, to escape death. He surely didn't want to be a hero or die for the "homeland." Yet this is what happened.

I It's as if we have an illogical explanation: the danger here compels us to stay rather than run away.

YAEL Yes. There is a strong feeling of being needed, that everyone is important for the common struggle. I remember that during the war, when my oldest brother was killed, my second-oldest brother was called back to the kibbutz to be with the family for a while. He was impatient to go back and join his unit. People tried to keep him in the kibbutz with various excuses, and he was very conflicted. He finally said that it was bad enough that our dead brother could no longer do his duty, and that there was no sense in his being absent from the front, too. We let him join his unit—there was no way to keep him with us. In his case, I'm sure that there was no need for heroism on his part, nor did he suffer the shame of those men who were not mobilized, since everybody knew why he was back home. He simply felt he was needed by his company at the front more than by us, and he went. B.'s feelings were of the same kind.

I   This might also have a positive side, you know. Our lives are perhaps more meaningful in Israel, since we feel personally needed.

YAEL   I frequently think about this meaning. The only question is how much we have this feeling in our daily lives, and whether this prevents people from leaving the country in spite of the troubles.

I   Well, you know the kibbutz and its outlook very intimately. What I believe, and you have reinforced today in our talk, is that the people there perhaps don't talk about it, but they live according to their ideology.

YAEL   Yes, that's true. With all the criticism heard about the kibbutzim lately, that they live shut off from the general society, they have as their guideline the supreme value of the State of Israel and its independence. This is a very central value, and it's worth any price to defend. They also have the strong conviction that it's their role or mission to do it. I wonder if the younger generation, those eighteen-year-olds joining the army today, have the same convictions we had at that age. When I joined the army, it was a relatively peaceful period. We felt the attraction of the uniforms and the status of national heroes, but the fears were not as pronounced as they are today.

I   Just one more question: Considering your deep personal loss, how do you feel about the Arabs?

YAEL   I am afraid of them, very clearly.

I   And hate?

YAEL   No, I don't feel any hate. Just fear.

•　•

Michal

I   Does the thought of war bother you a lot or doesn't it?

MICHAL   Usually it doesn't. During the elections I thought about the problem of war and what actions would lead us into another one. But it was thought without feeling. I don't feel any fear. I'm afraid or worried when people who are close to me are called up to reserve duty; or when I think of what will happen if the ones dear to me have to fight in a war, naturally it frightens me a great deal. Here, around town, away from the border areas, though, I usually don't think about it at all. Last week, for instance, when I took a trip to the north, I saw many army camps and fortifications, and I felt a pang of fear. It became concrete for me that we and the Arabs are enemies, sitting on two sides of a border. I went to the north through the Jordan Valley, and we drove along the border, with the wire fence to our right. I was watching the tiny Arab villages on the other side of the Jordan, and they looked so peaceful, and I thought to myself: My God, why do those nice people out there want to kill me? I don't feel that way with the Arabs of Jerusalem, as if here in Jerusalem it is my country and it's peaceful. As long as I don't move geographically, I'm not aware of any threat.

I   And for the men, does reserve duty bring war closer to their awareness?

MICHAL   I am sure it does, although it's difficult to generalize. My boyfriend, for instance, returned from the Yom Kippur War in a state of deep shock. The war had been extremely difficult for him. Only lately has he started to tell me about some of the horrors he saw and experienced almost four years ago. And war is still his greatest fear. He fought at the Canal and still has nightmares about those days. Through him I've begun to understand the enormous fears men have of the war. I know that his life has been deeply affected by it.

I   How?

MICHAL   Even today, when he gets an order by mail to report for reserve duty, he starts to shake and is covered with cold sweat. It's a reflex reaction. If he'll have to fight again, he'll do it, and do it well. But just the same, this is his automatic response.

I   And what do you think about that?

MICHAL   We simply have no choice. But, again, on a daily basis, I don't feel we exist here under "no-choice" conditions. Mostly I block the whole thing out of my awareness. Look, I'm afraid of cancer more than of war, and I don't think that our life here is similar to that of a sick patient, dying slowly, unaware of what's happening to him. [*laughs*] Though sometimes I do feel like this when talking to my boyfriend about his fears.

•   •   •   •

I   Do you feel that the relationships between men and women are affected by the war?

MICHAL   I never thought about it. I know that I prefer men who are combat soldiers to others who are just jobniks.* I am quite ashamed of this preference, which would be more appropriate for a high school girl than for a woman like myself. And, since I declare that I hate wars, it doesn't make sense to feel attracted specifically to the men who make them. Yet honestly, I do feel that way. Admiration is, perhaps, too strong a term, but my attitude toward the combat soldiers is something like it. It even reaches the extreme; namely, I would prefer that my boyfriend fight in the war rather than sit at home with me. [*laughs*] It's a stereotype that I can't get rid of. It isn't fair, since the rational person would rather sit at home; or if he were rational and not nationalistic, he would move to another place altogether. What rational reason is there to risk your life for a country? So I guess I am irrational. It's part of the Israeli identity, I believe.

I   Americans asked me if Israeli women are more sexually permissive with their men as a result of their admiration for the soldiers, in the same manner that parents here might be more

*People who hold non-combat jobs in the army

permissive with their children, since their future is so uncertain. Did you feel that way toward men?

MICHAL No, I don't accept that. It makes sense to indulge a man after the hard times he had in the army, but I never experienced that in my relationships. I don't feel I owe them something for their fighting or that I need to compensate them.

• • • •

I Do you feel that our education demands the blocking of emotions?

MICHAL No, not my education, at least. But all my friends are combat soldiers of elite units, and they have always played the role of the hero. They would criticize the army but would never complain about their difficulties, talk about or show their pains or fears, or even feel them at all. This, perhaps, is some sort of blocking. My education, however, didn't stress this. But, look, this whole question gets into the male-female stereotypes, which exist in other countries as well and may be unrelated to war. A man is required, for better or worse—I think for worse —to control his emotions more than a woman; he will neither cry nor express his feelings. Behavior seen as gentleness in women is looked upon as weakness in men. I don't think it's fair or justified. The military role of men, even the military future in store for high school boys, reinforces this distinction between the sexes. I think that all these phenomena start very early in life and are not suddenly produced at eighteen by the military life.

• • • •

I How do you feel about the Arabs?

MICHAL There is a gap between my thoughts and feelings. As far as my thoughts go, or my political philosophy, I am all for peaceful co-existence with the Arabs, and I can live under equal terms with them as citizens. But I would never go out socially with an Arab; or if I had a daughter, I would not like her to befriend Arab men. I am prejudiced as to their intelligence. As a Jew I feel superior. Yet I'm not hateful or resentful toward them. As for trust, I'm less trustful of an Arab, but I think it's possible to build mutual trust. That depends on the personality of the individual.

I have developed a friendship with an Arab merchant in the Old City who used to do business with my uncle. I frequently visit him in his store and feel very much at home there. I started going there during high school and continued during my army service and afterward. Apparently, I once went to shop or visit in uniform, I don't quite remember. Now every time I go there he asks me jokingly: "Are you still a soldier-girl?" We have a very special relationship; we drink coffee together, talk about our families, and every time I feel extra pleased about the fact that I was able to develop this kind of relationship with an Arab, which I didn't believe possible.

I   Is his question about your army service significant?

MICHAL   No, I don't think so. I think he considered my military service part of my process of growing up. Neither he nor I chose to see my uniform as signifying some sort of military relationship between the two of us.

•   •   •   •

I   Were you mobilized in the last war?

MICHAL   Yes. I served in a large civilian hospital, which, during the war and after it, received a large number of seriously wounded soldiers. My job was to take care of their families. It was my responsibility to provide transportation, food, and sleeping arrangements, to care for their various needs, and to give all sorts of support. There was another woman working with me, and we stayed in this hospital, day and night, for over six weeks.

I   Was it difficult?

MICHAL   Yes, it was hard, but there was something good about it. I felt I was contributing something, doing my share. I felt the difficulty later. At that time, I was in constant motion, running around day and night, almost without sleep. I have been with families in the most tragic conditions you can imagine. In the third week of my service, one of my friends arrived there, wounded. This was very difficult. One of our tasks was to receive and sort out the belongings of the wounded soldiers. So I was doing that in the office of the reception area when suddenly a bundle of uniforms and various objects was thrown in, soiled with blood and oil, and a name was called out, the name of this good friend of mine. I felt paralyzed. Someone had to help me leave the office and take me to the reception area, where the incoming wounded were lying on their stretchers. I found him there and checked that he was whole; hands, legs, eyes, were all there, so I calmed down. It was a moment of awful fear, but it passed quickly. Everything passed very quickly then. I was able to smile at people, tell jokes, and also perform all kinds of services, running between the wounded and their families. I didn't let myself feel any of the pain at that time.

Later, toward the end, I had a more difficult time. I was still at the hospital, and the names of friends who had been killed kept coming in. I felt as if I had been beaten, and inside I felt sort of empty and cut off from my surroundings. When I heard the name of the first dead soldier I knew, I cried a lot and was very upset. But later, I felt enveloped in some sort of numbness. I couldn't cry any more, even though I felt the pain. I couldn't cry at the funerals either, and it gave me a very heavy feeling. I felt I had to cry but couldn't. I remember looking for stimuli to make me miserable so I'd be able to cry, but I didn't succeed. I wrote, then, about my feelings, feelings for those who were gone.

•   •   •   •

MICHAL   When I returned to the university, I found these two laboratory workers sitting in the lab as if nothing had happened. This was very strange, after the long weeks I had spent in the hospital. But later, when the school year started, all the feelings vanished. I felt as if nothing remained in me from my whole war experience. We sent the lectures' notes to classmates who were still mobilized, and we sent packages to friends; but I had no empathy with their experience, the difficulties they were undergoing and the risks they were taking. I slept well at night, told jokes, and studied with my usual interest. This was strange. At the hospital I had experienced such intense, shocking events—and how easily I slipped back into the routine of the university, putting all those memories in a far corner, all packed up and locked away! This surprised me, as if I were superficial, since the traumas did not leave long-lasting traces on my life. Questions I had asked myself during the war—like: What for? Why? What will be?—questions about my existence and the existence of others, stopped bothering me immediately afterward. So I guess I am repressing a great deal, and that's also probably why I usually don't fear the next war.

•   •   •   •

I   With all the subjects we have brought up, how do you feel about living in Israel?
MICHAL   This is my home, it's a fact, and I'm a hundred percent sure I would not like to live elsewhere. I love this place. I am very patriotic toward this state, the city, and the culture. When I have foreign visitors, I am very much aware of our differences. I see them as foreigners; they are not like us. I feel more Israeli, especially vis-à-vis foreigners, but I can't define what my Israeli identity consists of.

•   •   •   •

I   Do you feel it's good or important to write about feelings concerning the war, the kind of book I am writing? Or is it dangerous for the morale of the people?
MICHAL   I think it's very important for people to talk, but to write it in a book—I don't think that's a way to help others express their own feelings. Writing these expressions is not that important, although I don't see it as dangerous either. Generally, I'm against spreading demoralizing stories. If people feel like sharing them at home, that's fine, but don't increase their circulation.
I   But talking about fear, for instance, like you and your boyfriend talk, or talking about mourning, is this demoralizing?

MICHAL No, by no means. But, you see, there are differences in that respect among people. I know a family who lost their son—they would be very angry whenever the radio or TV carried a program about the war or any kind of memorial. They said they remembered enough as it was and would like to be left in peace. As if these programs were reopening the wounds yet doing nothing about healing them. These people didn't feel that the sharing per se, or realizing that others had similar problems, helped them in any way. They didn't consider it as building their strength. They would have liked to lock their son's room with all their memories inside, far from their daily lives. Others, however, react in a totally different manner. They write books about their sons or collect their letters, photographs, and records of their activities; they reconstruct their rooms in the house, as if this keeps them among the living. I don't know which of these reactions is better or healthier, or whether there is one recommendation for all. Me, I'm in the middle, somewhere.

Dina

I I'm collecting material for a book, and I would like to find out about the effects the presence of war has had on our life in this country. I would like to know what you feel or think about this condition.

DINA Well, first of all, I don't think about it too much. From time to time I do think about the war, and naturally I don't like it. But I accept it, the way I accept the fact that winter comes every year. We have no choice; it's a fact. I don't see a way out of this condition; and when I do give it serious thought, I come to the conclusion that there will be no peace in my lifetime. I don't believe that there is any possibility of a simple, quick settlement being achieved. We just have to live with it.

I know several people who couldn't take it, though. They left the country. I have two people in mind who have emigrated, using the justification that they couldn't stand the threat of war or the thought of their children being mobilized. I must admit I don't especially admire them for this act. I see it as senseless, because even though we do have this problem, I'm convinced that there is no other place on earth which is as good for us to live in. Maybe I have this opinion because I've never lived elsewhere for a lengthy period of time; but I feel that when someone walks out and escapes from this country, it's like the legendary traveler who took a trip to Samarkand only to encounter Death waiting for him there. Doing such a thing seems absurd to me. Right here we are all in it together, in the same boat, so to speak. It seems to me that to separate oneself from the group in order to save one's skin is an act of treason.

I   And for those of us who stay in Israel, how does the strain of the political situation affect our personal life?

DINA   [*thinks for a while*] I don't know.

I   Do you think that our lives here are normal?

DINA   I think that, yes. Naturally.

•   •   •   •

I   People who participated in my groups talked about the image of the hero, which they perceived as central to their upbringing. They also talked about their guilt feelings when they couldn't conform with the image, when they felt weak or afraid. Do you see that as meaningful?

DINA   There is something to it, to the stereotype of the no-problem hero. But I think it isn't as rigid now as it was some years ago. In other words, the no-problem hero image used to be much stronger.

I   What caused this change?

DINA   Well, I don't know. Thinking back to the newspaper headlines on memorial days or during periods of hardship, I see them full of heroism, tales of heroes who never hesitated. No, this hasn't changed.

I   What happens to a young man who starts his military service and does not feel this way? I mean, suppose he is not very physically fit and he can't take the army life. What would he do about it?

DINA Well, I'm sure some people would feel better under easier conditions. But actually, my impression is that if we look at reality, not at what's written in books or papers, then there's general agreement that not everyone is a hero.

I So it's only a myth?

DINA Well, sure, there's nothing new about that. It seems to me highly improbable that a person who doesn't feel like a hero would be unable to find others with whom to share his feelings and would be compelled to bury them deep down inside himself. If someone would have come to tell me about his fears, I wouldn't have regarded him as crazy or disturbed. I am trying to recall the waiting period before the Six-Day War. At that time I knew several people who were afraid, very afraid.

I You had some connection with a military unit at that time, I remember. There were some stories about a flag.

DINA Oh, that's just nonsense; and it has been repeated and misrepresented so many times already.

I I don't remember the details. Let's repeat them once more.

DINA Well, we lived in Jerusalem in 1967, and there was an army camp near our neighborhood. One evening, the first night of the war, I think, we were sitting in the shelter, and there were soldiers on the streets. Suddenly they came in and asked whether any of the apartments had blackout arrangements so that they might put the lights on and study their maps. So they came into our flat, and we spent the time with them until they left for the attack on the Old City. When they left we gave them our Israeli flag, which we used every year for Independence Day. It was just a simple old flag we had around the house. Later, however, people started spreading legends about the flag, which actually didn't have any previous history.

I What were the legends?

DINA That my mother had saved this flag when she fled the Old City in 1948. This was even repeated in some books about the war. The funniest part is that people who personally participated in the event also repeated the legendary story rather than the factual one.

I And what did, in fact, happen during the war?

DINA   Well, this same unit was the one to liberate the Wailing Wall, and they flew our flag at the wall.

I   Did you ever get it back?

DINA   No, it's being kept in the Jerusalem Museum.

•   •   •   •

I   You started to talk about the waiting period before the '67 war, some people you knew who were very afraid.

DINA   Yes. One was a neighbor who lived next door to me. She had lived through the Second World War in Europe; and in those weeks of mounting tension before the Six-Day War, she told me that she was prepared to die, she and her small child. Her mother, who worked in some medical laboratory, asked her if she wanted to have some cyanide around the house, just in case. As for myself, I couldn't identify with this. Not that I expected the war to be a picnic for us. I was pessimistic in the sense that I thought it was going to be a long and difficult war, maybe like the War of Independence of 1948, but it didn't seem feasible to me that we should die or that something really horrible should happen. I thought my neighbor's reaction was a product of her previous experience in Europe and of the fact that she wasn't completely integrated into Israeli society the way we were.

I   This is very difficult to say, but it occurred to me while you were talking right now that the Jewish prisoners in the Nazi concentration camps also refused to believe that they were going to die, that the worst was really going to happen to them, until they were faced with the bitter end.

DINA   It may be that our situation really resembles theirs; but we might, on the other hand, resemble the early settlement in the country through the time of the establishment of the state, during which time we were always on the winning side. It might not be completely realistic to expect to remain victorious forever, but it's just more comfortable to stick to this belief.

I remember when I started to doubt this during the War of Attrition. I have two sons, and at that time it dawned on me that my oldest would be starting his service in the army in the near future and that peace was as remote as ever.

Here Dina starts to look very excited, as she continues:

DINA   I was not in actual physical danger, but I was very afraid of what might happen to my children when they grew up. This fear remains with me, and I think that this is one of the worst things you have to put up with, living here. We all know of so many families in which this threat really materialized. Well, thank God, I don't have anything to complain about, so far. From all the wars I've lived through, I, and the ones dearest to me, have emerged untouched. This certainly makes a difference.

I   You were born in Israel, weren't you?

DINA   Yes.

I   I heard once that your parents were personally involved in the riots of the thirties.

DINA   Well, yes, my father was killed in the riot of 1938. I was a very small child at the time. He was walking to work and was murdered by Arab terrorists. I never knew my father; I only experienced him as something that was missing in my life, although I never really felt like an orphan. My older brother was, however, more strongly affected by this event. He remembers our father, so he can relate more to his death. Our mother never talked about our father, so I have no image of him.

I   Do you experience, however, any feelings of vengeance or hostility toward the Arabs who committed this act? Do you think this could lead to certain rigid political attitudes on your part?

DINA   No, it doesn't work that way for me.

I   And for your brother, who has a deeper sense of loss?

DINA   I don't know. He's a very closed and introverted person. While he is more of a hawk than I am, I think that it's typical for men to be more hawkish than women. For a man, the idea of withdrawing and giving in, as well as any other sign of weakness, is much more difficult to accept than for a woman. Actually, I don't see women as having extremist political positions on either side; they are oriented toward the preservation of life rather than toward mounting ideological barricades.

I   Does war stand between men and women or somehow affect their relationships?

DINA I'll tell you about a couple I know. When her husband returned from the war, the wife expected him to finally give her some help and support. Not physical help, but it was as if she were saying: "See what a horrible period I lived through. I feel especially helpless, since I can't do much about the war. I suffer from loneliness and longings." So when he came home for a visit, he had to console his wife. That he himself had fought in the war, had spent the last couple of months sleeping in the sands near the Suez Canal, these were just petty details. I myself felt very bad about this. Well, it's true that the wife had a difficult time; and she had all my sympathy for it, especially since I didn't share her lot, as my husband wasn't mobilized in the last war; but just the same, her husband lived through more severe hardships. And from whom was she trying to get compensation for her suffering? From him, who was the cause of her suffering, since she had worried about him! This was ridiculous and also disturbing.

I remember many families that had similar complaints. The husbands came home on leave, and instead of being warmly received and provided with love and a well-earned rest, they were confronted with all the bills and problems that had accumulated during their absence, practical as well as non-practical matters.

•   •   •   •

I   What did you feel during the last war, the Yom Kippur War?

DINA First of all, we were still living under the impression of the victory era. This victor's psychology was not shaken right away but rather later, during the war. During the first few days of the Six-Day War, what we heard on the radio was not altogether true. Every hour the same version of the news was repeated. We couldn't understand a thing and imagined the worst catastrophes. Suddenly, these soldiers who came to our shelter told us that in the south, the battle was over, that they were planning an attack on Jerusalem, and that the air forces of the enemy had been destroyed. So, with this in mind, we thought that what the radio told us during the Yom Kippur War was an understatement, and we preferred to hear bad news, under which lies a favorable situation, than vice versa. Only much later did we realize the severe situation we were faced with. It was, for me, quite shocking, since I didn't expect a war at that time.

I Nobody did.

DINA Yes, but right after the 1967 war we had a euphoric feeling, that everything was settled once and for all. Gradually we realized that some sort of trouble would go on, and more people would necessarily be killed. But we didn't expect these events to undermine the fantastic superiority that was attained in the Six-Day War, and we certainly were not prepared to be caught in a situation of danger and despair. The image of the good world was blown to pieces. During the war I was alarmed by the number of casualties, and in this respect it was a very difficult time. And yet, not for one second did I doubt the future of Israel as a state.

I So you think that there has been a change in our sense of security since the war?

DINA Well, I don't know. We keep changing a little all the time, anyway. There is no dramatic change in my outlook on life in this country or in the world. But the war did change the sense of security, the feeling of omnipotence.

I Maybe it's a healthier position?

DINA It certainly is. To be with your feet on the ground and not above the clouds is much better.

Ronny

I May I start with some personal questions? When did you come to Israel?

RONNY   In 1969. I was eighteen at the time.

I   So you finished high school in France?

RONNY   Yes.

I   And have you been in the army?

RONNY   No.

I   Why is that?

RONNY   When I came here, I didn't speak a word of Hebrew. I was, however, willing to go into the army, but the army officials suggested that I defer my service for a year, so that I would have a chance to learn the language. I went to the university; and during that year, my desire to go into the army diminished. Consequently, I asked for a further deferment, which was granted for the period necessary to complete my studies.

I   And what is your status now?

RONNY   Well, as you know, I got married two years ago, and then I was released from the draft, as all married women are.

I   Tell me, why then did you immigrate to Israel?

RONNY   I like to say that being eighteen, this seemed to be a dramatic and interesting thing to do. But I believe there was more to my decision. My mother was born and grew up here, and the subject of Israel was always in the background when I was growing up in Paris. I knew I had family here, that I was even born here, although my parents left when I was very young. I think I wanted to leave France for various reasons, and coming to Israel was the most natural move.

I   Is it true that your grandfather was a very important Zionist?

RONNY   That's right.

I   Does this mean anything to you?

RONNY   As long as I lived in France, the fact that I had a famous grandfather didn't affect me. It was far away and meaningless. In Israel, however, I became aware of belonging to a "good family," and not always in the positive sense. Several of my relatives have important positions in the country; they are good Labor party supporters. I am sort of a black sheep among them.

I And your parents?

RONNY My father still lives in Paris. Mother came here after me. She's a different story. She spent many years in France, and they weren't happy years for her. She always felt a stranger there. She came back here full of hope as well as memories of Israel the way she knew it once, in the fifties, when she left. However, she was disappointed and had some serious adjustment problems, which I shared. For me she represents the myth that, in the past, Israel was a good and beautiful place, people were kind and decent, and somehow, who knows why, things have deteriorated. So all we have to do is turn the wheel backward, and everything will be fine.

●　　●　　●　　●

I Let's talk about your thoughts concerning the war, the fact that we continuously face the threat of war. How does this influence your feelings for the country, and what are the effects on other people?

RONNY Well, there have been some developments during the eight years I have been living here. My attitude toward the country has grown more complicated with time. Let me start with an incident that happened just a few days ago. In the school where I work, a booklet was published by the students for the occasion of "Ten Years After the Liberation of Jerusalem." Well, it's very difficult for me to read something like that. When children write about this subject, and some adults decide what material to include under the formal supervision of the school, the product is somehow a tribute to the total denial of the problematic aspects of our situation. The presentation centers on the idea that ten years ago, Jerusalem was liberated from the Arabs, and now we can all live here, and everything is fine. I'm used to the fact that, politically, most people see things in a different light than I do, but I was shocked to discover the incredibly poor quality of the children's writing. I believe that this is the outcome of the war. To my mind, there was nothing sincere in the booklet, nothing creative. It was a collection of clichés—in the poems as well as in the fiction. I feel that gradually, the way we perceive the world, and ourselves within it, is being shaped to become narrower and more constricted. The range of permissible ideas has become so limited that most of the wealth of expression existing within people is gradually pushed aside, repressed. I could find some excuses for the adults, but when I see this phenomenon in first graders, it depresses me.

You see, as to myself, I found my place here, and I'm content. But the idea of my children growing up in such an atmosphere is repulsive.

I   Because you'll not be able to control their total education?

RONNY   Not only that. I refer to the patterns we have here for the approaches to oneself and to others, which are deeply rooted in this society and which the schools keep reinforcing. But it is not only the schools.

I   How would you characterize these patterns?

RONNY   Very strong conformity. Very clear rules as to what is "right" or "wrong." Lack of tolerance of any idea or approach that is outside this limited range. And also the mechanisms of very strong defenses, aggression and fear of anything new that doesn't fit into the framework.

I   And do you see all this as the outcome of war?

RONNY   Not only the war. It goes further back. I don't deny the effects of anti-Semitism, of the holocaust in Europe, and such national traumas, which surely determine the psychological makeup of the people. Wars reinforce this structure; they provide legitimacy for all the negative aspects and the slogan of "no choice," "it's not good, but we have no choice."

I   Do you think we have choices? Besides leaving the country?

RONNY   Yes. The direction should be in looking truthfully for a peaceful settlement instead of fortification for the "no-choice" wars. To me a Palestinian state is welcome if peace will be assured. Another direction is from within the country, our attitudes toward the Arab minority, the struggle for a secular state, and so on. Anyway, I believe that the last wars in Israel could have been avoided by us. A "no-choice" war is, perhaps, an easier way than finding a peaceful solution.

I   Do you really believe so?

RONNY   Yes, I do. If the energy we put into fortifications were, instead, used to try out some political settlement, we might have been much better off. I know most people would disagree, but I still claim that we could, at least, make some opening moves, and I'm disturbed that we don't. These are other signs of the narrowness I was talking about before. People pick one way—war—with the belief that there's "no choice," and are sort of blind to the existing alternatives.

I   You're saying that people learn not to think, not to ask?

RONNY   Yes. But I want to make the distinction between wartime and peacetime. When war breaks out, your personal life and your country are endangered; that's no time for questioning. I'm for maximal discipline and the best performance in war. But between wars, why do people completely forget the severity of our situation? They avoid all thought of what will be; they dwell only on their daily lives and therefore don't try to remedy the basically sick condition we're in. When one is called to defend the country, that's no time for thought; then it's too late for planning. I have no cause to blame individuals for participating in wars, which would be especially unfair for me as a woman.

•   •   •   •

I   Do you see other effects of war on our lives?

RONNY   Well, on one level, the permanent threat of death for relatively young people. I am sure that the recurring wars bring that more and more into awareness. On another level, war affects male-female relationships in Israel. According to my own private little "survey," which also includes non-Israelis, the Israeli male is quite poor in his sexual performance. He is not oriented toward pleasure, not his own and certainly not his partner's; and this is, in my opinion, due to the wars, although it's indirect. The Israeli male is performance-oriented; he is programmed to perform, to make things—like wars—and to do it well. We remember the number of victories we had in the Six-Day War in 1967, but we deny all the complications resulting from them. In sexual relationships, as in war, men try to conquer. Numbers and performance are evaluated with very little internalization or emotional involvement. The same performance orientation is, by the way, characteristic of other areas, such as work, production, and studies. Whereas in other countries the male stereotype has been gradually changing, here a man still measures his masculinity in terms of the number of women he has taken to bed. The reserve service serves as some sort of an exclusive male club in which even so-called family men find their male outlets. All these facts lead to confirmation of the male stereotype, which centers on sex and aggression, and to the orientation toward women as objects for these needs.

On the other hand, women suffer from guilt feelings, since men do the fighting or, at least, serve much more in the reserves. This is an added risk and responsibility that women don't share with men. So women look for ways to compensate their men, their soldiers.

I   And men feel they deserve it?

RONNY   Sure, and this includes all the male population up to age fifty. Actually, I think that this complex interaction evolves with age, and older people sense it more that our high school students. Although they might have been affected by their approaching military service, I find high school kids to be normal adolescents in their sexual behavior. The problem starts later.

I   Do you include in the "problem" the suppression of the more gentle aspects of the male personality, such as expressing emotions, aspects which are incompatible with the role of the combat soldier?

RONNY   Yes, there is certainly suppression of the so-called feminine aspects of Israeli men. There is another level in the connection between sexual behavior and wars, and this is that in sex, people find a certain outlet for accumulated tensions. Here I find an analogy with driving. The Israelis are known to be reckless drivers, and many have suggested that this may be an outlet for mounting tension as well. I believe that most people repress or deny the sense of danger and tension in their lives, and these pressures are indirectly expressed in driving and, on a deeper level, in sexual behavior. Another manifestation of these pressures might be in the extreme competitiveness that I find in Israel, starting from the earliest school grades, which, I think, springs from the same source. All these are products of the war situation and also of the continuous military training in the reserves, which, for many, is a very dangerous activity even in peacetime. So men constantly live with fears, which accumulate to mounting tensions and are released in aggression and violence in daily life.

This was one of the strangest discoveries I made when I started to understand life in Israel. I observed how, on the one hand, we put tremendous stress on the solidarity of the people, the togetherness necessary for the immense task of defense; and on the other hand, at work, at the university, the moral level is of "dog eat dog." Nobody even notices any contradiction between the two. Perhaps there really isn't a contradiction, since we find outlets in everyday life for the tensions which cannot be released on the battlefield. As long as norms of the male, the hero, and of masculinity are not changed, there is, perhaps, no other way.

• • • •

RONNY I remember how deeply I was moved the first time I heard a man talking about his fear of war, since I wasn't used to hearing such things in Israel. From my point of view, as I was educated abroad, and also, as a woman who didn't experience combat and the need to repress feelings, I always searched for the missing link in the tales of war—the fear—and I didn't find it. Men told me about their positive excitement, some sort of a "high," during combat, but usually they just avoided any mention of feelings, justifying their avoidance with the phrases of "One must go back to business," or "There is no time to dwell on the past," and above all "Everything will be fine." So to find someone who admits his fears, who claims that his strongest experience in combat was terror, was some kind of a revelation for me.

I Interestingly enough, in the groups, alternative norms are developed. People talk about fears quite frequently, and they regret the fact that they block themselves from feeling more intensely.

RONNY   Well, there's no doubt in my mind about the existence of this anxiety, and somehow it has to be expressed. I don't think that the groups distort reality but that the external norms in these matters are strongly repressive, and only indirect channels remain for the expression of inner insecurity. I am pleased that in the groups this disguise isn't necessary.

I   Yes, but it also shows that the repression is not very severe, since in the group atmosphere people open up quite easily.

RONNY   Don't forget that many of these people are in the field of psychology, in which the norms are to make the unconscious conscious, to express feelings, and to be aware. But I fear that the average Israeli reader will be suspicious of these revelations. I believe in exposure. As long as people come across books like the one you're writing, see other ways to speak and feel about our life here, there is a chance of some change taking place.

About the Book _____

Introduction

How would Israelis like their reflection as depicted by the case material? What would be the reaction of group members confronted with the summary of their own experiences? What kind of process might evolve when people see their own experience in the context of the repetitive themes of the groups?

These and other related questions were explored in the last group of interviews, conversations with individuals who read the book or parts of it.

Avinoam (II)

After our first conversation ["Avinoam (I)"], I asked Avinoam to read some parts of The Unfinished Business of War in Israel, *and we met again for a conversation about it. In the following, a totally different aspect of Avinoam's personality is revealed—the professional mental-health worker rather than the hero-soldier.*

I   What do you feel about what you've read?
AVINOAM   My feeling is that it's very powerful and very human and very beautiful. It's a real-life book. I have read records of many groups or cases, and frequently they sounded false or untrue. Here, I felt it was really, completely true, very credible. I didn't detect anything that sounded fake. This is what I liked about the book.
I   I'm very pleased to hear that.
AVINOAM   I also liked the insertion of parts that the group

members wrote, although there the material is sometimes more refined, as if it were a secondary version of the primary experience expressed in the group sessions.

I Do people outside the university have these problems as well, or are they specific to students and professionals?

AVINOAM No, I don't think so. Some of the people you wrote about are more fluent and trained in expressing themselves verbally. But not all of them. Avi, with whom I identify easily, was as expressive as this stone here. He isn't any different from many of the soldiers I see daily. And Tamar is very tough, too, holding on to her mask. Your students seem more eloquent and sophisticated, but their rigidity, their masks, exist all the same. Their willingness to act out their fantasies is, perhaps, greater. But the type of problems they have could be found in many individuals after the war, notwithstanding their background. They are real issues, not just neurotic symptoms or make-believe problems.

I Some people think that Avi's problem of not feeling is not a "real" problem.

AVINOAM Well, it used to be my problem, so I know. But I'm also a psychotherapist, so I may be biased. I believe that people outside the mental-health profession, like the armored corp officers with whom I work, would also see Avi as having a real problem. They wouldn't think of it as an affectation. I've often encountered people who were outwardly very tough, but when cornered in a face-to-face situation, were found to be very sensitive and concerned human beings. They would be able to appreciate the problems dealt with in your cases.

It's not easy to read, though. I'm not easily upset emotionally, but everybody here in Israel would find in the cases something which reminds him of his own personal experience. It's very moving.

I Do you think an Israeli might feel insulted by reading the book, as if his weaknesses were exposed?

AVINOAM No, why should he be? I don't see the exposed parts as weaknesses. Also, when you report the feedback of the group to the one who worked, you show how people accepted the "heroes." I cannot see any people feeling slighted by your records; your own respect and appreciation of them, even love for them, are so apparent.

I   The main problem these people have to cope with is the national need for heroism and how it fits their private needs. Are you also aware of this problem?

AVINOAM   I myself, for many years, invested endless effort to becoming a hero. Perhaps I have wasted all those energies in that project; that's what I presently believe.

I   Could you enlarge on that?

AVINOAM   Look, before my studies I served for six years as an enlisted paratroop commander. They were beautiful years, I assure you; I loved them. But the amount of energy I invested in my image, in how other people would perceive me, and how I should behave so that they would be properly impressed; the amount of worrying I put into disguising my weaknesses, into covering up the fact that I, too, was sometimes helpless or didn't know, today I see all these as wasted efforts. I could have used those energies better, and I would certainly have enjoyed life more without this mask.

I   Do you see an alternative? Can one be a paratroop commander and show his men that he is sometimes weak or confused?

AVINOAM   That's a good question. I think, in the long run, you cannot deceive your men anyway. To behave without too many masks, to be completely honest and successful as an army commander, one would need to be, first of all, a mature person. If I went back to being a field commander today, I believe I could do it without games. But ten years ago I couldn't do it. I would have needed much more maturity and self-confidence.

There is something else. As Avi put it, a military psychiatrist had told him that his emotional indifference was "functional." I think this is somewhat true. In some situations—such as during the War of Attrition, when people were being killed continuously over a long period of time—the toughness, the black humor, the lack of emotions, were highly functional for us. You can act differently if you get a chance to work it out —the mourning, the fears—but this is impossible as long as the battle goes on. Even technically it's impossible; you have no time and no energy. One has to fight from hour to hour; to do some planning, if possible; and to cope with the real matters of food, sleep, and ammunition. When you have to deal with survival, it is functional to disregard the psychological aspects, the emotions, all that.

I   So you say it's a matter of timing?

AVINOAM   Certainly. Under fire you must put on a mask of bravery and courage, even if you don't feel that way. The least sign of my weakness would immediately lead to the spreading of weakness and panic among my men. I remember occasions when, as a field commander, I pretended, showed off my bravery, perfectly aware that I was playacting the hero while really feeling afraid inside. This had a tremendous calming effect on my men. These men depended on me as their commander, so I owed it to them to inspire security by all possible means.

The problem is to switch over, to change your behavior when circumstances have changed and the game is not functional any more. This is something I have seen already as a professional psychiatrist after the Yom Kippur War. When the actual fighting was over, officers had to shift their pattern of relating to their men in many ways. Those who could not make the shift, even though they were brilliant during combat, failed miserably in their role when the fighting was over.

I   What is the necessary change?

AVINOAM   Well, here is what I found important about your book. When the war is over, one of the roles of a good commander is to provide an atmosphere of talking about the experience and releasing the emotions involved in it—the mourning, the fears. I'm sure that this is of great importance for the smooth functioning of the army, as well as for the sanity of the individual.

I   This is exactly what I have been trying to say. Do people accept this attitude in the army?

AVINOAM   Well, among mental-health professionals, for sure. Actually, the army has implemented procedures that may provide this psychological release, although they have a different primary goal. After battle, the commander has to carry out a debriefing on all that has happened. This includes a complete reproduction of the battle in which the unit took part, and it may provide the perfect occasion for emotional work as well as intellectual understanding. You repeat the circumstances of friends getting killed, for instance, so you can talk about them, mourn for them with your men. The confrontations that may occur are very important, and it's the commander's role to deal with them. The whole setup changes after the war; you have to invest more energy in good human relations rather than in sheer survival.

Let me give you an example. In the armored corps' reorganization after the war, one tank company received tanks with bloodstains or even some remnants of human bodies that had remained in the tanks. Some soldiers refused to enter these tanks and clean them. I was called in when the problem arose. The commander of the company issued orders to wash the tanks—take soap and water and just do it! I believe that a different attitude was required, not just a technical, business-like attitude.

I   What would you do?

AVINOAM   I think I would gather the company for a talk . . . talk about the meaning of the bloodstains, their meaning for the soldiers as well as for myself. How I am affected as a person. I have seen commanders who could lead such a conversation, just as human beings. If a soldier sees his commander treating blood—the blood of his friend perhaps, or his own if he had been killed—as dirt to be promptly washed away, his whole attitude toward our wars and his duty may be affected. If, on the other hand, the commander expresses the feeling that it's blood, not just any dirt, that it's our fellow-fighters' blood, that it causes him pain to witness it because these tankists were his friends, but we must cope with the pain and prepare for tomorrow, the outcome would be completely different. And if the commander, instead of issuing orders, gets out with his men to wash the tanks and is the first to do so, it reinforces his words.

So what I claim very strongly is that there is a sharp shift in the functions that a commander has to fulfill from the war situation to post-war conditions; and in order to succeed in it, one has to be primarily human. That's why I think the message of the book is so central for us.

I   Could you formulate the message that you got from it?

AVINOAM   That weakness is part of human existence; that "muscles" are not strength, a mask is not power; that the expression of weakness is not weakness; and that there is always something to be done to help in coping, even by very simple means. I think the book is far from defeatism or lowering the morale. It shows how people who deal with their experience gain strength from it. In this sense it's very optimistic.

Dana

Dana is a widow of the Yom Kippur War. She has remarried and is now pregnant for the first time. Dana participated in my 1977 group. When she found out about the book I was writing, she requested to read the draft. I told her it wouldn't be easy, but she insisted, and I was keen to hear her reaction.

The interview took place after she read the clinical part. During the interview, even throughout the most difficult parts, she maintained a high degree of control over her emotions.

I   I was waiting to hear from you, to get your reaction to the book.

DANA   Well, it's a lot . . . it's so much, so many different aspects of the war and its effects. It's stunning to see it all in a book, all together in one long sequence. All the different aspects are pretty familiar to me [*smiles*], but I was shocked to find them specified, all together. It's all correct, I mean. I have experienced so much of it myself. But it's very difficult to take it all in now. And when you included some episodes about the holocaust as well, my reaction was: Well, this is too much! Also, I was deeply moved by the fact that you've arranged much of the material chronologically from 1970—such a long period of time—and the themes come up again and again. It made me feel that it is all part of one perpetual continuum.

I   Do you think it's good to write it all this way, or was it too painful for you to read, to re-experience?

DANA   I think it's very good for such a book to have been written and for many people to read it, here in Israel especially, so that people won't feel they are abnormal, so that they'll see that others have similar feelings, similar reactions. This is very helpful, because when you're suddenly bereaved, your whole world sort of caves in, and then you lose all perspective, you don't know whether your reaction is appropriate or what. Sometimes you think that you've lost your mind. Reading your cases is, therefore, some sort of revelation: lo and behold, others have experienced the same bizarre phenomena in their lives, I'm not at all alone in this, some people share my lot. Pain is very egocentric, you know; but here, by reading, your solitude is somewhat relieved.

I   What do you mean by egocentric pain?

DANA   In the first few weeks after Moti was killed, I was aware only of my own pain. Like Tamar in the book, I was sure nobody was as badly hit, was suffering as deeply, as I was. So, when I read about Tamar, it seemed very familiar.

Let me give you another example. I haven't talked about all this for years, you know. During the period right after Moti was killed, I couldn't force myself to make any necessary changes in our apartment. Since he wouldn't be coming any more—which I refused to believe for a long time—some of his things should have been removed from the closets. I kept them just the same. A whole shelf with his shirts, for instance. I couldn't do anything about them, give them away, throw them out, nothing. I kept Moti's shirts in our closet just as before. I thought I must be out of my mind, not being able to handle such simple objects. At that time I attended a widows' group, all recent widows of the Yom Kippur War. There I found out how other women also had hard times with objects that had belonged to their husbands, how difficult it was to get rid of these simple, personal objects, and what holding on to them signified to us.

So, to my amazement, I discovered that my problem with Moti's shirts was not that special, I wasn't all that crazy or frail. Other widows gave me back some confidence that I was normal. And your book may have a similar effect.

•   •   •   •

DANA   From a different point of view, although you wrote the book on an impressional level, without much interpretation, I think it would be very important for various professionals as well. I wish the professionals who deal with bereaved families —the social workers and psychotherapists and rehabilitation experts—would know more about how it feels—how *we* feel— when disaster hits us. From my experience, I sometimes had the feeling they were completely insensitive, indifferent, to what was going on emotionally. The social worker who was assigned to my "case" by the Defense Ministry sent me a mimeographed note, stating her reception hours in her office. I never went to see her.

I   That's incredible! Didn't she come for a home visit?

DANA   No, never. I could have collapsed at home and she wouldn't have known. And when Moti's mother had a breakdown, we couldn't face going through the bureaucracy of the ministry to get help, so we finally got a private specialist for her. But look, today I don't blame this social worker or the system. They were flooded, and some people really could not have managed on their own. Also, I heard that in other towns, they were more efficient and human. All I got from them were checks. It's very insulting. I wish they would be more understanding. What I wished for, then, was very basic: I simply wanted somebody to listen to me sympathetically—nothing more. I wanted my social worker to listen to me without any preconceived ideas or expectations; to be the person in front of whom I could be myself, not a stoic heroine, just me the way I felt; to not tell me how I ought to behave but accept me the way I was. These are the most important things right at the beginning; this is what's needed to preserve one's sanity. I know of people, professionals and others, who were able to perform this basic human task. But not in my hometown; they were simply flooded there.

Once I did go for help; it was after the widows' group had dissolved. They referred me to a psychotherapist, as I had requested; but unfortunately he was a behaviorist, and we didn't get along. In our first meeting he asked me how many times a day I cried and to chart this "reaction" for him over the next couple of days. This was ridiculous; it didn't make any sense. In the second session he told me about *his* problems. Again, he had his own difficulties, and couldn't cope with my sorrow or guess how I felt. So, I imagine that many professionals could profit from an honest presentation that tries to convey how people feel on the other side of the fence.

Another thing I was thinking about has to do with the world of invalids, something you touch upon in your 1974 group. Very few professionals try to empathize with the inner experience of the invalid, say a soldier whose leg or arm has been amputated and who is a paraplegic all of a sudden. It's extremely difficult, and only recently have people started to explore the complexity of this condition. Here again, to send him a check for one thousand dollars or what have you is worse than nothing; it prevents him from ever really rehabilitating himself.
I   You don't think people have this intention in mind, I'm sure.
DANA   Of course not. First, it's sheer incompetence. Then, it's also the result of overwork. And finally, it's perhaps necessary for these professionals to use some sort of formal approach that may seem indifferent, as a way of defending their own egos from being overwhelmed. Maybe, as you say in the book, it's "functional." I have a different opinion, as you see. Anyway, for a country like ours, which is constantly plagued with wars, too little attention has been given to this human aspect, too little has been written and said about it. It's part of the national repression, perhaps; and I'm glad your book is confronting the issue more openly.

•   •   •   •

I   Which part of the book seemed most relevant to you?

DANA   Several. The way I see it, the reaction to bereavement has two different facets. I found them both in the book. First, there is the emotional reaction, which, as I said before, is very egocentric. I felt the pain. I didn't believe the wound would ever heal. Then I felt anger—we all did in the widows' group—anger at *him* for deserting *me*. It's silly, I know, but I still felt deserted and angry, and I blamed Moti for my pain. Then there was regret, deep guilt feelings for the anger I had previously felt. Sometimes the circle started all over again. This is the emotional side. But it has another stage, which I don't remember finding in your book. It is, perhaps, the most difficult one.

For a long time I kept waiting for Moti to come back. I simply refused to believe that he was gone forever. I waited at home for him, believing he would suddenly show up. Then, when the prisoners of war were released, I hoped that he would somehow be returned with them. I looked forward to every new group of prisoners, waiting for Moti to be among them. So, you see, that's why I didn't remove his shirts from the closet. I had all sorts of fantasies about his return—you can't imagine how persistent they were. It's not like somebody being sick for a long time, where you see him getting weaker, until he's dead. Here you don't see a thing. I remember him tall and healthy, and the next thing I know, he's dead! It's very hard to believe, a person you lived with so long, and all of a sudden he's gone.

I   What did you expect to see?

DANA   I don't know. Next there is the military cemetery. Have you ever visited one?

I   Yes, of course.

DANA   So you know. Endless rows of small, square tombstones. With names on them. All are the same, completely identical. I was shocked to see Moti's name on one. But it's not that. Even seeing the tombstone was unreal; it didn't help me realize that Moti was, indeed, dead.

I   This takes a long time.

DANA   I know. Gradually I have accepted his death more. But to this very day I sometimes have fantasies of his return. This is one aspect I don't remember your writing about.

I You're right. Maybe it's because I saw the widows and the girlfriends a little later in the process. Yael used to tell me a lot about feeling that her boyfriend, who had been killed in the war, would one evening open the door and be back. But I don't think it was included in the book, so I'm glad you mentioned it. It's very important.

•   •   •   •

I A few minutes ago you referred to two different levels of reaction to death.

DANA Yes. One is emotional, which I experienced more than the other, the philosophical level. Moti's father reacted more philosophically. He grappled with the questions: "Why?" and "What for?" For the first few weeks he was the strongest of us, or so it seemed. He is an active Zionist who immigrated to Israel forty years ago to help build the country. The death of his first-born, he said, is part of the mission, the price of building a new country. He even said that this justifies the act of his immigration to Israel. He talked to me a lot about the Jewish destiny, the Bible, Job and his fate. He used the saying, "The Lord gave, and the Lord has taken away." I couldn't identify with him at the time. I felt he was covering up the pain with philosophy.

I And later?

DANA I think he was affected by his wife's breakdown. He changed his tune a bit, asking: "Why me?" This was more like the way I was feeling, too.

•   •   •   •

I You said you could identify with many things in the book. Did you identify with Tamar's self-accusation as well? Were her feelings also familiar?

DANA Not exactly, but I could understand them. I don't believe I could have prevented Moti's death by any means, and I think that's what Tamar had in mind. Frequently after his death I did feel regret, however, for minor disagreements between us—the kind of little conflicts that are an integral part of every marriage. I regret some things we didn't do his way.

If I had known he was going to be killed, I would have given him the moon and the stars. Such an event completely over-turns one's perspective about wishes, rights, compromises, etc. But all the same, I never felt I caused his death, even indirectly, or could have prevented it.

•　　•　　•　　•

DANA   Another section that was meaningful for me was the one on the man who didn't fight. I think this is a central issue of our life in Israel, and you and your groups have, in a way, presented it too weakly or forgivingly. I remember how I re-sented all men who didn't fight, especially those who didn't have any good excuse for it. I don't think their problem is that they blame themselves—we help them in it a great deal! I felt very resentful and accusing of the Israeli men who, if they were abroad, didn't jump on the first plane to come home to take part in the fighting. I saw them as cowards—or worse, as traitors. I found it hard to forgive them. When some of them, men we used to know, came to visit me later, to offer their condolences for my loss, I felt like throwing them out of my home and back to where they came from.

I   Well, you're right. My groups were more accepting. First, because of the group atmosphere, and second, because these men were, perhaps, of the kind you termed as having good excuses.

DANA   Yes, I know I'm very harsh in that respect. I also heard of men who did return on the first available plane and were killed on their way to the battlefield. Uselessly, one might say. But, on the other hand, some men already here were killed uselessly, too. That's not an excuse for not joining the war.

•　　•　　•　　•

I   Well, there was something else I wanted to ask you about. You got married again. How long after the war was it?

DANA   Two years. Two and a half years, to be precise.

I   Did you have conflicts about that?

DANA   And how! To this very day I hardly believe I did it. Let me explain this, it's a very complicated matter. I think Ester also presented it in her work in the group. Every widow feels both an obligation to remember the dead and guilt for any signs of forgetting. On the other hand, when I see another widow rehabilitating herself—creating new social contacts, becoming intimate with someone else—I'm very happy for her! When my friend, a widow I met in the group, confided in me, some time ago, that she was in love with a man, that he made her happy, I was thrilled for her and for her two children. Yet, at the same time, she was trembling with anxiety, afraid that I'd be angry or critical in any way! She was so relieved to see my reaction. So, this is a guilt trip we give ourselves; all the same, it's very difficult to handle.

I How did you handle it?

DANA One of the things that helped me was moving to another town, to another university, and to a new set of friends. The change of the flat was very important. I could never bring another man to our apartment, Moti's and mine, to face the closets still filled with Moti's personal belongings. I had to clean it all up, to start anew, so to speak, in order to leave town. I also could never become attached to another man as long as I lived so close to my in-laws, Moti's parents, although they said they wanted me to re-marry.

I How did they react when you did?

DANA Very well, but it hurt them all the same [*smiles*]. My present husband joins me now when I visit them, and they have adjusted to my new situation. They are happy I'm going to have a baby. We all have some sort of balanced relationship now.

I Would you advise other widows to move, too?

DANA No, not at all. I think everyone has different responses and a very unique healing process. For me, the move was necessary, that's all.

• • • •

I I have only a few more questions that I'd like to ask you about the book. Could you anticipate anyone feeling hurt or insulted by it?

DANA By no means. One has to acknowledge both the strength and the weakness, the stoic heroism and the pain.

I   But in the book it might seem as if weakness and pain prevail.

DANA   Well, yes, but the strength and the heroism stand out in our reality, they're on the surface. You see, I feel that the number of people who dare cope with the pain and weakness is too small for the size of our problem here.

I   Did you really feel like reading the book, all the cases, or did you do it partly for my sake?

DANA   No, I really wanted to find out how other people live with these problems we all have in common, to a lesser or a greater extent. And I'm pretty sure every single person in Israel would find someone in the book to identify with. As for me, I'm curious about the topic and unfinished with my own problem.

I   I'm very glad and thankful for all you've said to me today.

DANA   Well, I am pleased, too. You see, I wouldn't have talked to you or to anyone if we hadn't established our relationship before. Right after the war, some people conducted research on widows, and I received lots of questionnaires in the mail to fill out. I didn't respond; it just made me angry that I was approached in this way. Later, I read in the papers the result of that survey, which was based on only 10 percent of the widows who were contacted! The remaining 90 percent probably felt as I did. So it takes time and trust for me to be able to talk about the war and all that has happened to me since. If I go for additional therapy, I hope to be able to talk about it more.

I   You mentioned Ester's session before ["Four People at the Doorstep"]. I remember your strong reaction to her work. How do you see it now?

DANA   To this day I am very surprised at the intensity of my reaction then, my uncontrollable weeping. I didn't realize how painful this wound still is. I thought I had more or less recovered. I hardly ever talk about it at all. At the same time I was glad, you know, to find out that I didn't forget Moti. I carry this obligation to remember, as I said before; so in a perverse way, I'm glad I'm sensitive to this pain. Can you understand this?

That moved the tin soldier. He was nearly weeping
tin tears, but that would not have been proper. . . .
Then the tin soldier melted down, and the next day . . .
found him in the shape of a little tin heart.

—Hans Christian Andersen, *The Steadfast Tin Soldier*

Recommended Readings

On Gestalt Therapy

Baumgardner, Patricia. *Gifts from Lake Cowichan*. Palo Alto, Calif.: Science and Behavior Books, 1975.

Fagan, Joen, and Shepard, Irma L., eds. *Gestalt Therapy Now*. Palo Alto, Calif.: Science and Behavior Books, 1970.

Hatcher, Chris, and Himmelstein, Philip, eds. *The Handbook of Gestalt Therapy*. New York: Jason Aronson, 1976.

Latner, Joel. *The Gestalt Therapy Book*. New York: Julian Press, 1973.

Loew, C. A., Grayson, H., and Loew, G. H. *Three Psychotherapies: A Clinical Comparison*. New York: Brunner-Mazel, 1975.

Naranjo, Claudio. *The Techniques of Gestalt Therapy*. Berkeley, Calif.: SAT Press, 1973.

Perls, Frederick S. *Ego, Hunger, and Aggression: The Beginning of Gestalt Therapy*. New York: Random House, 1969.

———. *Gestalt Therapy Verbatim*. Lafayette, Calif.: Real People Press, 1969.

———. *In and Out the Garbage Pail*. Lafayette, Calif.: Real People Press, 1969.

———, Hefferline, R. F., and Goodman, P. *Gestalt Therapy*. New York: Julian Press, 1951.

Perls, Fritz. *The Gestalt Approach and Eyewitness to Therapy*. Palo Alto, Calif.: Science and Behavior Books, 1973.

Polster, Erving, and Polster, Miriam. *Gestalt Therapy Integrated: Contours of Theory and Practice*. New York: Brunner-Mazel, 1973.

Shepard, Martin. *Fritz: An Intimate Portrait of Fritz Perls and Gestalt Therapy*. New York: Saturday Review Press, 1975.

Simkin, James S. *Gestalt Therapy Mini-Lectures*. Millbrae, Calif.: Celestial Arts, 1976.

Smith, Edward W., ed. *The Growing Edge of Gestalt Therapy*. New York: Brunner-Mazel, 1976.

Stephenson, F. Douglas. *Gestalt Therapy Primer: Introductory Readings in Gestalt Therapy.* Springfield, Ill.: C. C. Thomas, 1975.

Stevens, John O., ed. *Gestalt Is.* New York: Bantam, 1977.

On Wars in Israel*

The following list is far from complete. First, the majority of books in this area were published in Hebrew and were not translated into foreign languages. Second, most of the books on this topic were written from military and/or political points of view, disregarding the personal, experiential aspects. Therefore, the following are only books in English that focus on the human experience of war.

The War of Independence

Knohl, D., ed. *Siege in the Hills of Hebron.* New York: Yoseloff, 1958.

Larkin, Margaret. *The Hand of Mordecai.* London: V. Gollancz, 1968.

Levin, H. *Jerusalem Embattled: A Diary of the City Under Siege.* London: V. Gollancz, 1948.

Rose, P. *The Siege of Jerusalem.* London: Patmos Publishers, 1949.

Sugrue, T. *Watch for the Morning.* New York: Harper & Brothers, 1950.

The Sinai Campaign

Barer, S. *The Weekend War.* Tel Aviv: Karni, 1959.

Bernet, M. M. *The Time of the Burning Sun.* New York: New American Library, 1968.

Bondy, R., Zmora, O., and Bashan, R., eds. *Mission Survival: People of Israel's Story: From Threat to Annihilation.* New York: Sabra Books, 1968.

Dayan, Yael. *Yael Dayan Israel Journal: June 1967.* New York: McGraw-Hill, 1967.

Feldman, E. *The Twenty-Eighth Year of Iyar.* New York: Bloch, 1968.

Shapira, A., ed. *The Seventh Day: Soldiers' Talk About the Six-Day War.* New York: Charles Scribner's Sons, 1970.

Teveth, S. *The Tanks of Tammuz.* New York: Viking Press, 1969.

The War of Attrition

Sherman, Arnold. *In the Bunkers of Sinai.* New York: Sabra Books, 1971.

---

*This part of the bibliography was prepared with the aid of *The State of Israel*, vols. I, II, by A. Neuberg. Jerusalem: Center for Public Libraries in Israel, 1970–76. This work is an annotated bibliography.

The Yom Kippur War

Dan, U. *Sharon's Bridgehead.* Tel Aviv: E. L. Special Edition, 1975.

Davis, Moshe, ed. *The Yom Kippur War: Israel and the Jewish People.* New York: Arno Press, 1974.

Hart, Harold H., ed. *Yom Kippur Plus 100 Days: The Human Side of the War and Its Aftermath, As Shown in the Columns of the Jerusalem "Post."* New York: Hart Publishers, 1974.

Raviv, Judah. *Last Stand at Firdan.* Jerusalem: Keren Kayemeth Leisrael, 1974.

About the Author

Amia Lieblich is a professor of psychology at the Hebrew University in Jerusalem. She also does clinical work, primarily as a group therapist working with students. She has spent two years in the United States: one training in Gestalt therapy with Dr. James Simkin of Los Angeles; the other visiting at the University of Massachusetts in Amherst. Dr. Lieblich has published numerous articles in academic psychology journals. She lives in Jerusalem with her husband and two children.